Xylor Jane
Notebooks

Essays by Em Rooney
and John Yau

CANADA

parrasch heijnen

Contents

8
Printout of prime numbers, notating twin primes and palindromes

9
Printout of prime numbers

10
Sketch for *Sooner*, Ink on 1mm graph paper, 2012

11
8th order Magic Square, moves in an L like a knight, Sketch for *Shadow Dancer*, 2018

13
Sketch for *Via Crucis VI Hi Mom*, 2009

14
Friday, Right-handed, 2006

15
Chelsea Starr, Friday, Left-handed, SF, CA, 2006

17
Font studies for *Via Crucis II*

18
Friday, Right-handed, 2006

19
Printout list of Solstice and Equinox dates and times 1999–2020

20
Untitled, 1,1,2,2,3,3,4,4, Expansion starts on orange, Left-handed, 2006

21
Layout for *Heart* paintings, 2007

23
Prime times columns study, 2013

24
Freehand lines, Prismacolor pens on paper, 19 × 17.5 inches, 2005

25
Study for *Stripped*, 2009

27
"RollerBall" font sketch for *Via Crucis XII & XIV*, 2010

28
94 of my favorite 11-digit prime palindromes arranged in 4 columns. Sketch for *Zahav* and *Mani-Pedi*, 2017

29
Blue/Red expansion for Z, 30 × 22 inches, 2005

30
Phi printout

31
Sketch for *Princess*, 2011

33
List of triangular numbers

34
Fibonacci sequence, 2002

35
Sketch for *Family Vacation*, 2016

37
Sketch for *Sevens*, 2017

38
Jody S., Left-handed, expansion on green, San Francisco, CA, 2005

39
Sketch for *Departing*, 2008

41
Sketch for 101-digit nesting prime palindromes, 2013

42
Fibonacci sequence printout

43
Fibonacci sequence printout

44
Triangles arranged in sixes rotating on hexagon wheels, notated with ROYGBIV starting position. Sketch for *Via Crucis V*, 2010

45
Ones font constructed with triangles sketch for repunit painting *RXGWCW*, 2012

47
Sketch for *Magic Square for 5775*, Twentynine Palms, CA, 2014

48
Sketch for *3rd Order Magic Square for Finding Lost People*, 2014

49
Matt P., Costa Rica, 2017

50
Study of Julian Day Numbers in ROYGBIV based on day of the week for painting *RNBWBS*. Ink on 1mm graph paper, 2008

51
Sketch for *Via Crucis X*, 2009

53
Nesting prime palindromes font study, 2013

54
Border study for a portrait of a 2, 2015

55
Sketch of ROYGBIV border expansions, Map for *Magic Square for Maine Coon*. Ink on 1mm graph paper, 2016

56
List of 11-digit prime palindromes including their order number within the complete set of 42,100. Notes for *Threes, Sevens, and Nines*, 2017

57
Sketch for *Dancefloor*, 2007

59
Calendar configurations

60
2457604, Ink on paper, 2016

61
8th Order Magic Square in binary. Sketch for *Pall*, 2015

63
Ink drawing, 2005

65
Double unit postal font, 2017

66
Fibonacci printout

67
Pythagorean triangles in ROYGBIV in a double snake arrangement, 2007

68
Triangular numbers under 100, Ink drawing on block print, 2018

69
Sketch for *Portrait of a 5*, 2014

71
Sketch for *Portrait of a Two*, 2017

72
3rd Order Magic Square for Deep Sleep. Map for 3 color plates. Aquatint print edition with Wingate Studio, 2013

73
List of palindromic triangular numbers and 5-digit primes, 2006

75
List of prime times of day, 12-hour version, Ink on "note-ables" stationary tablet, 2012

77
727-digit tetradic Sophie Germain prime number. Sketch for *Via Crucis VIII*, 2009

78
Very first ROYGBIV drawing in 8 Directions. *Sherrie*, 2005

79
Sketch for *Brood*, 2007

80
2458357, Sunday, Truro, MA, 2018

81
List of 11-digit prime palindromes including their order number within the complete set of 42,100, 2017

83
101-digit nesting prime palindrome. Sketch for failed paintings, 2013

84
Colored pencil on 1mm graph paper, 2006

85
Jill Ann, Ink on paper, 2005

86
Font sketch for *Snow Globe for Roman Olpalka*, 2011

87
Nesting prime palindrome printout. ROYGBIV sketch for failed paintings, 2013

89
Nesting prime palindromes CYM font glazing guide, 2013

90
List of prime numbers in base 7

91
Phil Ross, Ink on paper, drawn with a straight edge, 2005

92
Drawing on 1mm graph paper used for printed card announcement of solo show *3:07* at CANADA, 2012

93
Days Alive countdown 16661-16386, Ink on 1mm graph paper, 2007. Section used for a button edition by Jack Hanley Gallery.

95
ROYGBIV in 8 directions with 2 centers. Line number map for Sophie Germain primes paintings, 2010

97
Spiral rotations, Galway, Ireland, 2005

99
Glazing guide, 2013

100
11-digit prime numbers list in 2 columns

101
M.M. 12/21, Ink on paper, drawn with a straight edge, 2005

102
Fibonacci Sequence, colored pencil on black Xerox paper, 2002

103
Fibonacci sequence printout

104
Drawing for Shaydl. Colored pencil on 1mm graph paper, 2016

105
Sophie Germain prime palindromes printout

106
Pythagorean triangle border in expanding ROYGBIV. Sketch on 1mm graph paper for *Magic Square for Earthlings*, 2017

107
2458366, Wednesday, Truro, MA. Ink on 1mm graph paper, drawn with a straight edge, 2018

108
Folded list of 133 11-digit prime palindromes

109
2458365, Tuesday, Truro, MA. Ink on paper, 2018

111
Glazing guide, 2013

112-114
Give It A Go list of ideas to attempt in paintings 2007–10

115
Colored pencil grid on black Xerox paper, 2001

116
Sketch for *Nox Rex 23*, a map of the starting spoke and direction of wheel rotation, 2012

117
Sketch for *Family Vacation*, 2016

118
2457605, ink on paper, 2016

119
List of dates and days of the week of palindromic Julian Day Numbers. Notes for the drawing *1,000,000 days away*, 2009

120
Sketch for failed painting of seven 11-digit prime palindromes, 17776667771-17779997771, 2011

121
2457469, Tuesday, Puako, HI, 2016

122
A sectioned list of 7-digit prime palindromes. Sketch for *5:55*, 2010

123
Trianglehearts how to, 2017

125
ROYGBIV in 4 directions with 2 centers. Line number map for *Mood Chart*, 2010

126
2458228, Amtrak Train #379, Rocky Hill-Raleigh, 2018

127
Sketch for *Bomb Jr*, 2012

128
The sixty numbers that repeat in the ones column of the Fibonacci sequence, colored pencil study for a mural in Clarion Alley, SF, CA. 30 × 22 inches, 2003

130
Portrait of 1st four prime numbers, 2, 3, 5, 7, in Robert Indiana–style font, 2017

131
2456836 #2, Truro, MA, 2018

133
Content can be the subject of itself, drawing made during an artist lecture by Richard Tuttle

135
Sketch for *Black Rose*, 2009

137
3,727 digit prime palindromes, the third (in green) is the sum of first and second, 2010

139
Glazing guide and alarm clock font, 2014

140
The sixty numbers that repeat in the ones column of Fibonacci sequence arranged in a quadrant pinwheel. Sketch for *Candy Cake*, 2012

141
Number e

142
The sixty numbers that repeat in the ones column of the Fibonacci sequence. Quadrant Snakes search maps for zeros and fives alignments. Sketch for *Morpheus*, 2012

143
2458387, Tuesday, Truro, MA, 2018

145
Leap Second sketch, 2015

146
Grid guide for *Bombinating*, 2009

147
Chapters Alive

148
List of fourteen 7-digit prime palindrome favorites, 2013

149
7-digit prime numbers, ink on 1mm graph paper, 2012

150
Problems w/ painting list

151
Untitled for Planned Parenthood, 24 × 18 inches, 2016

152
Typewritten questionaire of *Time Survey* coinciding with my 20-year wrap-up in SF, 2009

153
Testate, 15769, 2007

155
Ones and Zeros sketch for *8th Order Magic Square in binary*, 2018

156
Nesting prime palindromes. Sketch for B.A. R.I.P., 2013

157
Sketch for wall drawing #22, 2006

159-161
Prime Julian Day numbers and their corresponding dates, created for *K48 #7 Starship Counterforce* produced by Scott Hug. Ink on 1mm graph paper, 2008

162
Double dot counting on a spiral, 2006

163
Map study for *Portrait of a Two*, 2016

165
Postal font study, 2014

167
Alarm clock font study, 2014

168
List of 7-digit prime palindromes 3400043-3222223 arranged in backward snake

169
3rd Order Magic Square, 2012

171
Sketch for Sophie Germain prime palindromes

13513	13523	13537	13553	13567	13577	13591	13597	13613	13619
13627	13633	13649	13669	13679	13681	13687	13691	13693	13697
13709	13711	13721	13723	13729	13751	13757	13759	13763	13781
13789	13799	13807	13829	13831	13841	13859	13873	13877	13879
13883	13901	13903	13907	13913	13921	13931	13933	13963	13967
13997	13999	14009	14011	14029	14033	14051	14057	14071	14081
14083	14087	14107	14143	14149	14153	14159	14173	14177	14197
14207	14221	14243	14249	14251	14281	14293	14303	14321	14323
14327	14341	14347	14369	14387	14389	14401	14407	14411	14419
14423	14431	14437	14447	14449	14461	14479	14489	14503	14519
14533	14537	14543	14549	14551	14557	14561	14563	14591	14593
14621	14627	14629	14633	14639	14653	14657	14669	14683	14699
14713	14717	14723	14731	14737	14741	14747	14753	14759	14767
14771	14779	14783	14797	14813	14821	14827	14831	14843	14851
14867	14869	14879	14887	14891	14897	14923	14929	14939	14947
14951	14957	14969	14983	15013	15017	15031	15053	15061	15073
15077	15083	15091	15101	15107	15121	15131	15137	15139	15149
15161	15173	15187	15193	15199	15217	15227	15233	15241	15259
15263	15269	15271	15277	15287	15289	15299	15307	15313	15319
15329	15331	15349	15359	15361	15373	15377	15383	15391	15401
15413	15427	15439	15443	15451	15461	15467	15473	15493	15497
15511	15527	15541	15551	15559	15569	15581	15583	15601	15607
15619	15629	15641	15643	15647	15649	15661	15667	15671	15679
15683	15727	15731	15733	15737	15739	15749	15761	15767	15773
15787	15791	15797	15803	15809	15817	15823	15859	15877	15881
15887	15889	15901	15907	15913	15919	15923	15937	15959	15971
15973	15991	16001	16007	16033	16057	16061	16063	16067	16069
16073	16087	16091	16097	16103	16111	16127	16139	16141	16183
16187	16189	16193	16217	16223	16229	16231	16249	16253	16267
16273	16301	16319	16333	16339	16349	16361	16363	16369	16381
16411	16417	16421	16427	16433	16447	16451	16453	16477	16481
16487	16493	16519	16529	16547	16553	16561	16567	16573	16603
16607	16619	16631	16633	16649	16651	16657	16661	16673	16691
16693	16699	16703	16729	16741	16747	16759	16763	16787	16811
16823	16829	16831	16843	16871	16879	16883	16889	16901	16903
16921	16927	16931	16937	16943	16963	16979	16981	16987	16993
17011	17021	17027	17029	17033	17041	17047	17053	17077	17093
17099	17107	17117	17123	17137	17159	17167	17183	17189	17191
17203	17207	17209	17231	17239	17257	17291	17293	17299	17317
17321	17327	17333	17341	17351	17359	17377	17383	17387	17389
17393	17401	17417	17419	17431	17443	17449	17467	17471	17477
17483	17489	17491	17497	17509	17519	17539	17551	17569	17573
17579	17581	17597	17599	17609	17623	17627	17657	17659	17669
17681	17683	17707	17713	17729	17737	17747	17749	17761	17783
17789	17791	17807	17827	17837	17839	17851	17863	17881	17891
17903	17909	17911	17921	17923	17929	17939	17957	17959	17971
17977	17981	17987	17989	18013	18041	18043	18047	18049	18059
18061	18077	18089	18097	18119	18121	18127	18131	18133	18143
18149	18169	18181	18191	18199	18211	18217	18223	18229	18233
18251	18253	18257	18269	18287	18289	18301	18307	18311	18313
18329	18341	18353	18367	18371	18379	18397	18401	18413	18427
18433	18439	18443	18451	18457	18461	18481	18493	18503	18517
18521	18523	18539	18541	18553	18583	18587	18593	18617	18637
18661	18671	18679	18691	18701	18713	18719	18731	18743	18749
18757	18773	18787	18793	18797	18803	18839	18859	18869	18899

18911 18913 18917 18919 18947 18959 18973 18979 19001 19009
19013 19031 19037 19051 19069 19073 19079 19081 19087 19121
19139 19141 19157 19163 19181 19183 19207 19211 19213 19219
19231 19237 19249 19259 19267 19273 19289 19301 19309 19319
19333 19373 19379 19381 19387 19391 19403 19417 19421 19423
19427 19429 19433 19441 19447 19457 19463 19469 19471 19477
19483 19489 19501 19507 19531 19541 19543 19553 19559 19571
19577 19583 19597 19603 19609 19661 19681 19687 19697 19699
19709 19717 19727 19739 19751 19753 19759 19763 19777 19793
19801 19813 19819 19841 19843 19853 19861 19867 19889 19891
19913 19919 19927 19937 19949 19961 19963 19973 19979 19991
19993 19997 20011 20021 20023 20029 20047 20051 20063 20071
20089 20101 20107 20113 20117 20123 20129 20143 20147 20149
20161 20173 20177 20183 20201 20219 20231 20233 20249 20261
20269 20287 20297 20323 20327 20333 20341 20347 20353 20357
20359 20369 20389 20393 20399 20407 20411 20431 20441 20443
20477 20479 20483 20507 20509 20521 20533 20543 20549 20551
20563 20593 20599 20611 20627 20639 20641 20663 20681 20693
20707 20717 20719 20731 20743 20747 20749 20753 20759 20771
20773 20789 20807 20809 20849 20857 20873 20879 20887 20897
20899 20903 20921 20929 20939 20947 20959 20963 20981 20983
21001 21011 21013 21017 21019 21023 21031 21059 21061 21067
21089 21101 21107 21121 21139 21143 21149 21157 21163 21169
21179 21187 21191 21193 21211 21221 21227 21247 21269 21277
21283 21313 21317 21319 21323 21341 21347 21377 21379 21383
21391 21397 21401 21407 21419 21433 21467 21481 21487 21491
21493 21499 21503 21517 21521 21523 21529 21557 21559 21563
21569 21577 21587 21589 21599 21601 21611 21613 21617 21647
21649 21661 21673 21683 21701 21713 21727 21737 21739 21751
21757 21767 21773 21787 21799 21803 21817 21821 21839 21841
21851 21859 21863 21871 21881 21893 21911 21929 21937 21943
21961 21977 21991 21997 22003 22013 22027 22031 22037 22039
22051 22063 22067 22073 22079 22091 22093 22109 22111 22123
22129 22133 22147 22153 22157 22159 22171 22189 22193 22229
22247 22259 22271 22273 22277 22279 22283 22291 22303 22307
22343 22349 22367 22369 22381 22391 22397 22409 22433 22441
22447 22453 22469 22481 22483 22501 22511 22531 22541 22543
22549 22567 22571 22573 22613 22619 22621 22637 22639 22643
22651 22669 22679 22691 22697 22699 22709 22717 22721 22727
22739 22741 22751 22769 22777 22783 22787 22807 22811 22817
22853 22859 22861 22871 22877 22901 22907 22921 22937 22943
22961 22963 22973 22993 23003 23011 23017 23021 23027 23029
23039 23041 23053 23057 23059 23063 23071 23081 23087 23099
23117 23131 23143 23159 23167 23173 23189 23197 23201 23203
23209 23227 23251 23269 23279 23291 23293 23297 23311 23321
23327 23333 23339 23357 23369 23371 23399 23417 23431 23447
23459 23473 23497 23509 23531 23537 23539 23549 23557 23561
23563 23567 23581 23593 23599 23603 23609 23623 23627 23629
23633 23663 23669 23671 23677 23687 23689 23719 23741 23743
23747 23753 23761 23767 23773 23789 23801 23813 23819 23827
23831 23833 23857 23869 23873 23879 23887 23893 23899 23909
23911 23917 23929 23957 23971 23977 23981 23993 24001 24007
24019 24023 24029 24043 24049 24061 24071 24077 24083 24091
24097 24103 24107 24109 24113 24121 24133 24137 24151 24169
24179 24181 24197 24203 24223 24229 24239 24247 24251 24281

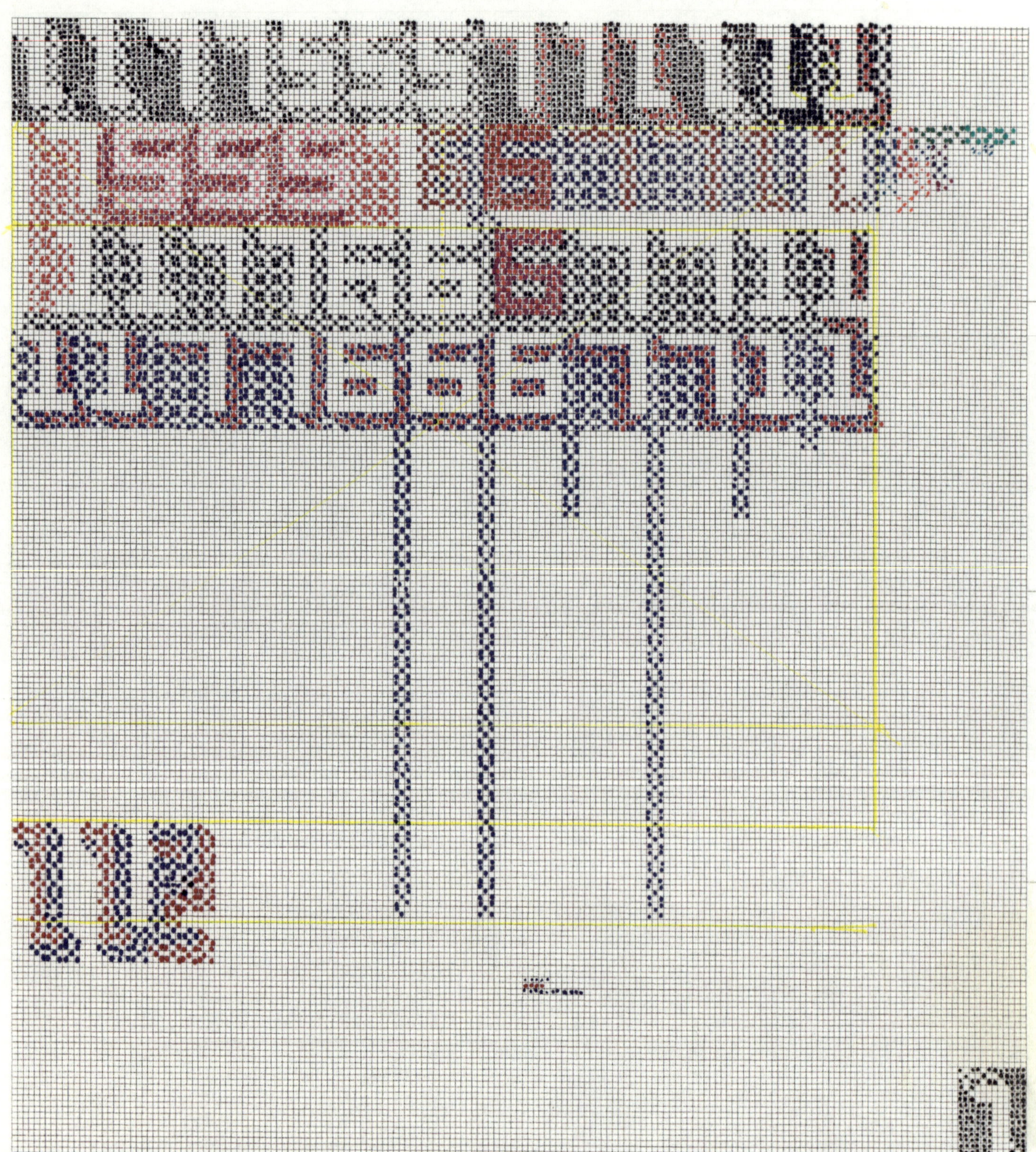

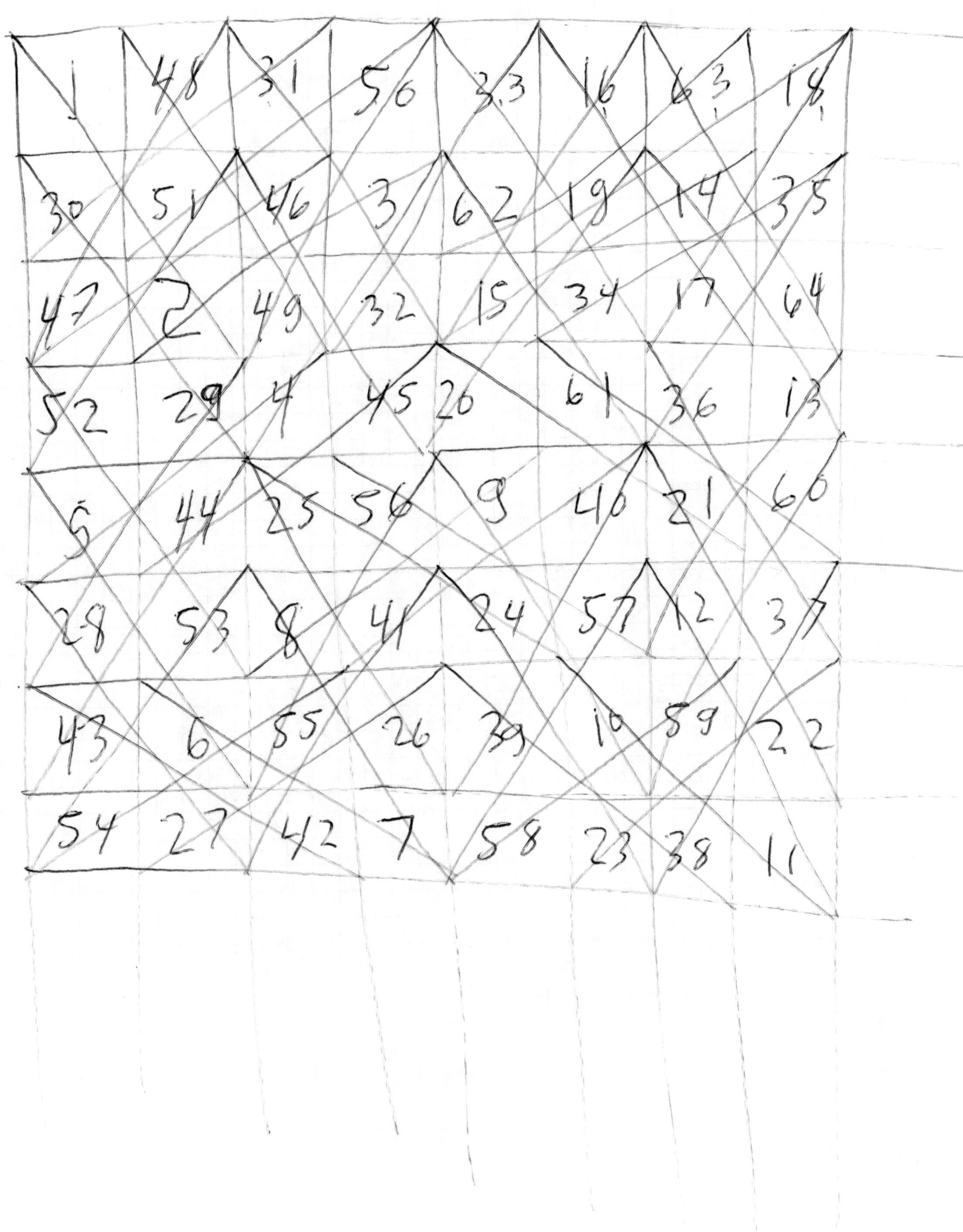
1 48 31 56 33 16 63 18
30 51 46 3 62 19 14 35
47 2 49 32 15 34 17 64
52 29 4 45 20 61 36 13
5 44 25 56 9 40 21 60
28 53 8 41 24 57 12 37
43 6 55 26 39 10 59 22
54 27 42 7 58 23 38 11

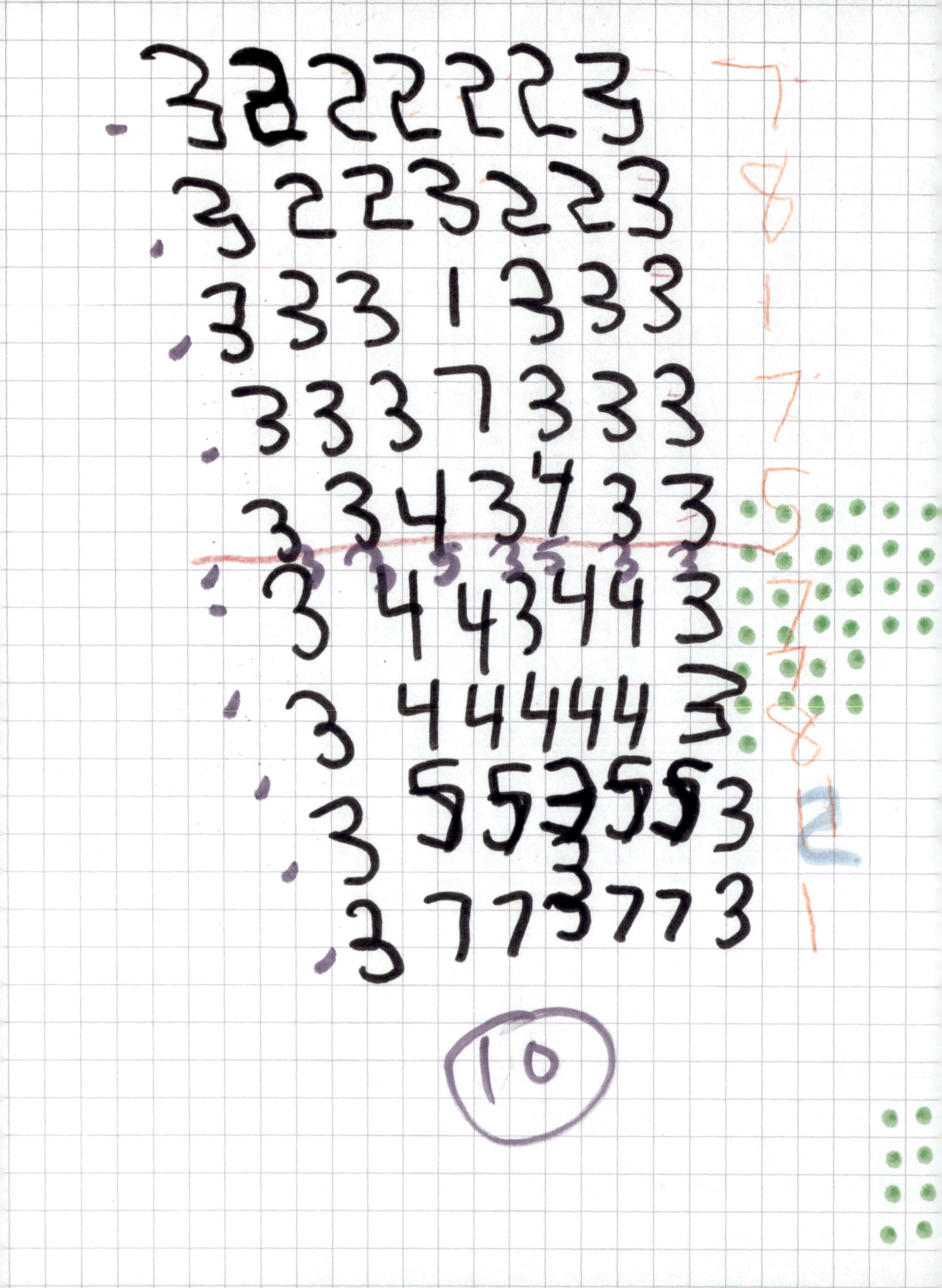

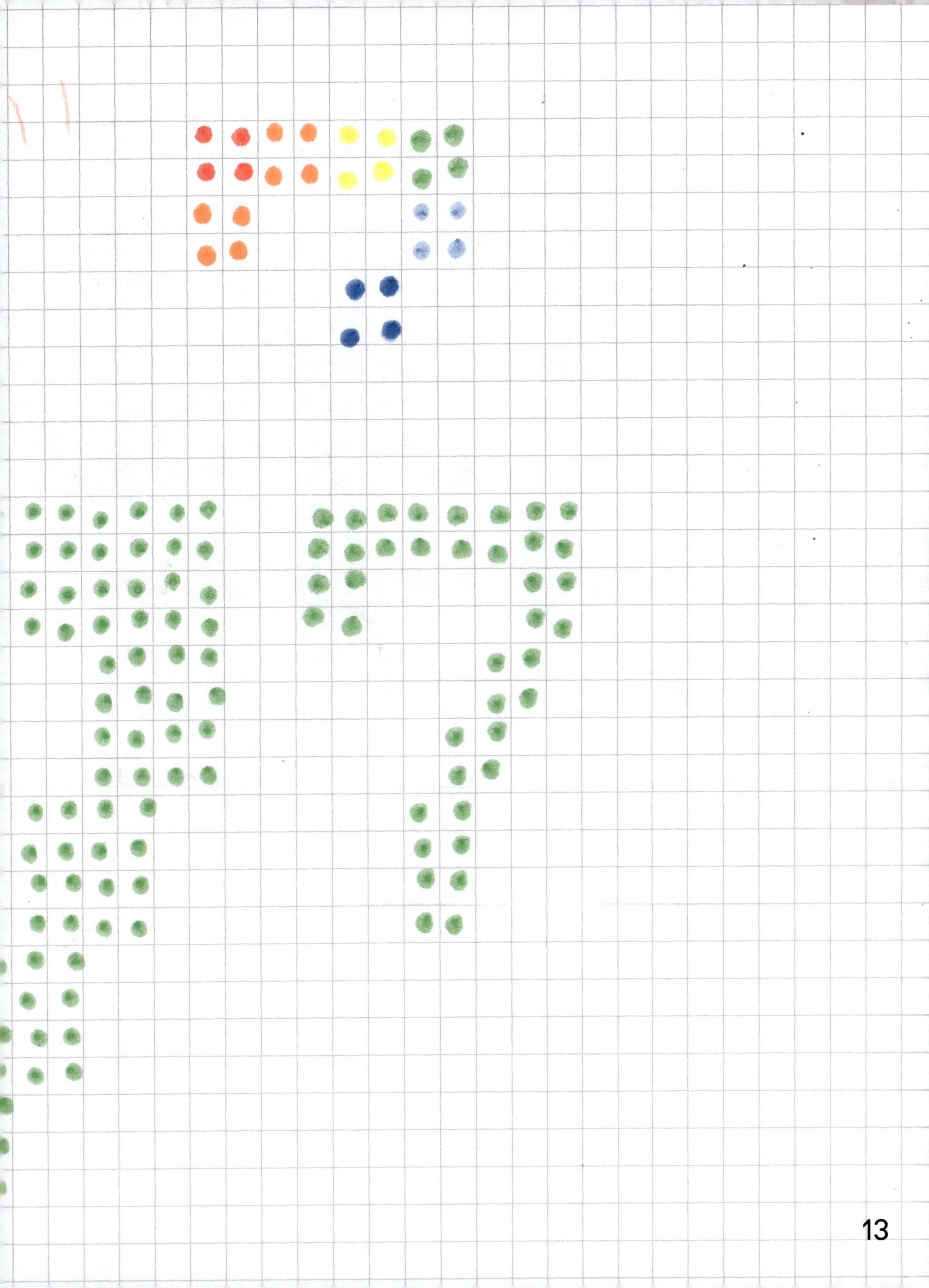

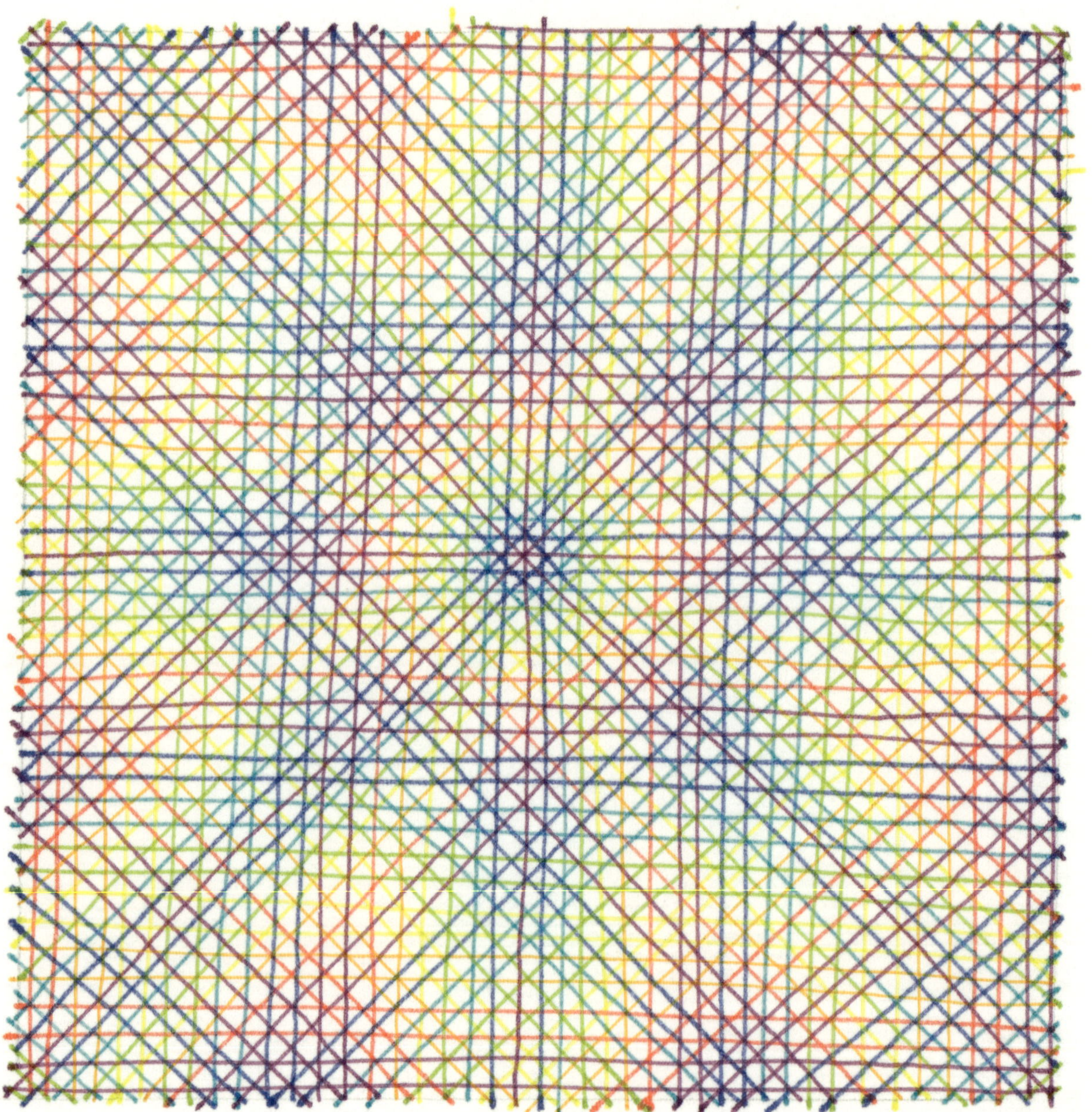

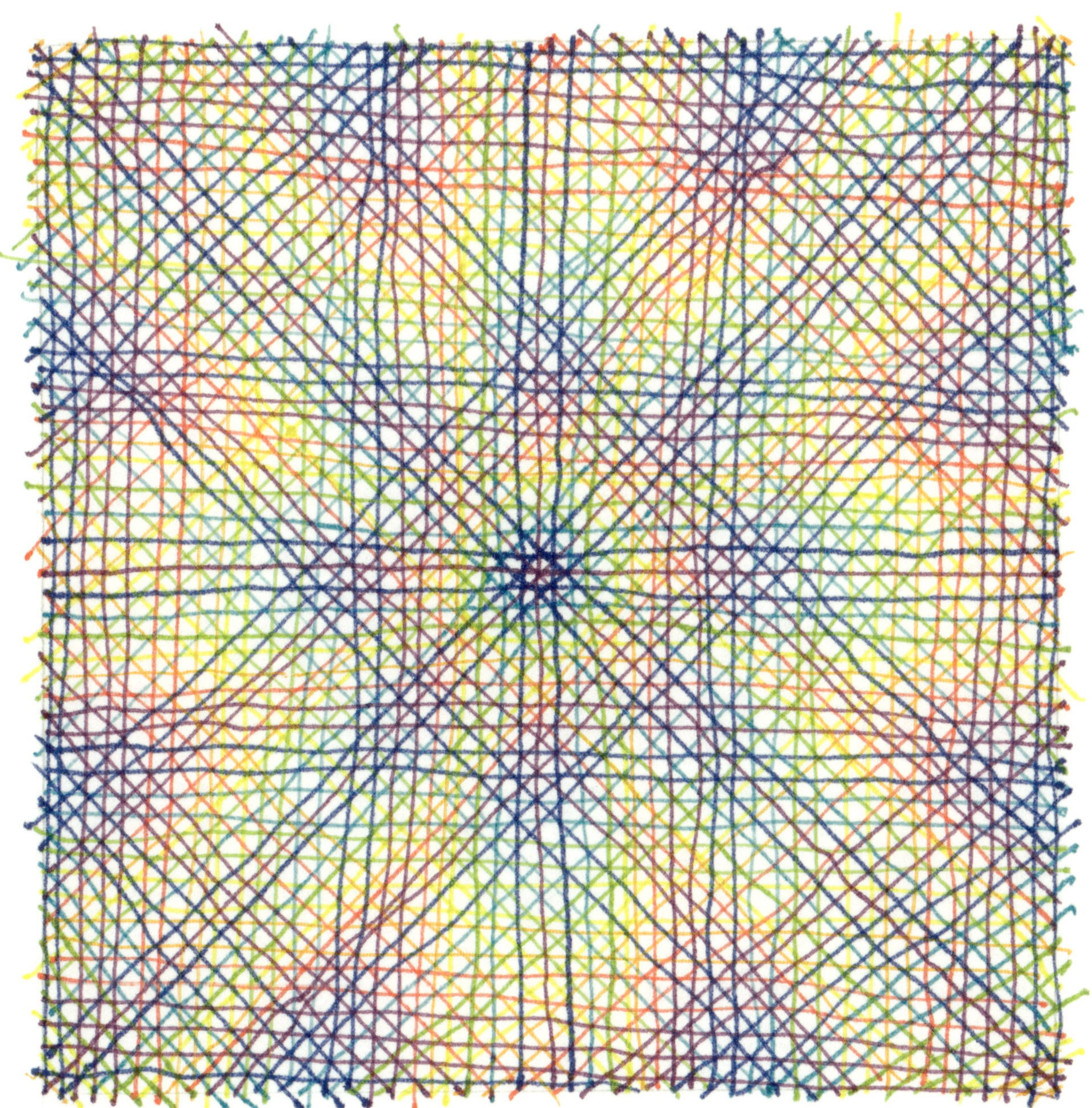

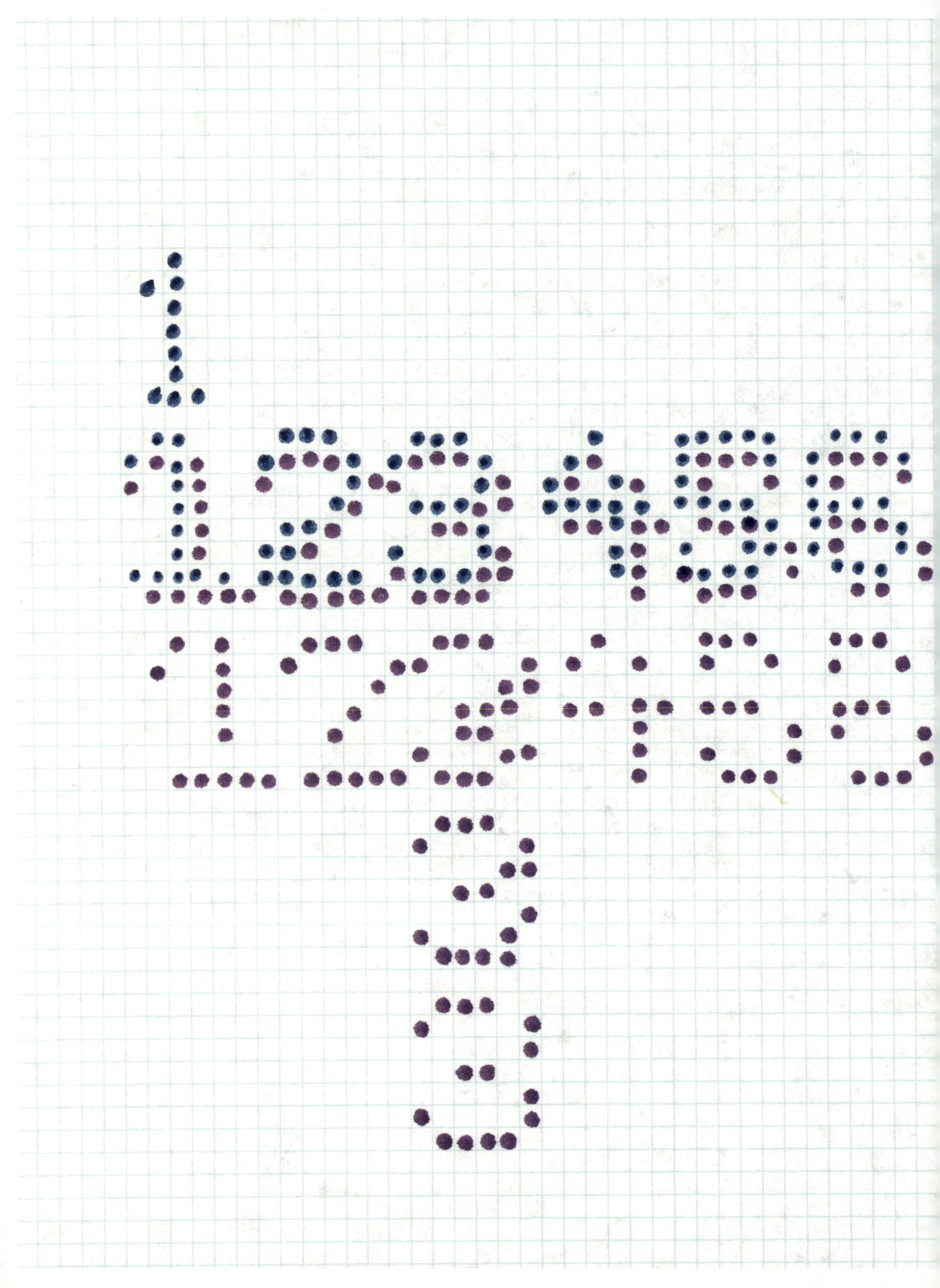

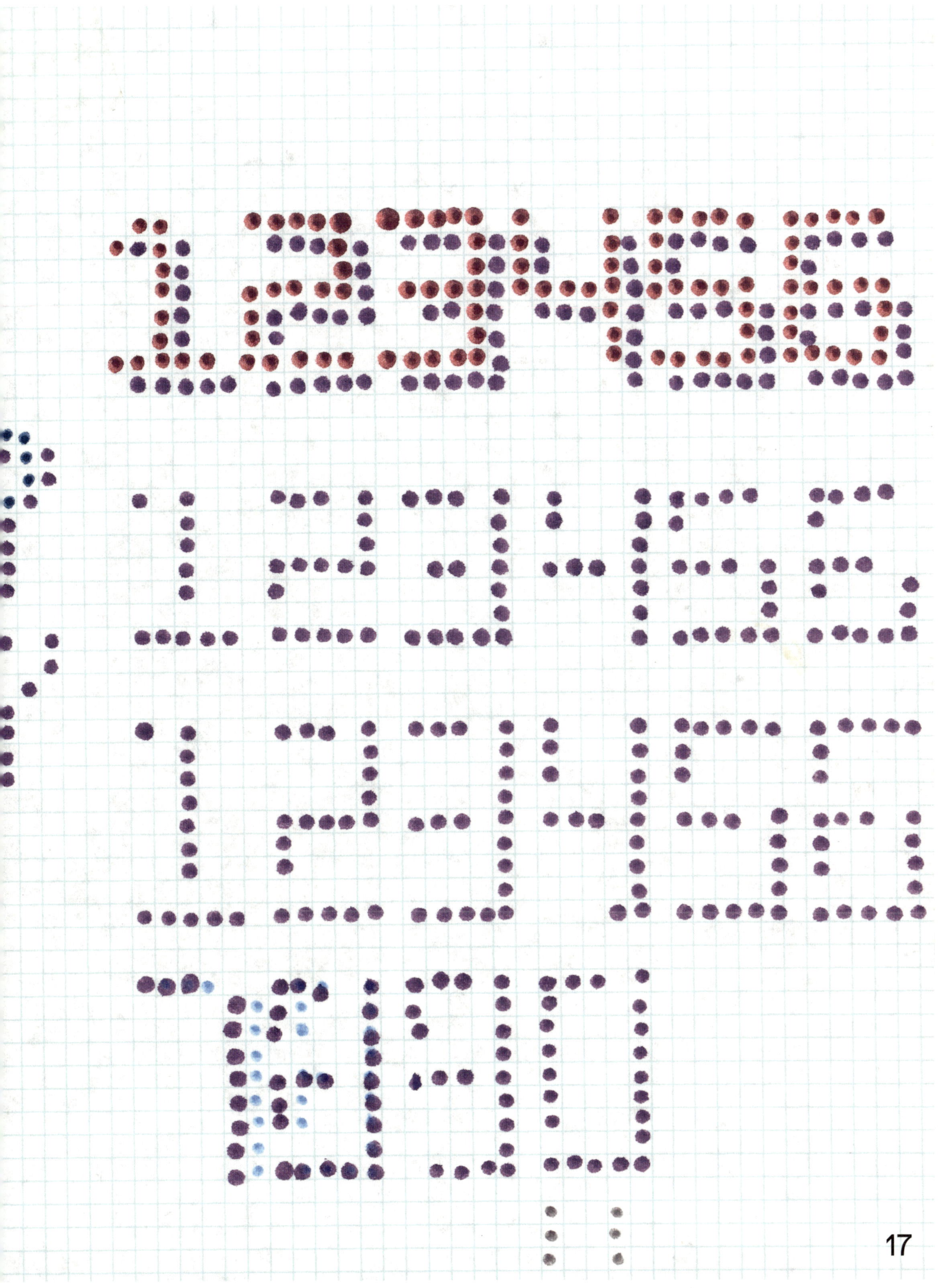

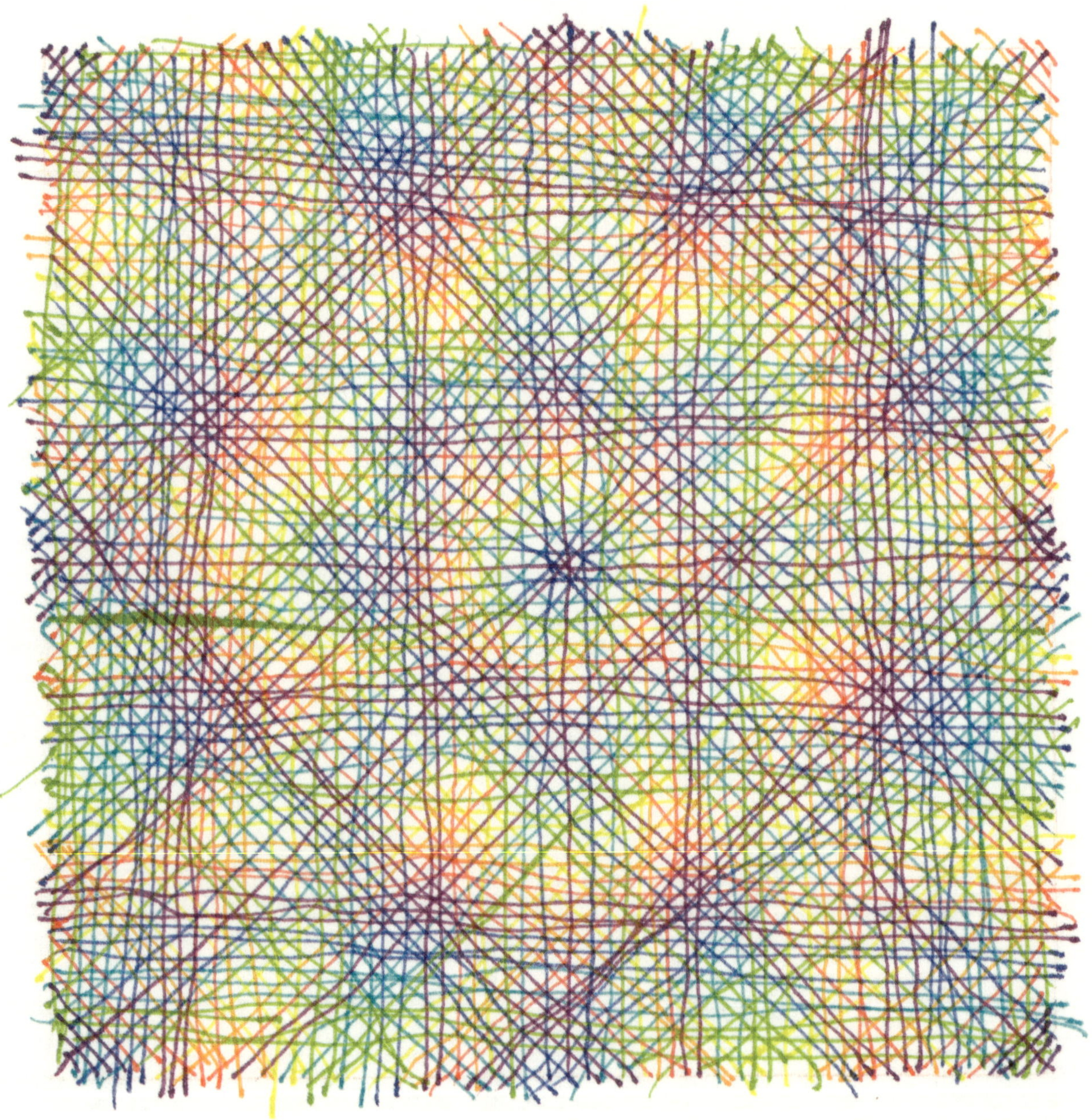

1999 03 21 01:46:53 TD 1999 03 21 01:45:49 UT	1999 06 21 19:50:11 TD 1999 06 21 19:49:07 UT	1999 09 23 11:32:34 TD 1999 09 23 11:31:31 UT	1999 12 22 07:44:52 TD 1999 12 22 07:43:49 UT
2000 03 20 07:36:19 TD 2000 03 20 07:35:15 UT	2000 06 21 01:48:47 TD 2000 06 21 01:47:43 UT	2000 09 22 17:28:39 TD 2000 09 22 17:27:35 UT	2000 12 21 13:38:30 TD 2000 12 21 13:37:26 UT
2001 03 20 13:31:47 TD 2001 03 20 13:30:40 UT	2001 06 21 07:38:47 TD 2001 06 21 07:37:41 UT	2001 09 22 23:05:32 TD 2001 09 22 23:04:26 UT	2001 12 21 19:22:34 TD 2001 12 21 19:21:27 UT
2002 03 20 19:17:13 TD 2002 03 20 19:16:05 UT	2002 06 21 13:25:29 TD 2002 06 21 13:24:21 UT	2002 09 23 04:56:28 TD 2002 09 23 04:55:20 UT	2002 12 22 01:15:27 TD 2002 12 22 01:14:19 UT
2003 03 21 01:00:50 TD 2003 03 21 00:59:41 UT	2003 06 21 19:11:32 TD 2003 06 21 19:10:23 UT	2003 09 23 10:47:53 TD 2003 09 23 10:46:44 UT	2003 12 22 07:04:53 TD 2003 12 22 07:03:43 UT
2004 03 20 06:49:42 TD 2004 03 20 06:48:32 UT	2004 06 21 00:57:56 TD 2004 06 21 00:56:46 UT	2004 09 22 16:30:54 TD 2004 09 22 16:29:44 UT	2004 12 21 12:42:41 TD 2004 12 21 12:41:30 UT
2005 03 20 12:34:30 TD 2005 03 20 12:33:18 UT	2005 06 21 06:47:12 TD 2005 06 21 06:46:00 UT	2005 09 22 22:24:14 TD 2005 09 22 22:23:02 UT	2005 12 21 18:36:01 TD 2005 12 21 18:34:49 UT
2006 03 20 18:26:39 TD 2006 03 20 18:25:26 UT	2006 06 21 12:26:56 TD 2006 06 21 12:25:43 UT	2006 09 23 04:04:27 TD 2006 09 23 04:03:13 UT	2006 12 22 00:23:10 TD 2006 12 22 00:21:57 UT
2007 03 21 00:08:30 TD 2007 03 21 00:07:15 UT	2007 06 21 18:07:30 TD 2007 06 21 18:06:16 UT	2007 09 23 09:52:18 TD 2007 09 23 09:51:04 UT	2007 12 22 06:08:54 TD 2007 12 22 06:07:39 UT
2008 03 20 05:49:23 TD 2008 03 20 05:48:07 UT	2008 06 21 00:00:27 TD 2008 06 20 23:59:11 UT	2008 09 22 15:45:34 TD 2008 09 22 15:44:18 UT	2008 12 21 12:04:51 TD 2008 12 21 12:03:34 UT
2009 03 20 11:44:44 TD 2009 03 20 11:43:26 UT	2009 06 21 05:46:37 TD 2009 06 21 05:45:19 UT	2009 09 22 21:19:41 TD 2009 09 22 21:18:23 UT	2009 12 21 17:47:53 TD 2009 12 21 17:46:36 UT
2010 03 20 17:33:18 TD 2010 03 20 17:31:59 UT	2010 06 21 11:29:31 TD 2010 06 21 11:28:11 UT	2010 09 23 03:10:08 TD 2010 09 23 03:08:48 UT	2010 12 21 23:39:34 TD 2010 12 21 23:38:15 UT
2011 03 20 23:21:50 TD 2011 03 20 23:20:29 UT	2011 06 21 17:17:36 TD 2011 06 21 17:16:16 UT	2011 09 23 09:05:44 TD 2011 09 23 09:04:23 UT	2011 12 22 05:31:09 TD 2011 12 22 05:29:48 UT
2012 03 20 05:15:32 TD 2012 03 20 05:14:09 UT	2012 06 20 23:09:55 TD 2012 06 20 23:08:32 UT	2012 09 22 14:50:05 TD 2012 09 22 14:48:43 UT	2012 12 21 11:12:43 TD 2012 12 21 11:11:21 UT
2013 03 20 11:03:02 TD 2013 03 20 11:01:38 UT	2013 06 21 05:05:04 TD 2013 06 21 05:03:40 UT	2013 09 22 20:45:15 TD 2013 09 22 20:43:51 UT	2013 12 21 17:12:07 TD 2013 12 21 17:10:44 UT
2014 03 20 16:58:12 TD 2014 03 20 16:56:48 UT	2014 06 21 10:52:21 TD 2014 06 21 10:50:56 UT	2014 09 23 02:30:11 TD 2014 09 23 02:28:46 UT	2014 12 21 23:04:08 TD 2014 12 21 23:02:43 UT
2015 03 20 22:46:16 TD 2015 03 20 22:44:49 UT	2015 06 21 16:39:02 TD 2015 06 21 16:37:36 UT	2015 09 23 08:21:40 TD 2015 09 23 08:20:14 UT	2015 12 22 04:49:04 TD 2015 12 22 04:47:38 UT
2016 03 20 04:31:19 TD 2016 03 20 04:29:51 UT	2016 06 20 22:35:18 TD 2016 06 20 22:33:51 UT	2016 09 22 14:22:15 TD 2016 09 22 14:20:47 UT	2016 12 21 10:45:18 TD 2016 12 21 10:43:50 UT
2017 03 20 10:29:46 TD 2017 03 20 10:28:17 UT	2017 06 21 04:25:17 TD 2017 06 21 04:23:48 UT	2017 09 22 20:02:56 TD 2017 09 22 20:01:26 UT	2017 12 21 16:29:05 TD 2017 12 21 16:27:35 UT
2018 03 20 16:16:35 TD 2018 03 20 16:15:05 UT	2018 06 21 10:08:26 TD 2018 06 21 10:06:55 UT	2018 09 23 01:55:14 TD 2018 09 23 01:53:43 UT	2018 12 21 22:23:52 TD 2018 12 21 22:22:22 UT
2019 03 20 21:59:34 TD 2019 03 20 21:58:02 UT	2019 06 21 15:55:23 TD 2019 06 21 15:53:51 UT	2019 09 23 07:51:18 TD 2019 09 23 07:49:46 UT	2019 12 22 04:20:34 TD 2019 12 22 04:19:02 UT
2020 03 20 03:50:45 TD	2020 06 20 21:44:49 TD	2020 09 22 13:31:47 TD	2020 12 21 10:03:28 TD

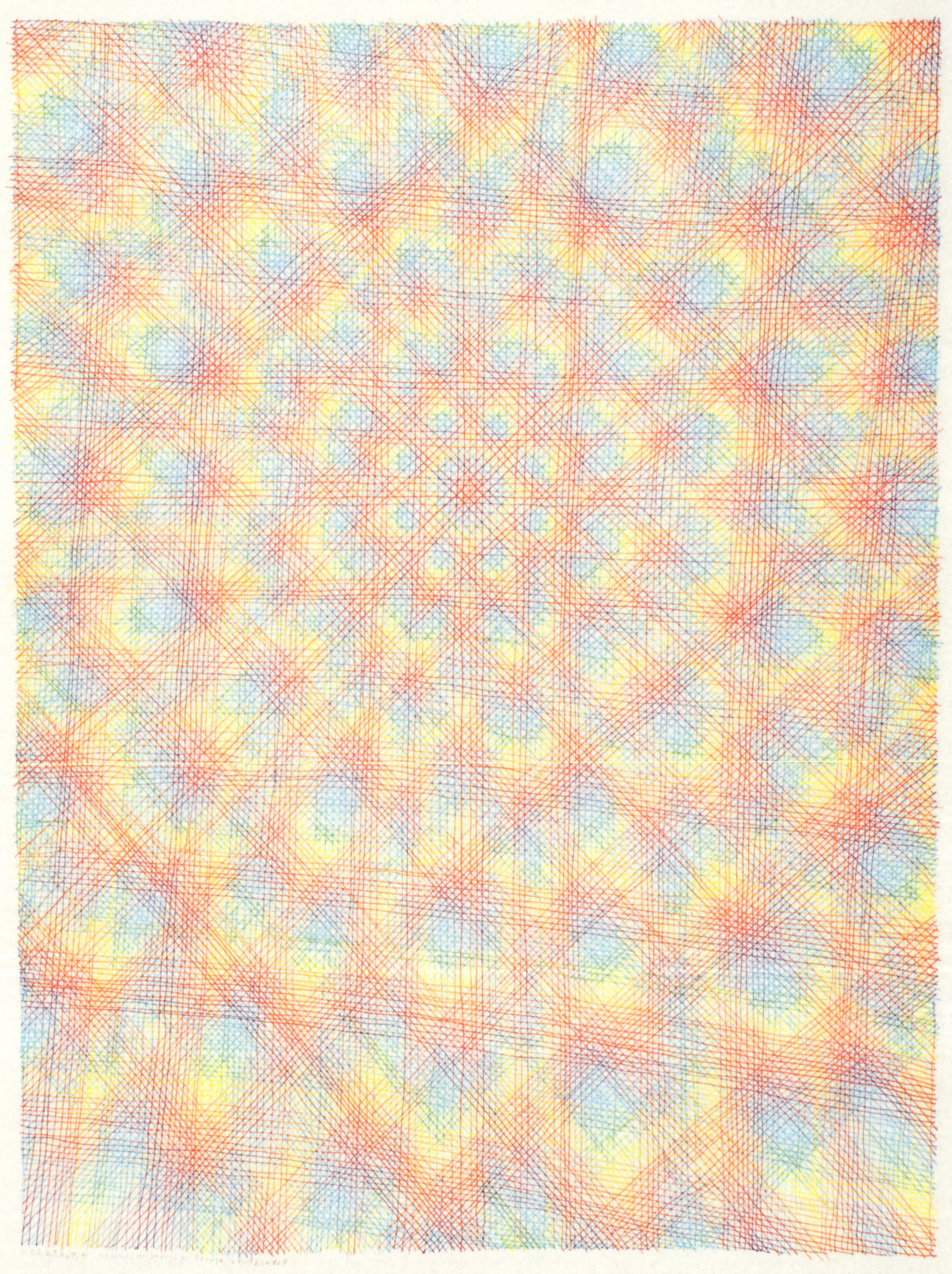

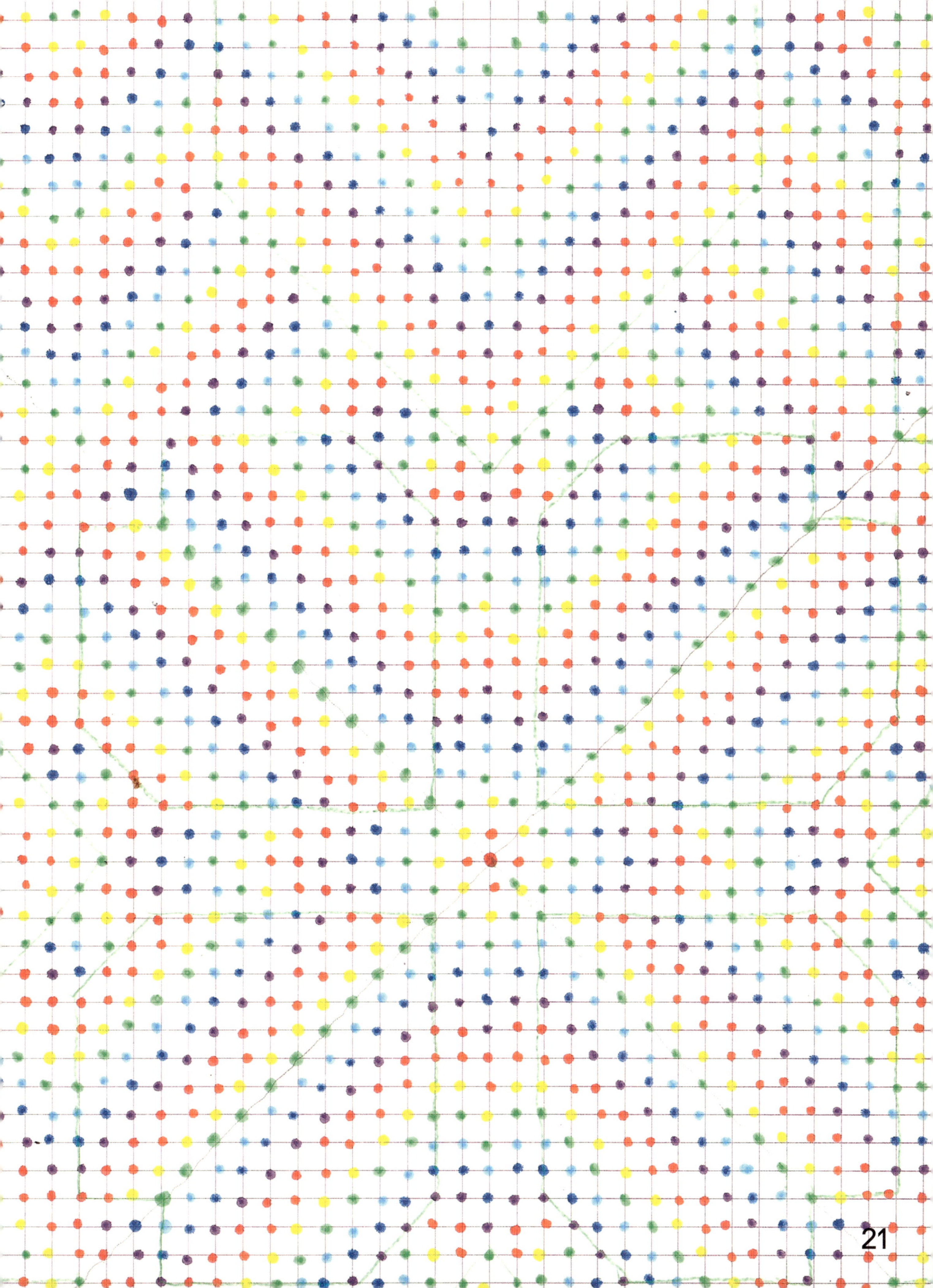

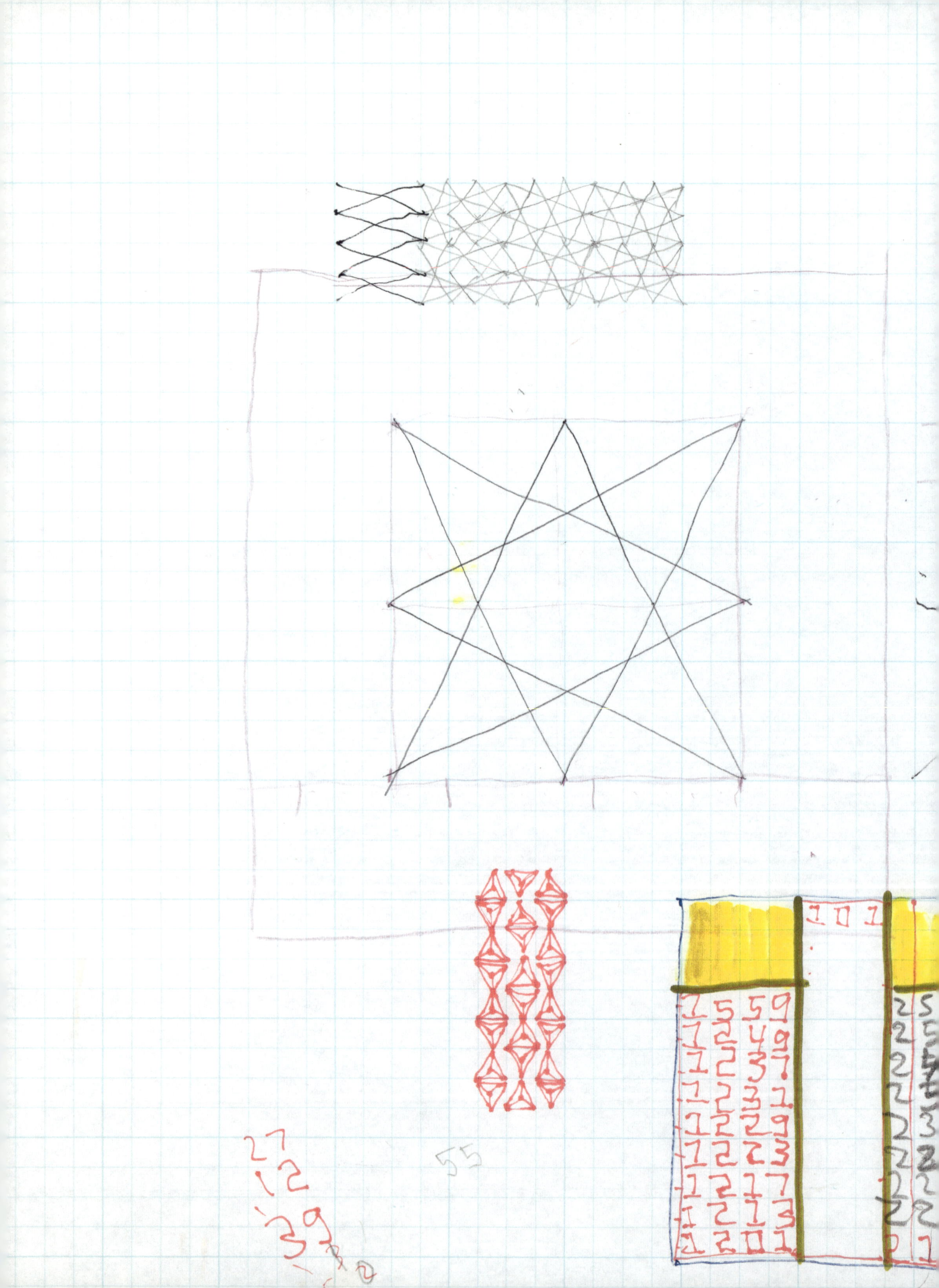

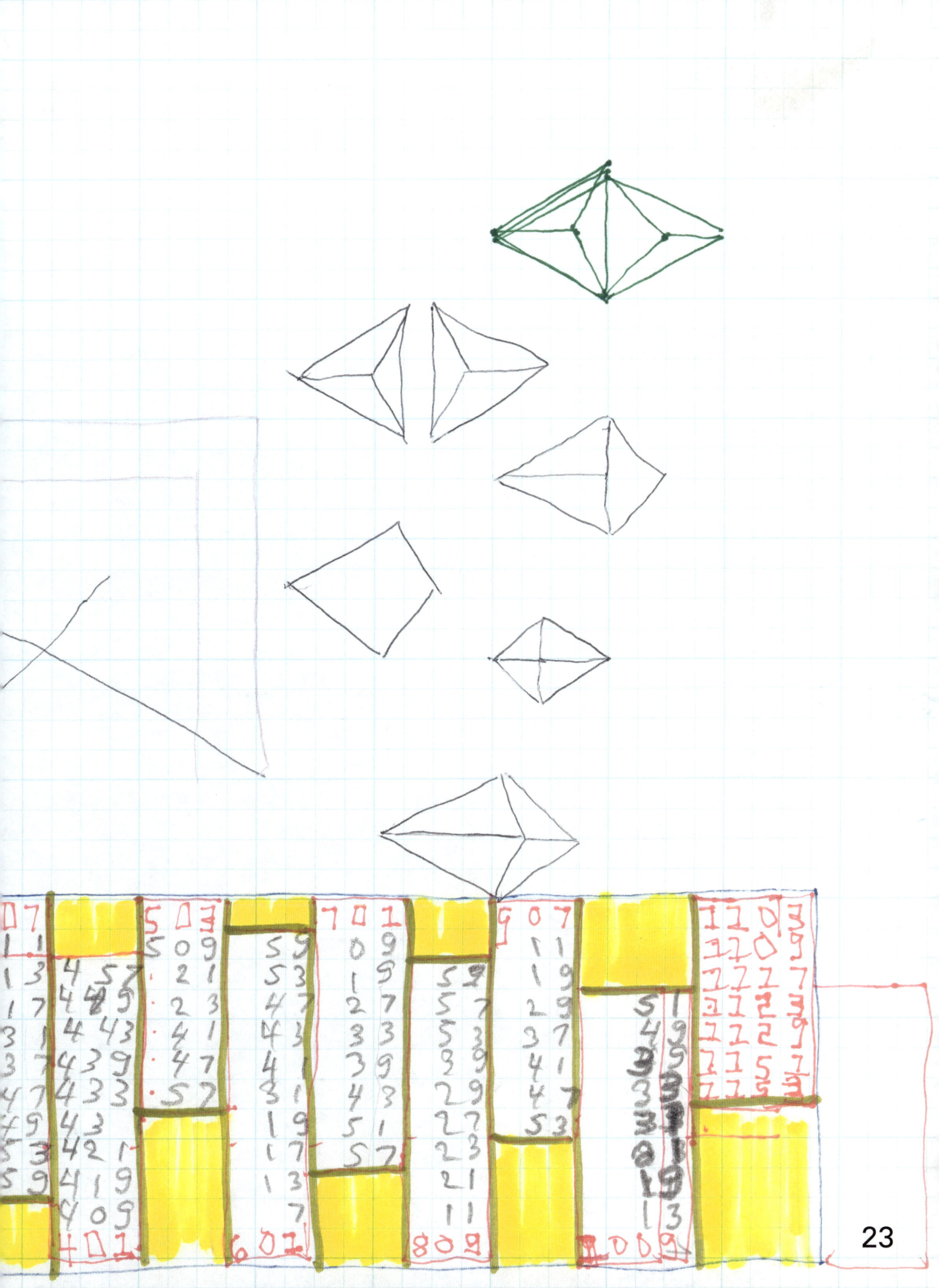

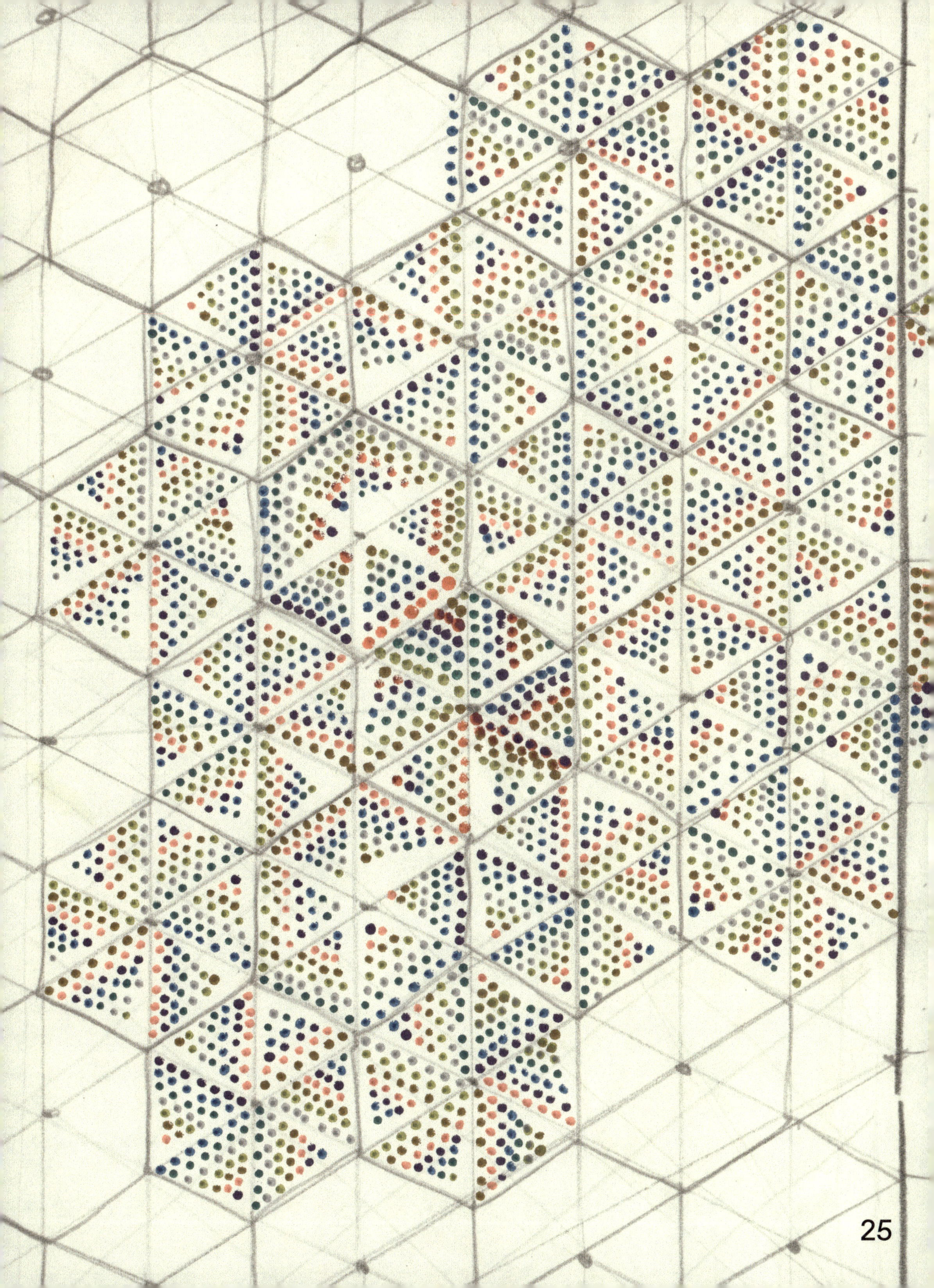

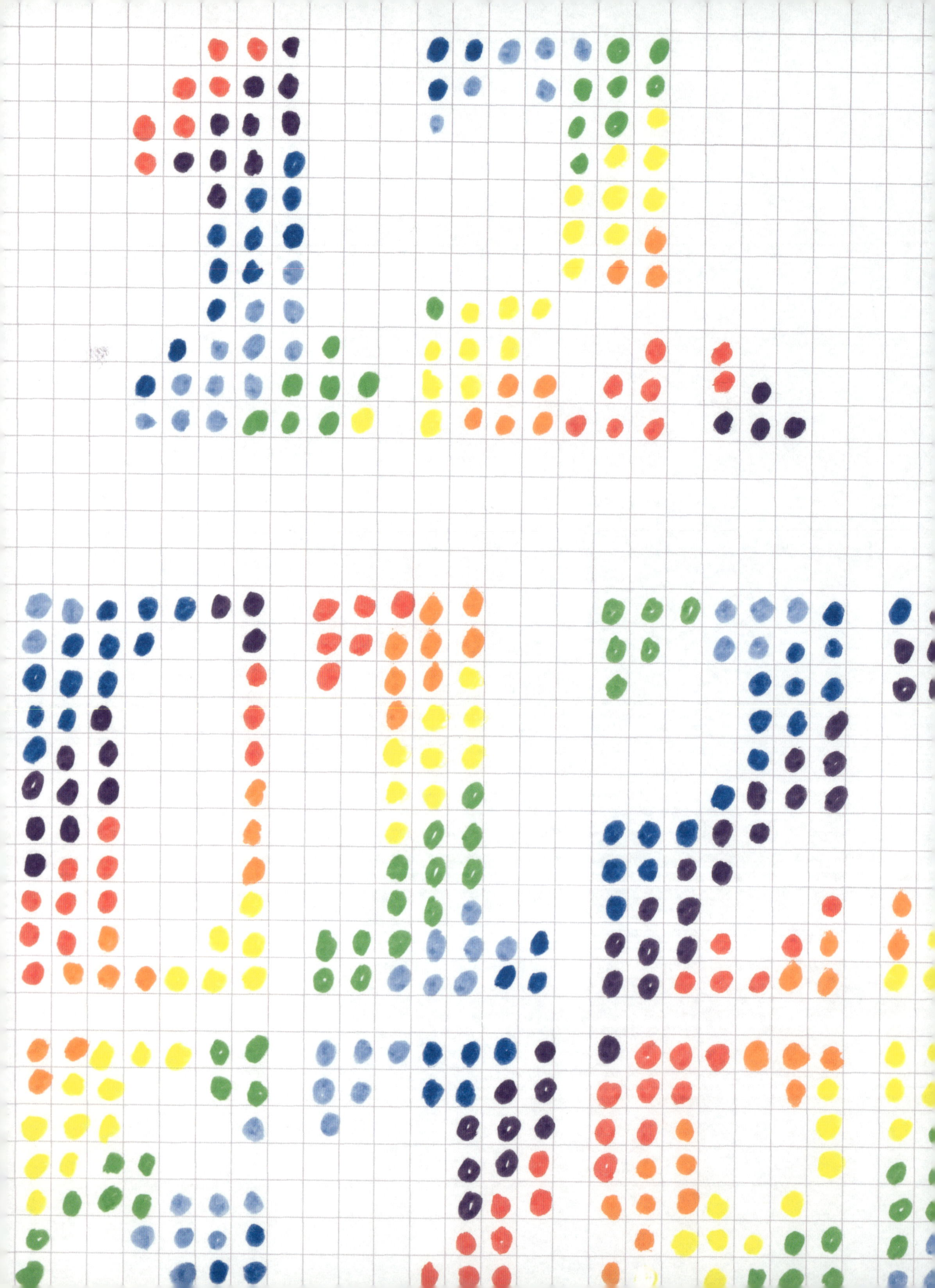

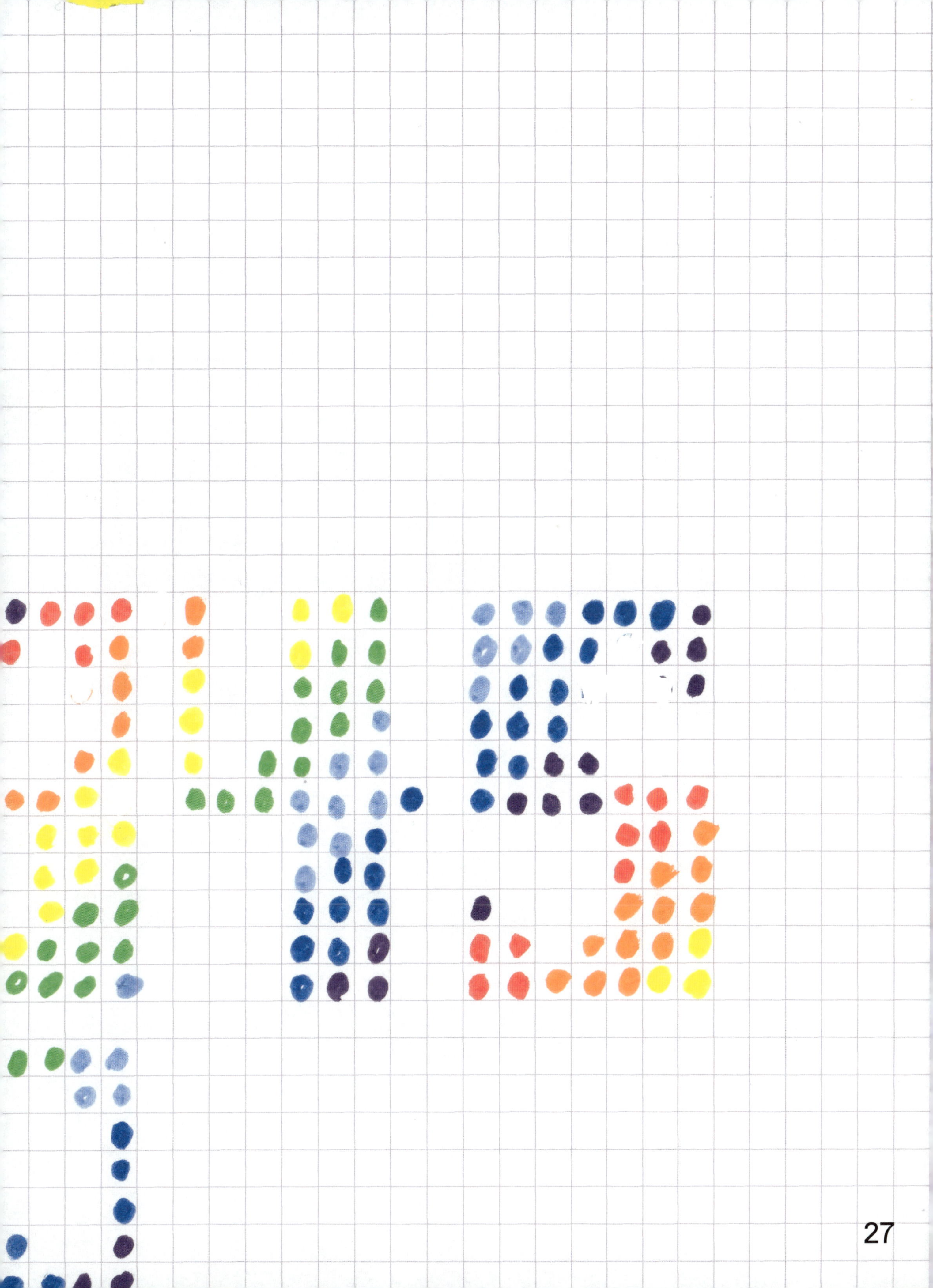

11:11 515 1111 ·3113 3133 3113 ·7117 7177 7117 ·9191 9191919

1111 777 1111 ·3133 3333 3313 ·7117 7777 7117 ·9199 1119919

1111 999 1111 ·3232 323 2323 ·7222 2722 2227 ·9222 2922 2229

1114 141 4111 ·3311 313 1133 ·7277 7777 727 ·9229 9299229

1115 111 5111 ·3333 535 3333 ·7333 7773 337 ·9444 494 4449

1115 555 5111 ·3337 737 7333 ·7337 3337 337 ·9494 444 4949

1118 888 8111 ·3355 333 5533 ·7373 3733 737 ·5499 494 9949

1115 919 9111 ·3434 3334343 ·7444 444 4447 ·9555 959 5559

1141 444 1411 ·3443 444 3443 ·7474 777 4747 ·9559 959 9559

1151 111 1511 ·3444 434 4443 ·7555 555 5557 ·9599 999 9959

1188 181 8811 ·3553 333 3553 ·7557 757 7557 ·9777 979 7779

1199 111 9911 ·3555 353 5553 ·7667 676 7667 ·9888 898 8889

1159 91999 11 ·3737 3337 373 ·771111 1177 ·9898 888 8989

1212 1 2121 21 ·3777 737 7773 ·7717 71771 77 ·9922 222 2299

1222 212 2221 ·3833333383 ·7733 777 3377 ·9944 999 4499

1311 131 1131 ·3838 888 8383 ·774 7474 7477 ·9955 555 5599

1311 313 1131 ·3888 383 8883 ·7747 7777 477 ·9959 555 9599

1313 111 3131 ·7767 7767 77 ·9959 9999 599

1333 111 3331 ·7777 272 7777 ·9988 8888 899

1411 111 1141 ·7777 767 7777 ·9991 1911 1999

1414 141 4141 ·7777 878 7777 ·9992 9992 999

1777 717 7771 ·7777 999 7777 ·9994 999 4999

1811 111 1181 ·7788 7878 877 ·9995 5955 599

1811 [illegible]88 1181 7878878787 ·9998 8988 999

1881 8181 881 7888 878 8887 9995 8989 999

1919 9999 191

9999 9199 999

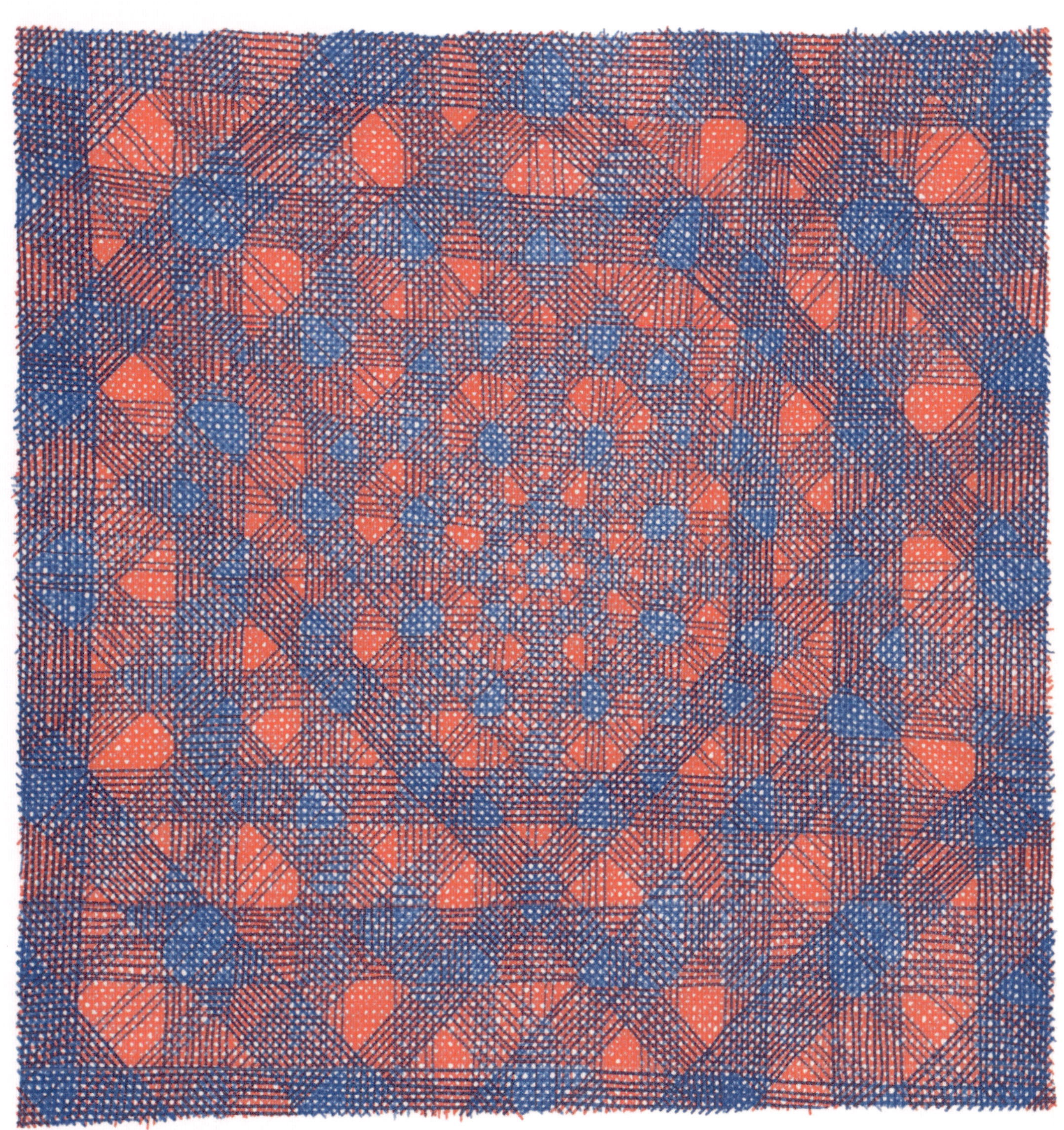

First 10,000 Digits of the Golden Ratio

This is the first publication of the Golden Ratio to 10,000 digits. If you know of an earlier one, please . How was this done? There's

We're now listed as a (search for "gold")!

```
1.61803 39887 49894 84820 45868 34365 63811 77203 09179 80576
  28621 35448 62270 52604 62818 90244 97072 07204 18939 11374
  84754 08807 53868 91752 12663 38622 23536 93179 31800 60766
  72635 44333 89086 59593 95829 05638 32266 13199 28290 26788
  06752 08766 89250 17116 96207 03222 10432 16269 54862 62963
  13614 43814 97587 01220 34080 58879 54454 74924 61856 95364
  86444 92410 44320 77134 49470 49565 84678 85098 74339 44221
  25448 77066 47809 15884 60749 98871 24007 65217 05751 79788
  34166 25624 94075 89069 70400 02812 10427 62177 11177 78053
  15317 14101 17046 66599 14669 79873 17613 56006 70874 80710
  13179 52368 94275 21948 43530 56783 00228 78569 97829 77834
  78458 78228 91109 76250 03026 96156 17002 50464 33824 37764
  86102 83831 26833 03724 29267 52631 16533 92473 16711 12115
  88186 38513 31620 38400 52221 65791 28667 52946 54906 81131
  71599 34323 59734 94985 09040 94762 13222 98101 72610 70596
  11645 62990 98162 90555 20852 47903 52406 02017 27997 47175
  34277 75927 78625 61943 20827 50513 12181 56285 51222 48093
  94712 34145 17022 37358 05772 78616 00868 83829 52304 59264
  78780 17889 92199 02707 76903 89532 19681 98615 14378 03149
  97411 06926 08867 42962 26757 56052 31727 77520 35361 39362
  10767 38937 64556 06060 59216 58946 67595 51900 40055 59089
  50229 53094 23124 82355 21221 24154 44006 47034 05657 34797
  66397 23949 49946 58457 88730 39623 09037 50339 93856 21024
  23690 25138 68041 45779 95698 12244 57471 78034 17312 64532
  20416 39723 21340 44449 48730 23154 17676 89375 21030 68737
  88034 41700 93954 40962 79558 98678 72320 95124 26893 55730
  97045 09595 68440 17555 19881 92180 20640 52905 51893 49475
  92600 73485 22821 01088 19464 45442 22318 89131 92946 89622
  00230 14437 70269 92300 78030 85261 18075 45192 88770 50210
  96842 49362 71359 25187 60777 88466 58361 50238 91349 33331
  22310 53392 32136 24319 26372 89106 70503 39928 22652 63556
  20902 97986 42472 75977 25655 08615 48754 35748 26471 81414
  51270 00602 38901 62077 73224 49943 53088 99909 50168 03281
  12194 32048 19643 87675 86331 47985 71911 39781 53978 07476
  15077 22117 50826 94586 39320 45652 09896 98555 67814 10696
  83728 84058 74610 33781 05444 39094 36835 83581 38113 11689
  93855 57697 54841 49144 53415 09129 54070 05019 47754 86163
  07542 26417 29394 68036 73198 05861 83391 83285 99130 39607
  20144 55950 44977 92120 76124 78564 59161 60837 05949 87860
  06970 18940 98864 00764 43617 09334 17270 91914 33650 13715
  76601 14803 81430 62623 80514 32117 34815 10055 90134 56101
  18007 90506 38142 15270 93085 88092 87570 34505 07808 14545
  88199 06336 12982 79814 11745 33927 31208 09289 72792 22132
```

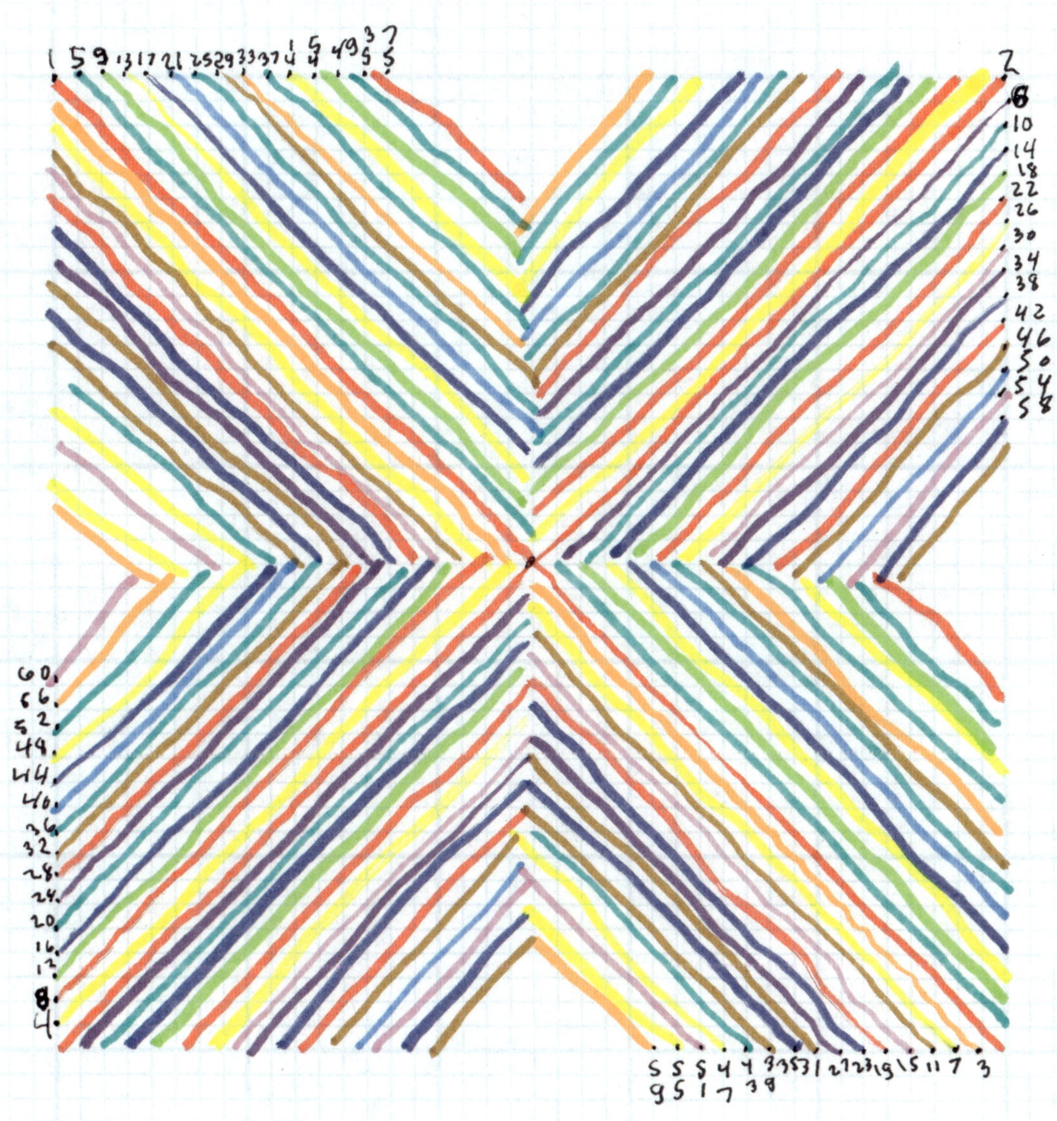

0123456789

0
1
3
6
10
15
21
28
36
45
55
66
78
91
105
120
136
153
171
190
210
231
253
276
300
325
351
378
406
435
465
496
528
561
595
630
666
703
741
780
820
861
903
946
990
1035
1081
1128
1176
1225

1830
1891
1953
2016
2080
2145
2211
2278
2346
2415
2485
2556
2628
2701
2775
2850
2926
3003
3081
3160
3240 3321
3403
3486
3570
3655
3741
3828
3916
4005
4095
4186
4278
4371
4465
4560
4656
4753
4851
4950
5050
5151
5253
5356
5460
5565
5671
5778
5886
5995

7260
7381
7503
7626
7750
7875
8001
8128
8256
8385
8515
8646
8778
8911
9045
9180
9316
9453
9591
9730
9870
10011
10153
10296
10440
10585
10731
10878
11026
11175
11325
11476
11628
11781
11935
12090
12246
12403
12561
12720
12880
13041
13203
13366
13530
13695
13861
14028

15931
16110
16290
16471
16653
16836
17020
17205
17391
17578
17766
17955
18145
18336
18528
18721
18915
19110
19306
19503
19701
19900
20100
20301
20503
20706
20910
21115
21321
21528
21736
21945
22155
22366
22578
22791
23005
23220
23436
23653
23871
24090
24310
24531
24753
24976
25200
25425

27966
28203
28441
28680
28920
29161
29403
29646
29890
30135
30381
30628
30876
31125
31375
31626
31878
32131
32385
32640
32896
33153
33411
33670
33930
34191
34453
34716
34980
35245
35511
35778
36046
36315
36585
36856
37128
37401
37675
37950
38226
38503
38781
39060
39340
39621
39903
40186

62481	84666	110215	140185
62835	85078	110685	140715
63190	85491	111156	141246
63546	85905	111628	141778
63903	86320	112101	142311
64261	86736	112575	142845
64620	87153	113050	143380
64980	87571	113526	143916
65341	87990	114481	144453
65703	88410	114960	144992
66066	88831	115440	145530
66430	89253	115921	146070
66795	89676	116403	146611
67161	90100	116886	147696
67528	90525	117370	148240
67896	90951	117855	148785
68265	91378	118341	149331
68635	91806	118828	149878
69006	92235	119316	150426
69378	92665	119805	150975
69751	93096	120295	151525
70125	93528	120786	152076
70500	93961	121278	152628
70876	94395	121771	153181
71253	94830	122265	153735
71631	95266	122760	154290
72010	95703	123256	154846
72390	96141	123753	155403
72771	96580	124251	155961
73153	97020	124750	156520
73536	97461	125250	157080
73920	97903	125751	157641
74305	98346	126253	158203
74691	98790	126756	158766
75078	99235	127260	
75466	99681	127765	
75855	100128	128271	
76245	100576	129286	
76636	101025	129795	
77028	101475	130305	
77421	101926	130816	
77815	102378	131328	
78210	102831	131841	
78606	103285	132355	
79003	103740	132870	
79401	104196	133386	
79800	104653	133903	
80200	105111	134421	

Jane

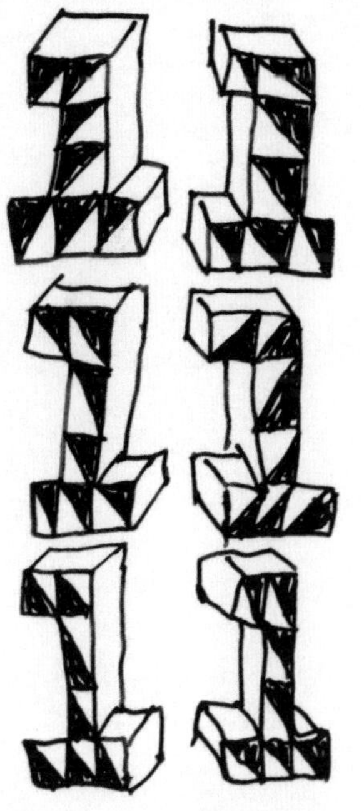

22642 | 71177177117. | 7474777474
22643 | 71177777117. | 7555555555
23783 | 72222722227. | 7557757755
24384 | 72777777727. | 7667676766
24966 | 73337773337. | 7711111117
24994 | 73373337337. | 7717717717
7733777337
24345 | 73733733737. | 7747474747
26057 | 74444444447. | 7747777747
 | | ~~7767767767~~

26381
27203
27230
28360
28829
28898
29074
29214
29216
~~29421~~

7
77677677677 29421
77772727777 29511
7
77777677777 29513
77778787777 29514
77779997777 29516
77878787887 29624
78788788787 30568
78888788887 30658

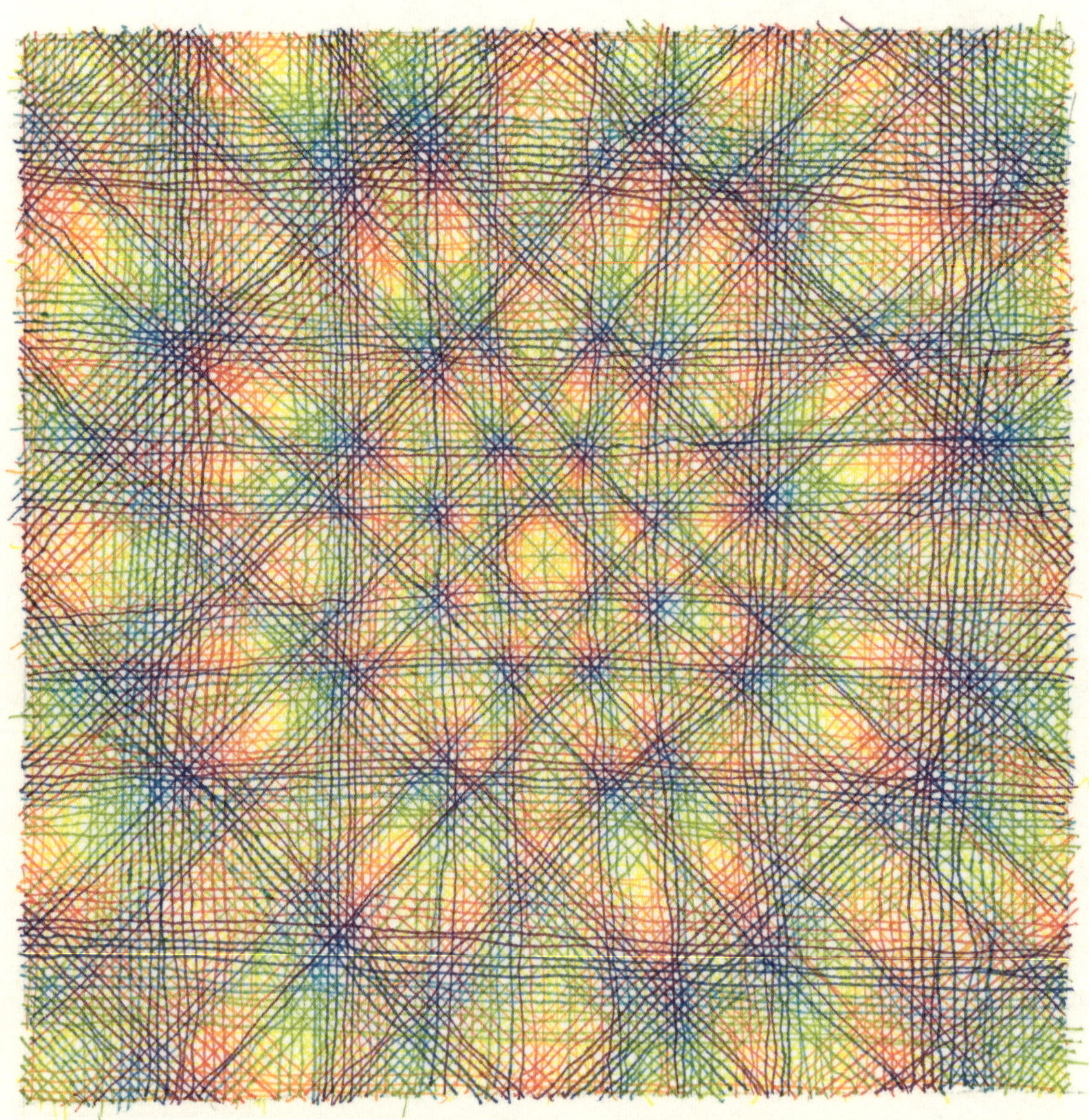

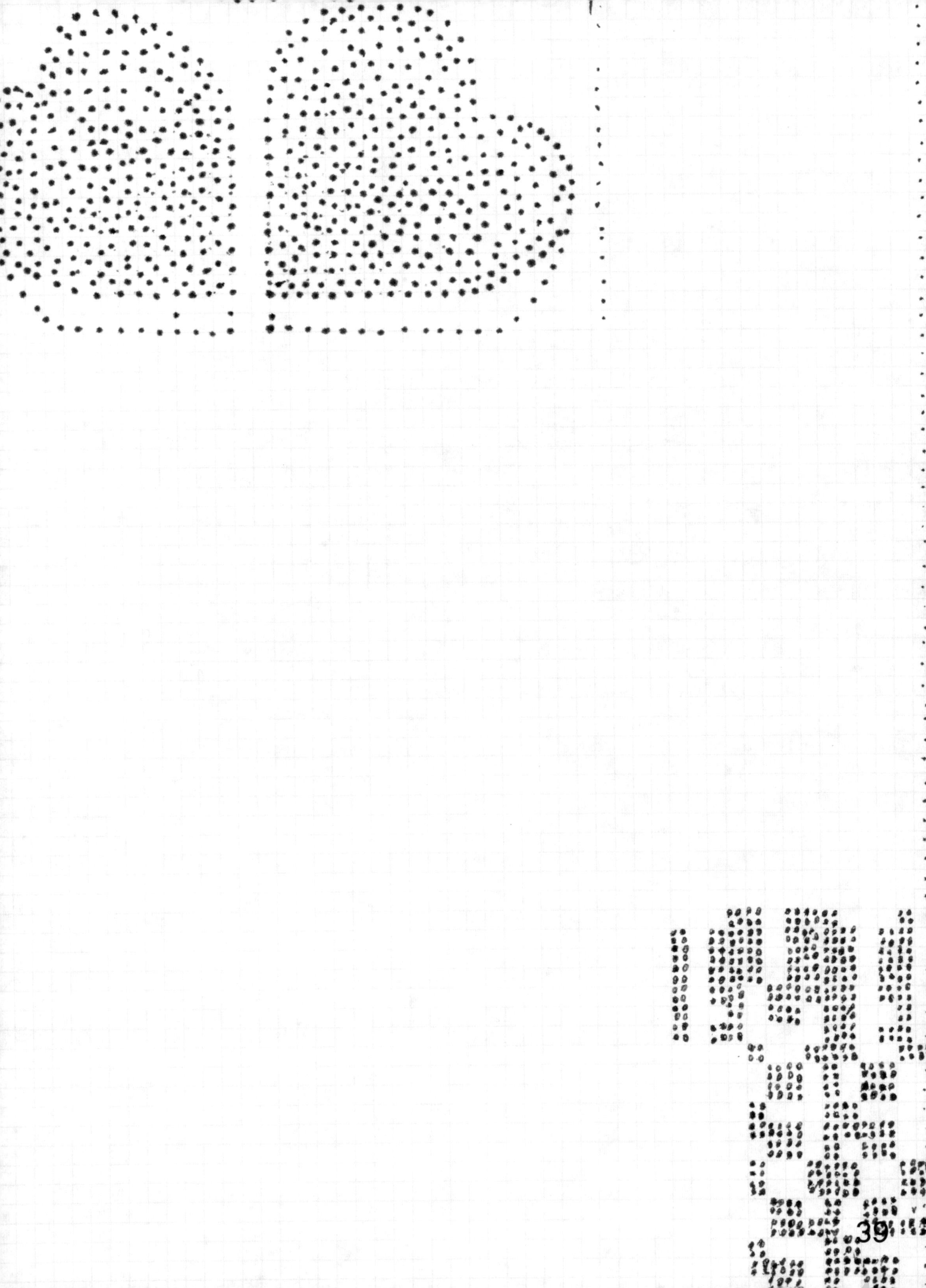

993433363539703098727375177977949099729996983

3433363539703098727375177977949099729996983

33363539703098727375177977949099729996983

363539703098727375177977949099729996983

3539703098727375177977949099729996983

39703098727375177977949099729996983

703098727375177977949099729996983

3098727375177977949099729996983

98727375177977949099729996983

727375177977949099729996983

7375177977949099729996983

75177977949099729996983

177977949099729996983

7977949099729996983

77949099729996983

949099729996983

9099729996983

99729996983

729996983

9996983

96983

983

3

302030973896999279909497797715737278903079353633434399
30203097389699927990949779771573727890307935363343
302030973896999279909497797715737278903079536333
3020309738969992799094977977157372789030795363
302030973896999279909497797715737278903079993
30203097389699927990949779771573727890307993
302030973896999279909497797715737278903079
302030973896999279909497797715737278903
302030973896999279909497797715737278 9
302030973896999279909497797715737 27
3020309738969992799094977977157 37
3020309738969992799094977977157
30203097389699927990949779771
302030973896999279909497797
3020309738969992799094977
302030973896999279909 49
30203097389699927990 94
3020309738969992799
30203097389699927
302030973896999
30203097389 69
30203097389
302030973
3020309 7
30203
2

Fibonacci numbers Fib(n) for n from 101 to 300

Unless a number is explicitly marked "Prime", it is composite (and has other factors apart from 1 and itself), but its factorization is not given here.
Produced by Maple

101 : 573147844013817084101
102 : 927372692193078999176
103 : 1500520536206896083277
104 : 2427893228399975082453
105 : 3928413764606871165730
106 : 6356306993006846248183
107 : 10284720757613717413913
108 : 16641027750620563662096
109 : 26925748508234281076009
110 : 43566776258854844738105
111 : 70492524767089125814114
112 : 114059301025943970552219
113 : 184551825793033096366333
114 : 298611126818977066918552
115 : 483162952612010163284885
116 : 781774079430987230203437
117 : 1264937032042997393488322
118 : 2046711111473984623691759
119 : 3311648143516982017180081
120 : 5358359254990966640871840
121 : 8670007398507948658051921
122 : 14028366653498915298923761
123 : 22698374052006863956975682
124 : 36726740705505779255899443
125 : 59425114757512643212875125
126 : 96151855463018422468774568
127 : 155576970220531065681649693
128 : 251728825683549488150424261
129 : 407305795904080553832073954
130 : 659034621587630041982498215
131 : 1066340417491710595814572169 Prime
132 : 1725375039079340637797070384
133 : 2791715456571051233611642553
134 : 4517090495650391871408712937
135 : 7308805952221443105020355490
136 : 11825896447871834976429068427
137 : 19134702400093278081449423917 Prime
138 : 30960598847965113057878492344
139 : 50095301248058391139327916261
140 : 81055900096023504197206408605
141 : 131151201344081895336534324866
142 : 212207101440105399533740733471
143 : 343358302784187294870275058337
144 : 555565404224292694404015791808
145 : 898923707008479989274290850145
146 : 1454489111232772683678306641953
147 : 2353412818241252672952597492098
148 : 3807901929474025356630904134051
149 : 6161314747715278029583501626149
150 : 9969216677189303386214405760200

151 : 16130531424904581415797907386349
152 : 26099748102093884802012313146549
153 : 42230279526998466217810220532898
154 : 68330027629092351019822533679447
155 : 110560307156090817237632754212345
156 : 178890334785183168257455287891792
157 : 289450641941273985495088042104137
158 : 468340976726457153752543329995929
159 : 757791618667731139247631372100066
160 : 1226132595394188293000174702095995
161 : 1983924214061919432247806074196061
162 : 3210056809456107725247980776292056
163 : 5193981023518027157495786850488117
164 : 8404037832974134882743767626780173
165 : 13598018856492162040239554477268290
166 : 22002056689466296922983322104048463
167 : 35600075545958458963222876581316753
168 : 57602132235424755886206198685365216
169 : 93202207781383214849429075266681969
170 : 150804340016807970735635273952047185
171 : 244006547798191185585064349218729154
172 : 394810887814999156320699623170776339
173 : 638817435613190341905763972389505493
174 : 1033628323428189498226463595560281832
175 : 1672445759041379840132227567949787325
176 : 2706074082469569338358691163510069157
177 : 4378519841510949178490918731459856482
178 : 7084593923980518516849609894969925639
179 : 11463113765491467695340528626429782121
180 : 18547707689471986212190138521399707760
181 : 30010821454963453907530667147829489881
182 : 48558529144435440119720805669229197641
183 : 78569350599398894027251472817058687522
184 : 127127879743834334146972278486287885163
185 : 205697230343233228174223751303346572685
186 : 332825110087067562321196029789634457848
187 : 538522340430300790495419781092981030533
188 : 871347450517368352816615810882615488381
189 : 1409869790947669143312035591975596518914
190 : 2281217241465037496128651402858212007295
191 : 3691087032412706639440686994833808526209
192 : 5972304273877744135569338397692020533504
193 : 9663391306290450775010025392525829059713
194 : 15635695580168194910579363790217849593217
195 : 25299086886458645685589389182743678652930
196 : 40934782466626840596168752972961528246147
197 : 66233869353085486281758142155705206899077
198 : 107168651819712326877926895128666735145224
199 : 173402521172797813159685037284371942044301
200 : 280571172992510140037611932413038677189525
201 : 453973694165307953197296969697410619233826
202 : 734544867157818093234908902110449296423351
203 : 1188518561323126046432205871807859915657177
204 : 1923063428480944139667114773918309212080528
205 : 3111581989804070186099320645726169127737705
206 : 5034645418285014325766435419644478339818233
207 : 8146227408089084511865756065370647467555938
208 : 13180872826374098837632191485015125807374171
209 : 21327100234463183349497947550385773274930109
210 : 34507973060837282187130139035400899082304280

718 802 4035
BFN Realty
Neil Dolgin
718 388 7700

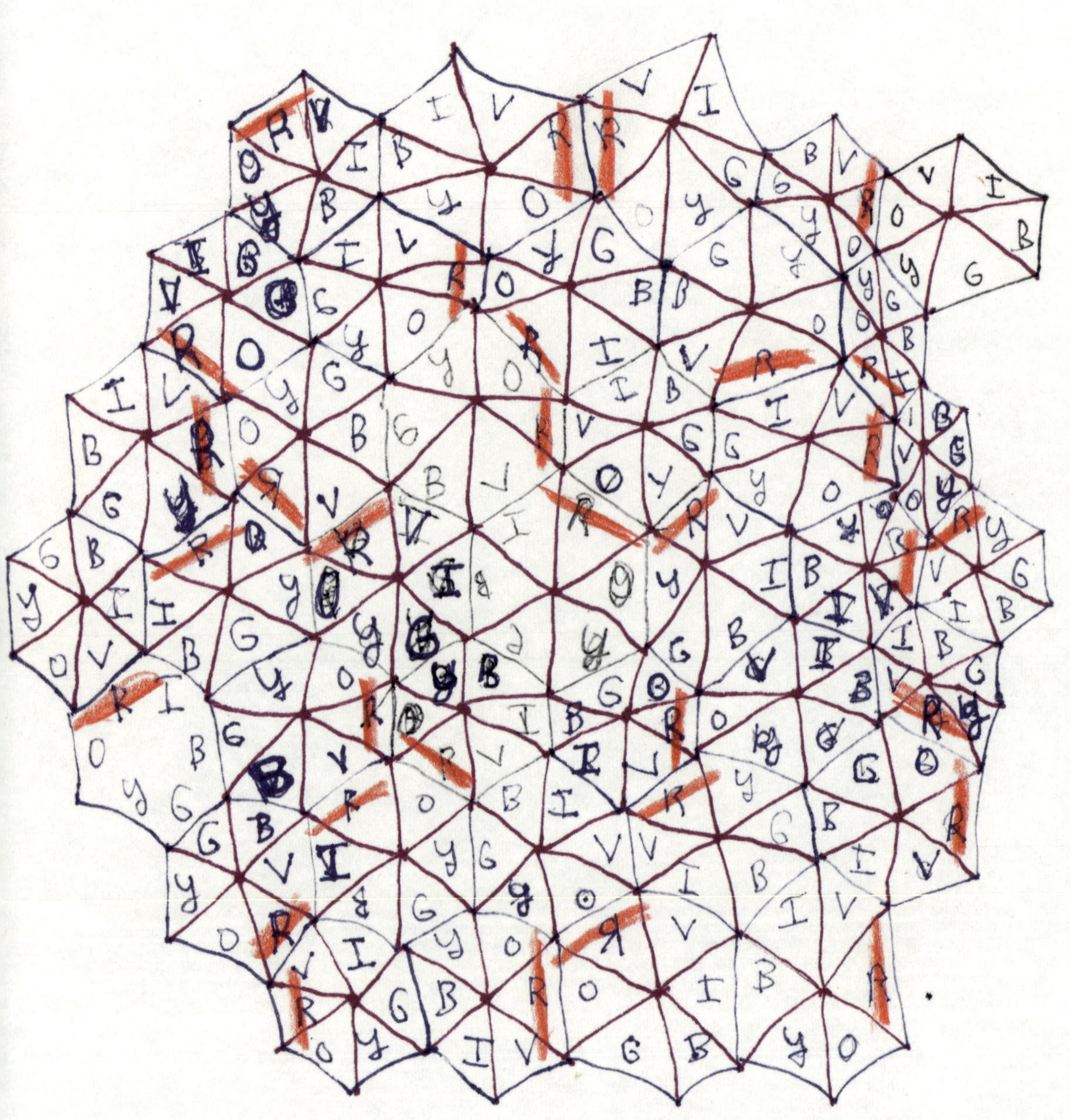

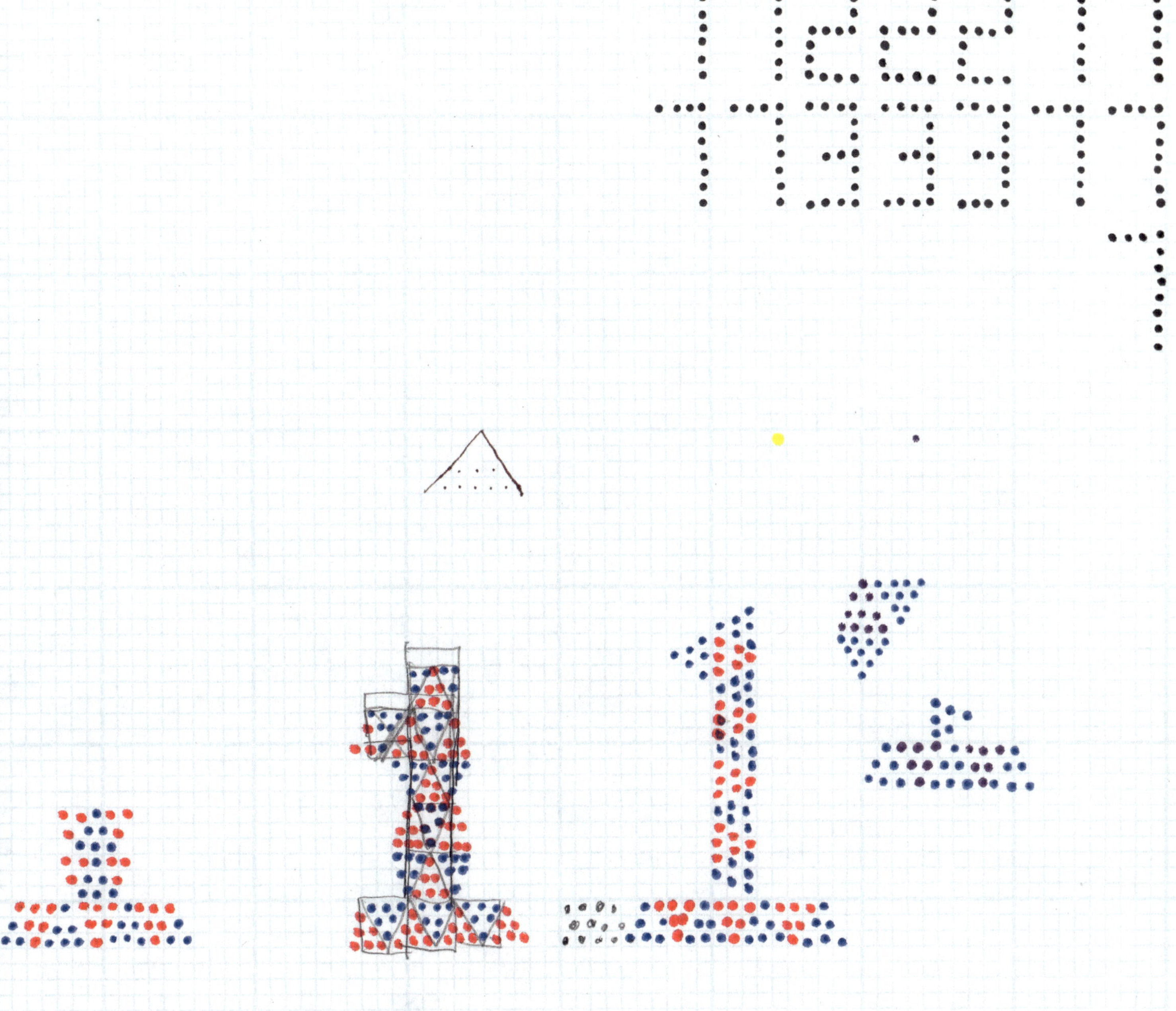

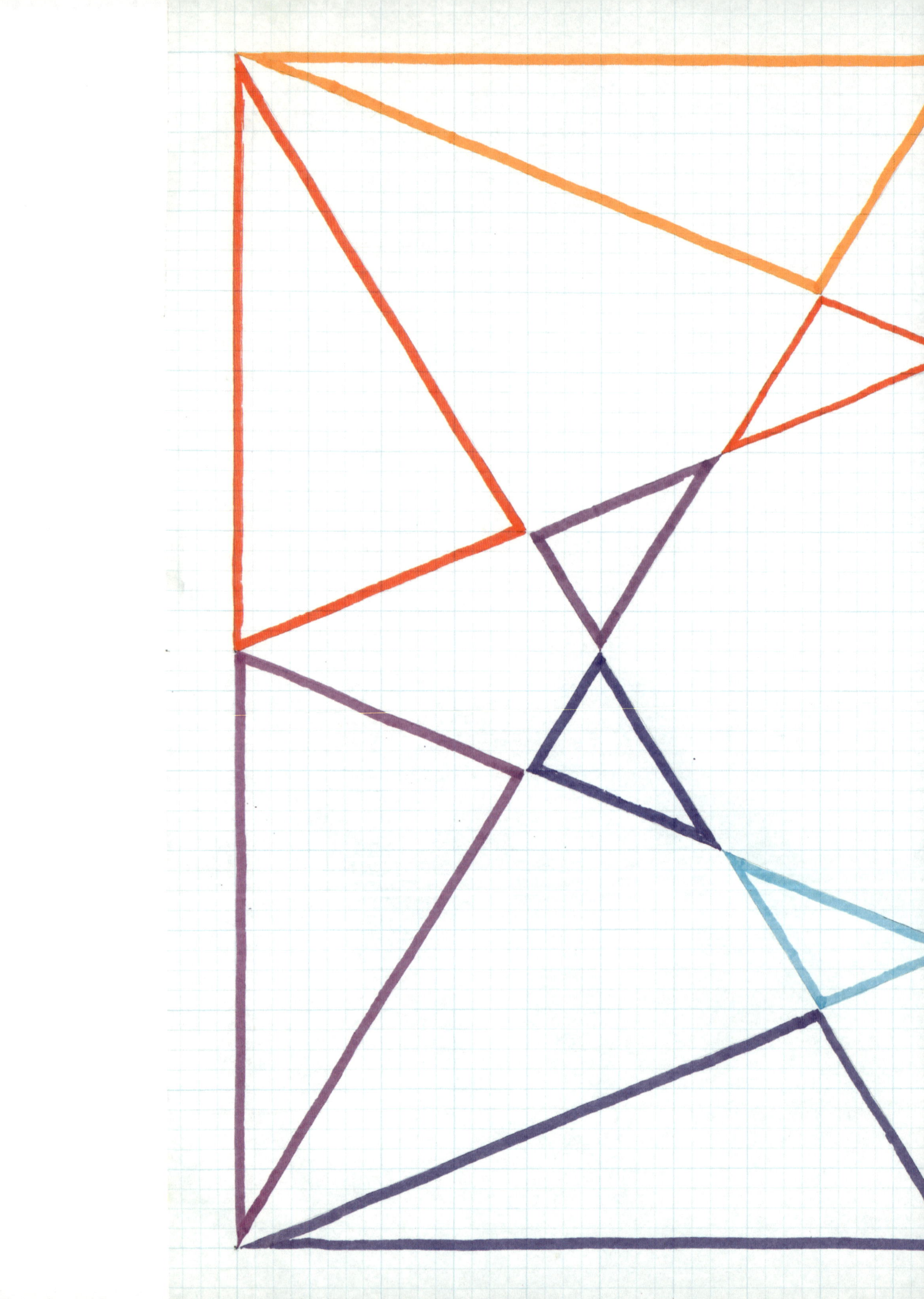

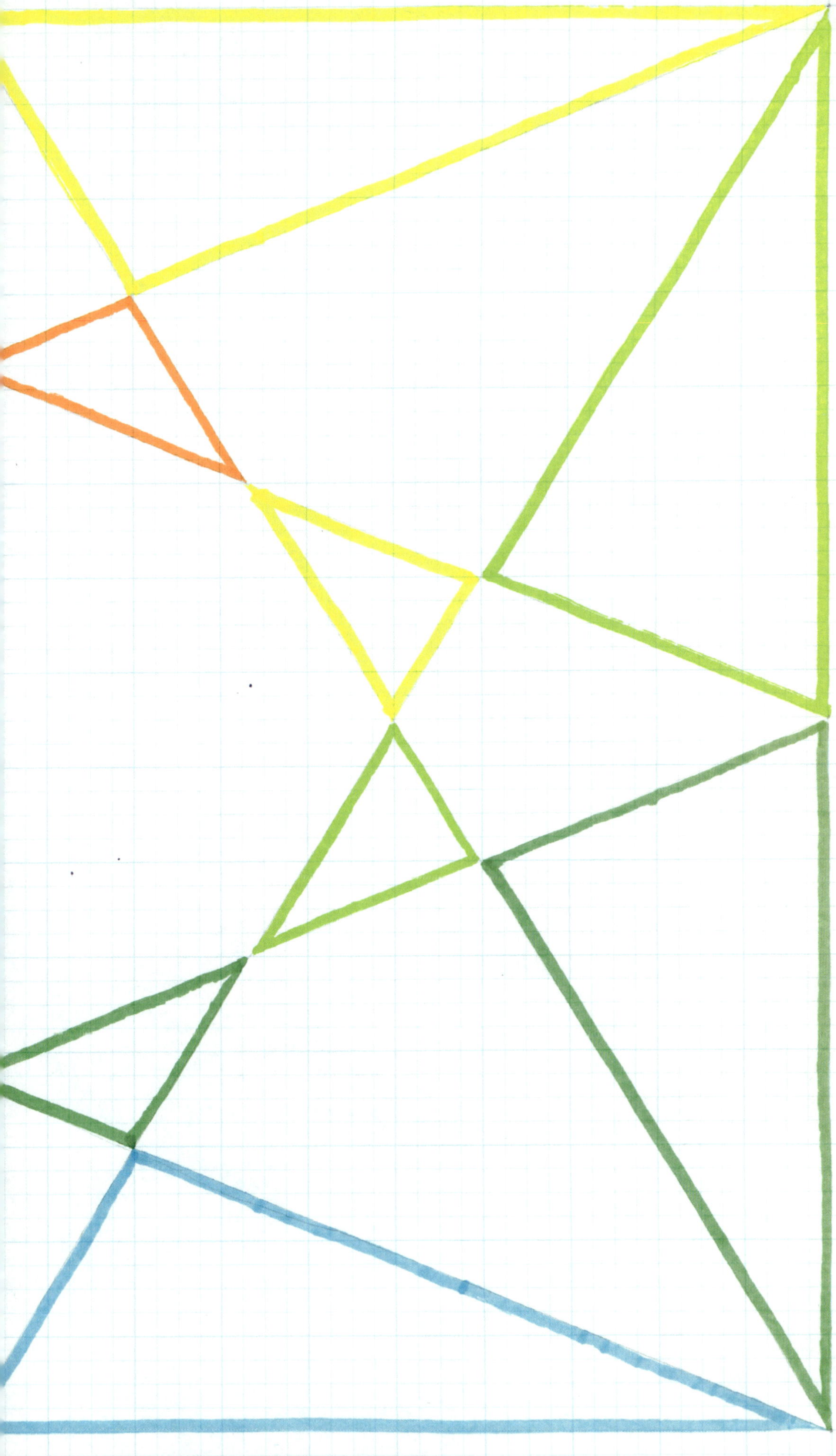

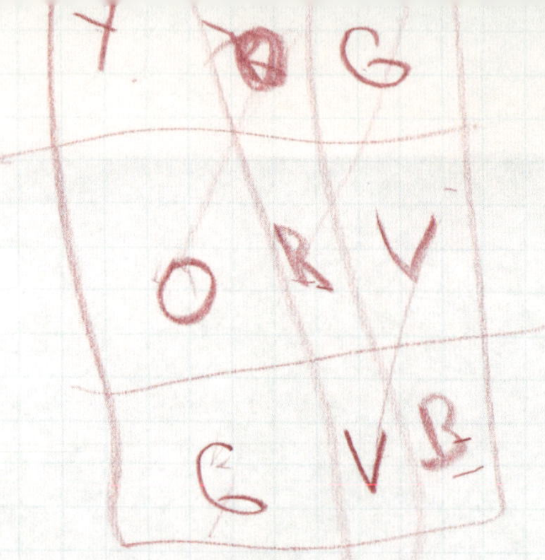

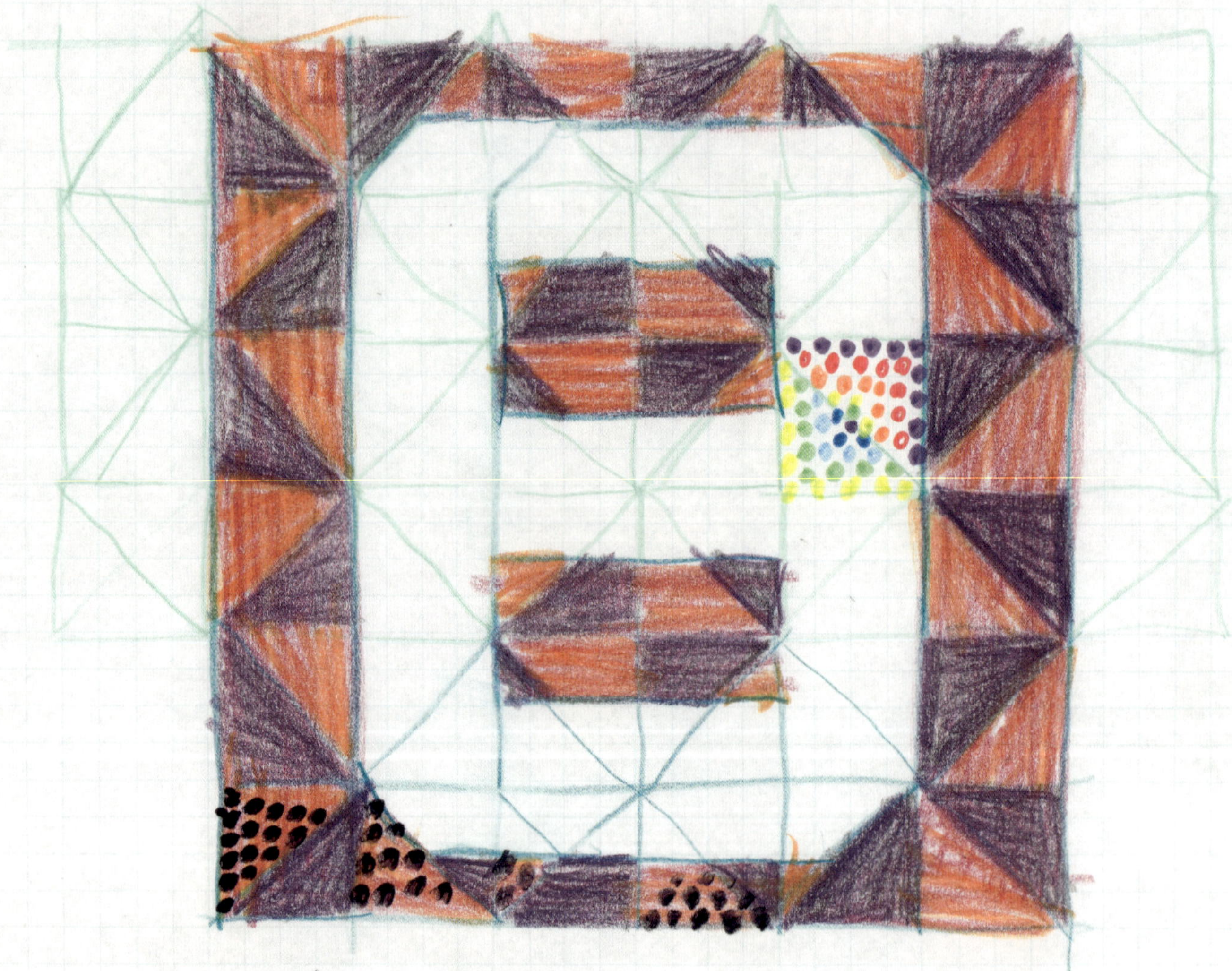

YO OR GB

OR VR BG

GY OR VB

B

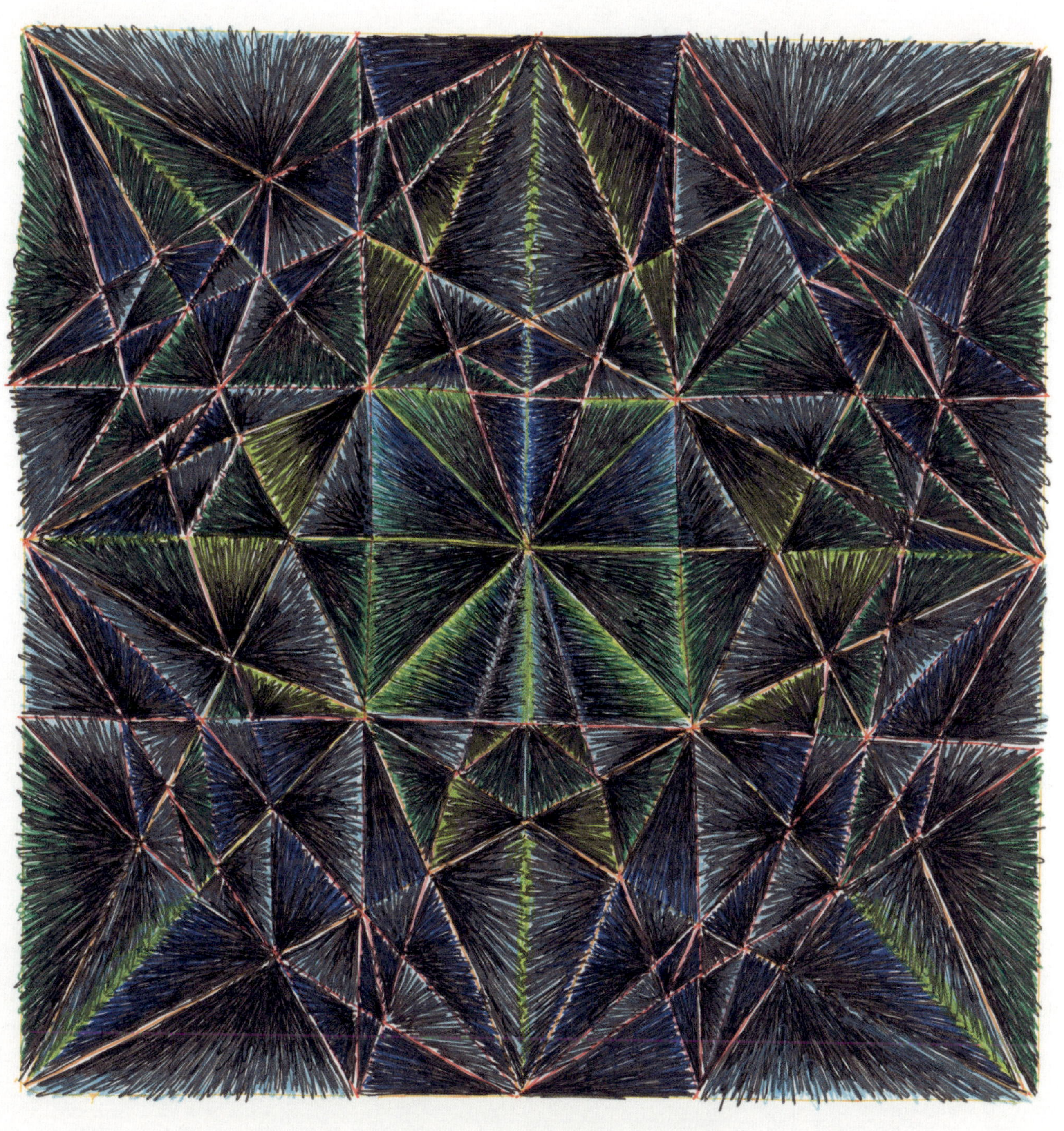

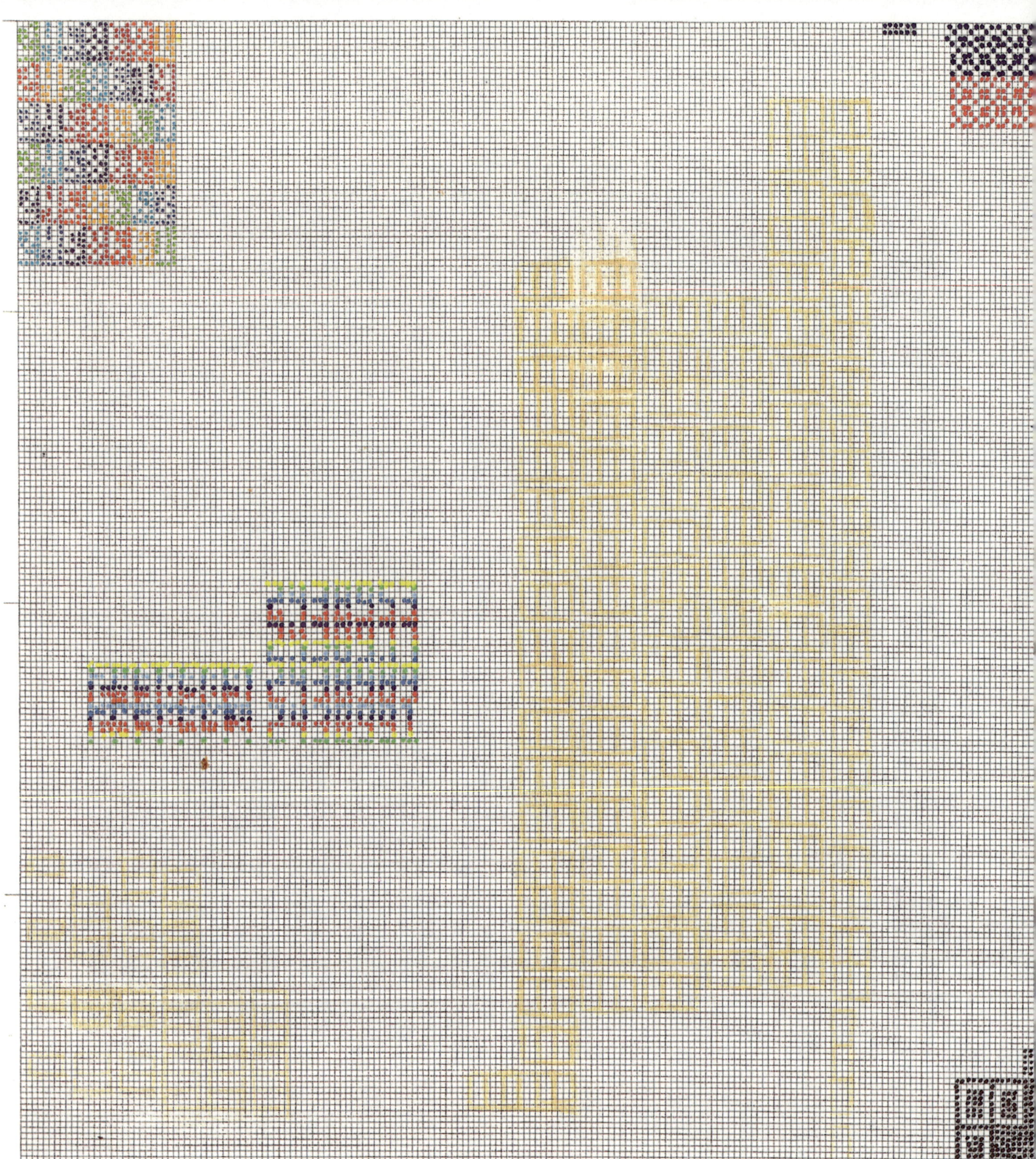

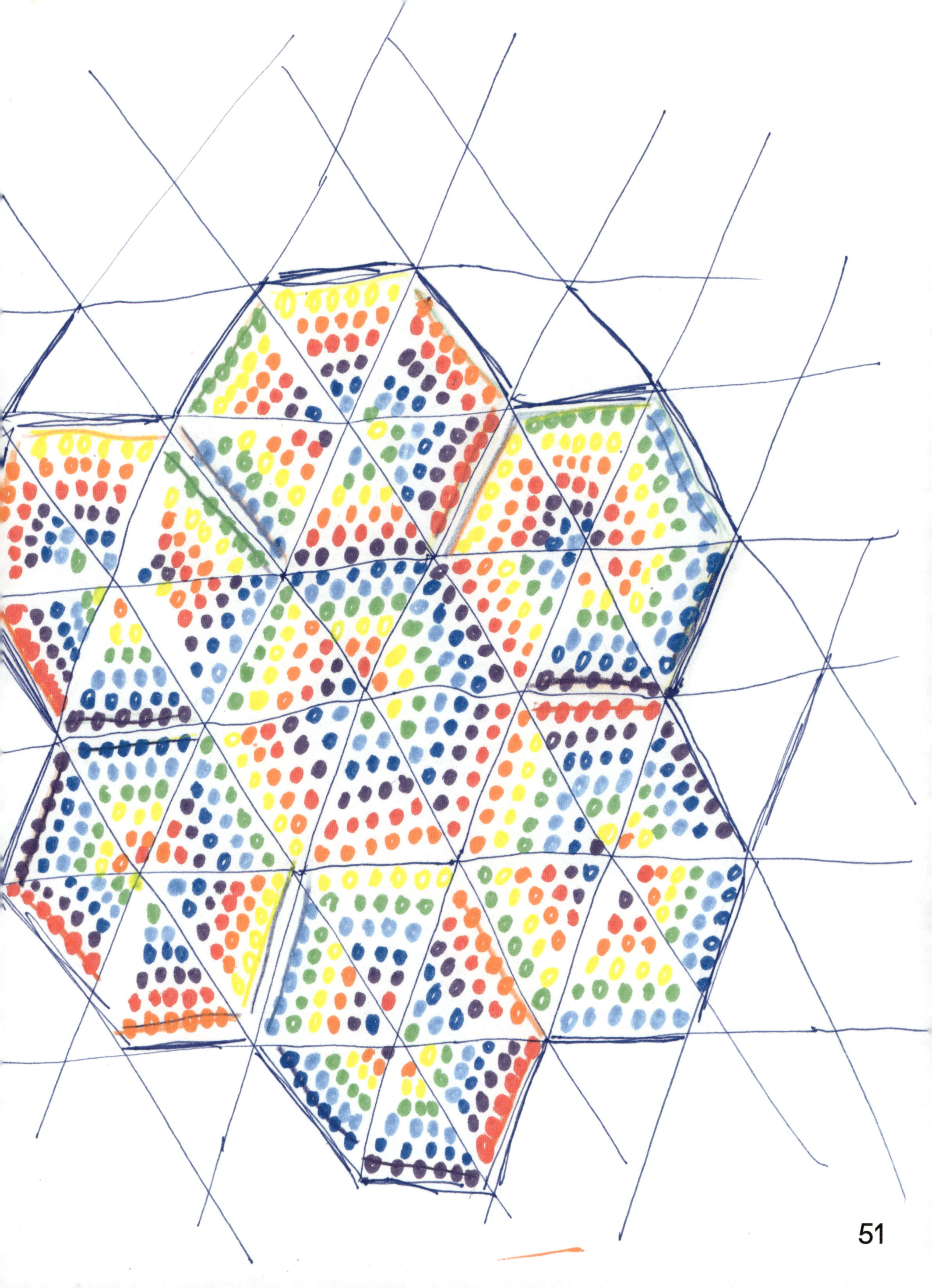

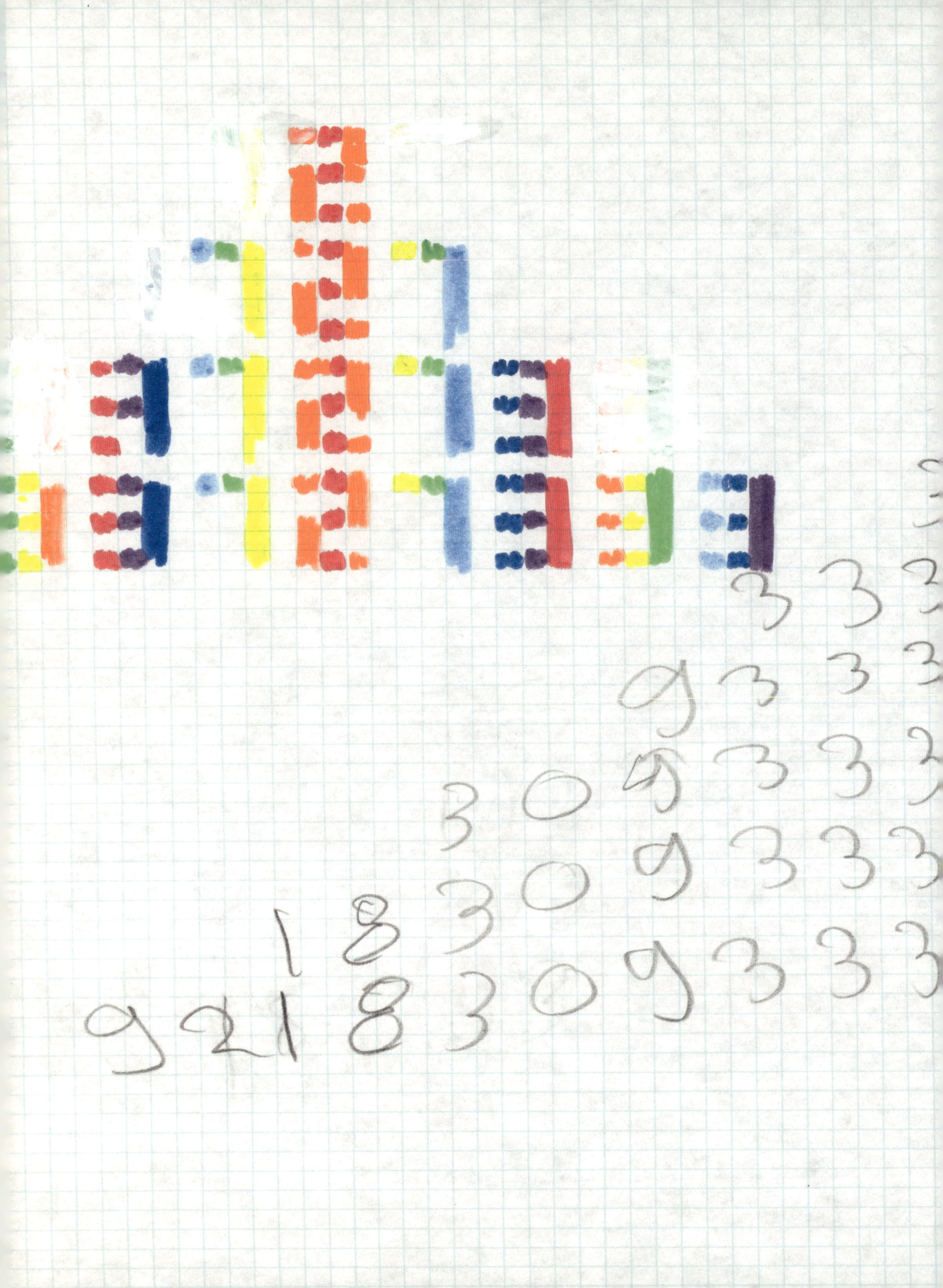

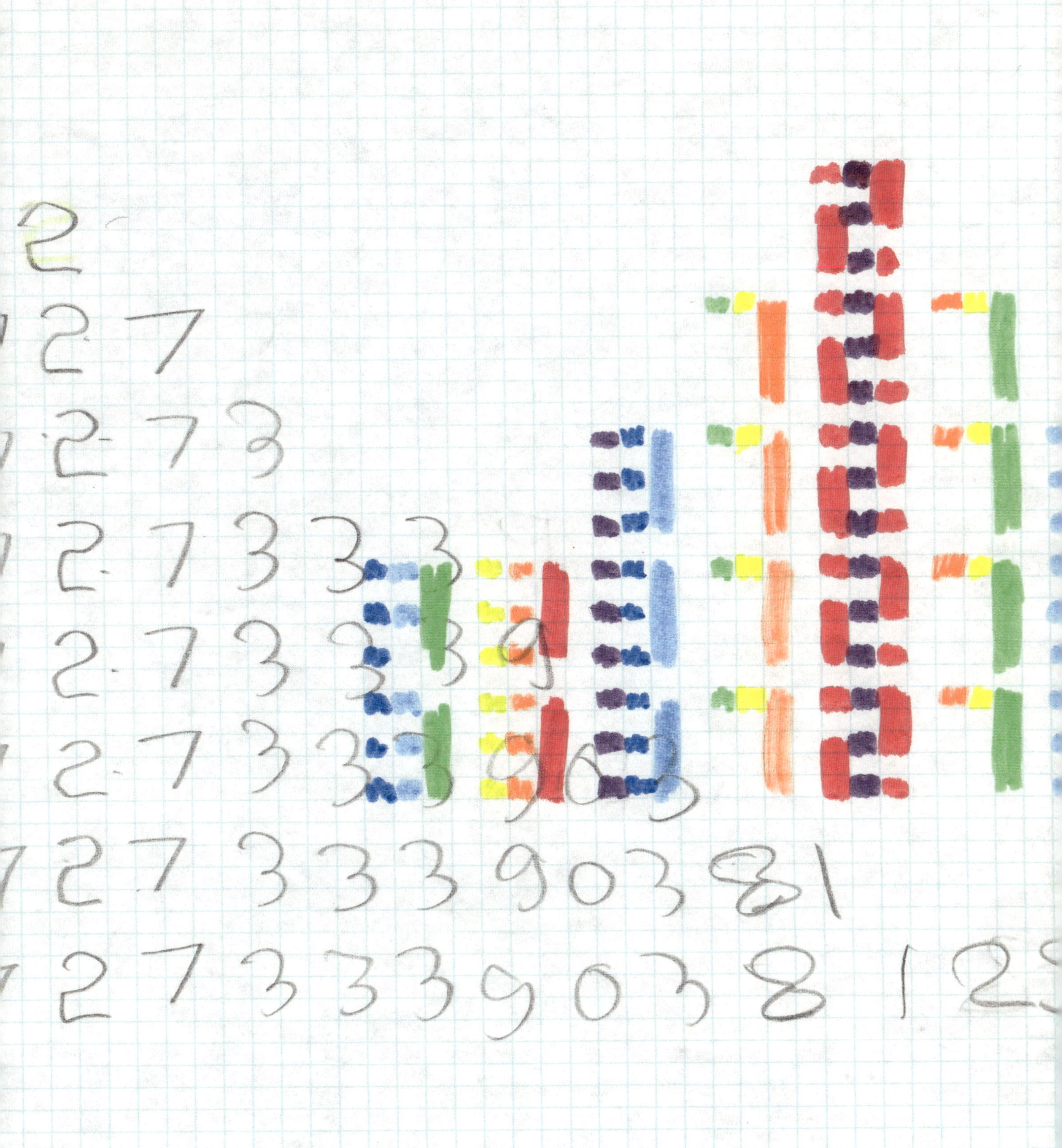
2
2 7
2 7 3
2 7 3 3 3
2 7 3 3 3 9
2 7 3 3 3 9 0 3
2 7 3 3 3 9 0 3 8 1
2 7 3 3 3 9 0 3 8 1 2

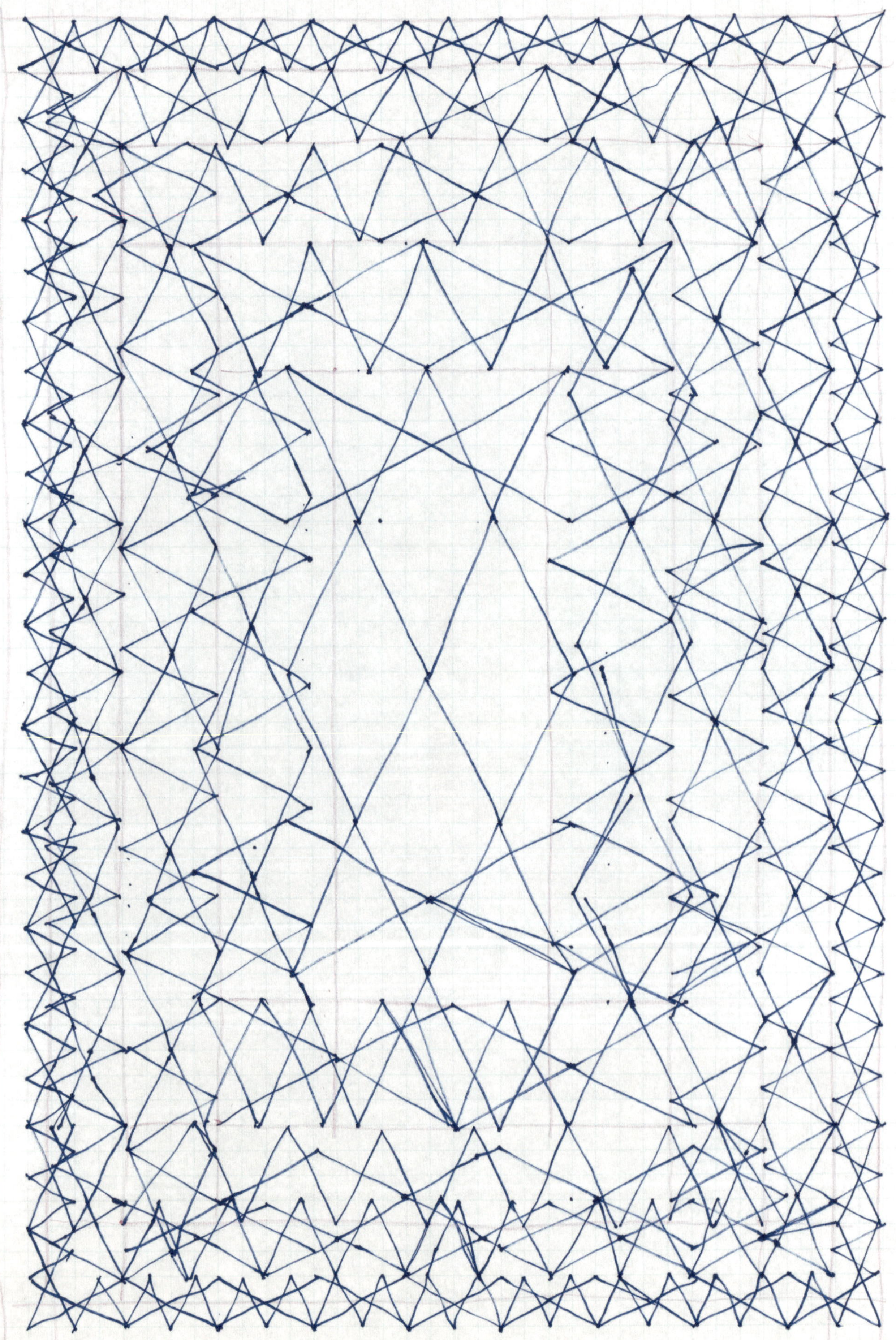

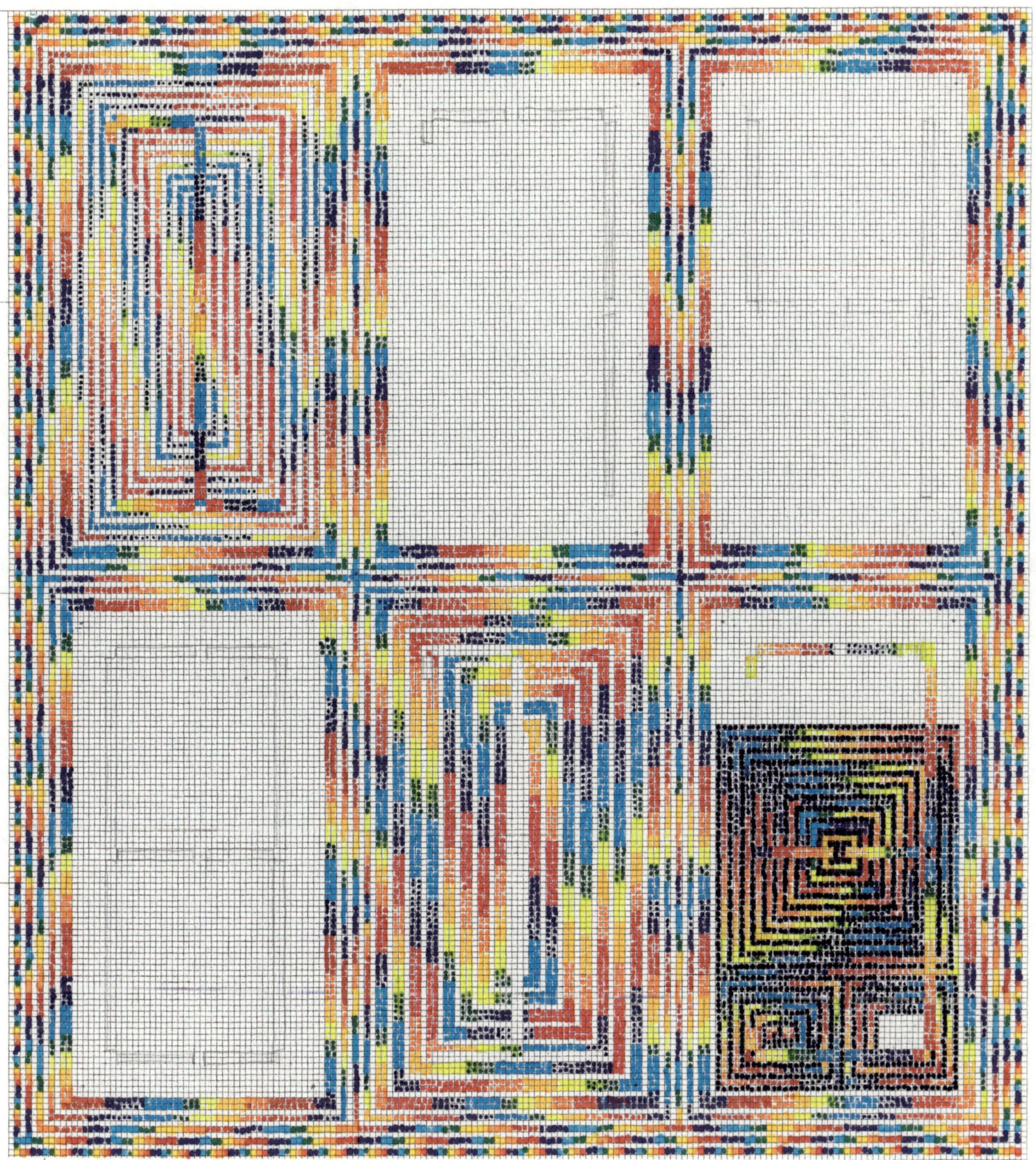

12113. 31133133113
12327. 31333333313
13397 32323232323
14189. 33113131133
14423. 33335353333
14469 33377377333
14660. 33553335533
15544. 34343334343
15636 34434443443
15648. 34444344443
16774. 35533333553
16803. 35553535553
18748. 37373337373
19151. 37777377773
19724. 38333333383
19798 38388838383
20265 38883838883

(17)

22642. 71177177117
22643 71177777117
23783. 72222722227
24384 72777777727
24966. 73337773337
24994 73373337337
25345 73733733737
26057 74444444447
26381 74747774747
27203 75555555557
27230 75577577557
28360 76676767667
28829 77337773377
28898
29014 77474747477
29214
29216 77477777477

33889 91919191919
33880 91991119919
34105 92222922229
34183 92292929229
36352 94444944449
36887 94944444949
36939 94994949949
37530 95559595559
37980. 95999999959
39808. 97777977779
40958. 98888988889
41301. 99222222299
41637. 99555555599
41680. 99595559599
41994 99888888899
42034 99929992999
29421. 77677677677
29624. 77878787877
30568 78788788787
30658 78888788887
29511 77772727777
29513 77777277777
29514 77777677777
29516 77778787777
77775959777
42052. 99949994999
42094. 99988988999
42099. 99998989999
42100. 99999199999

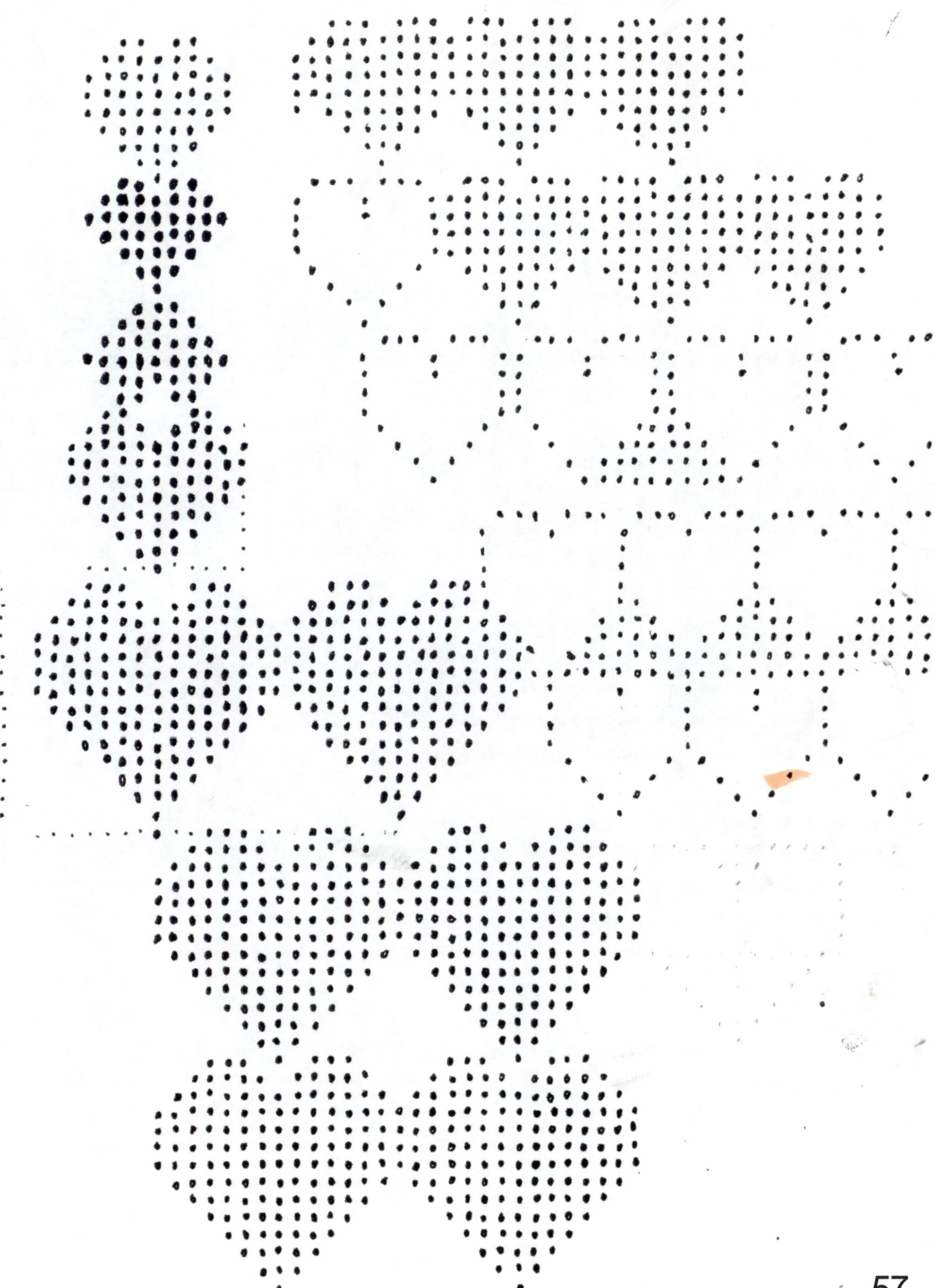

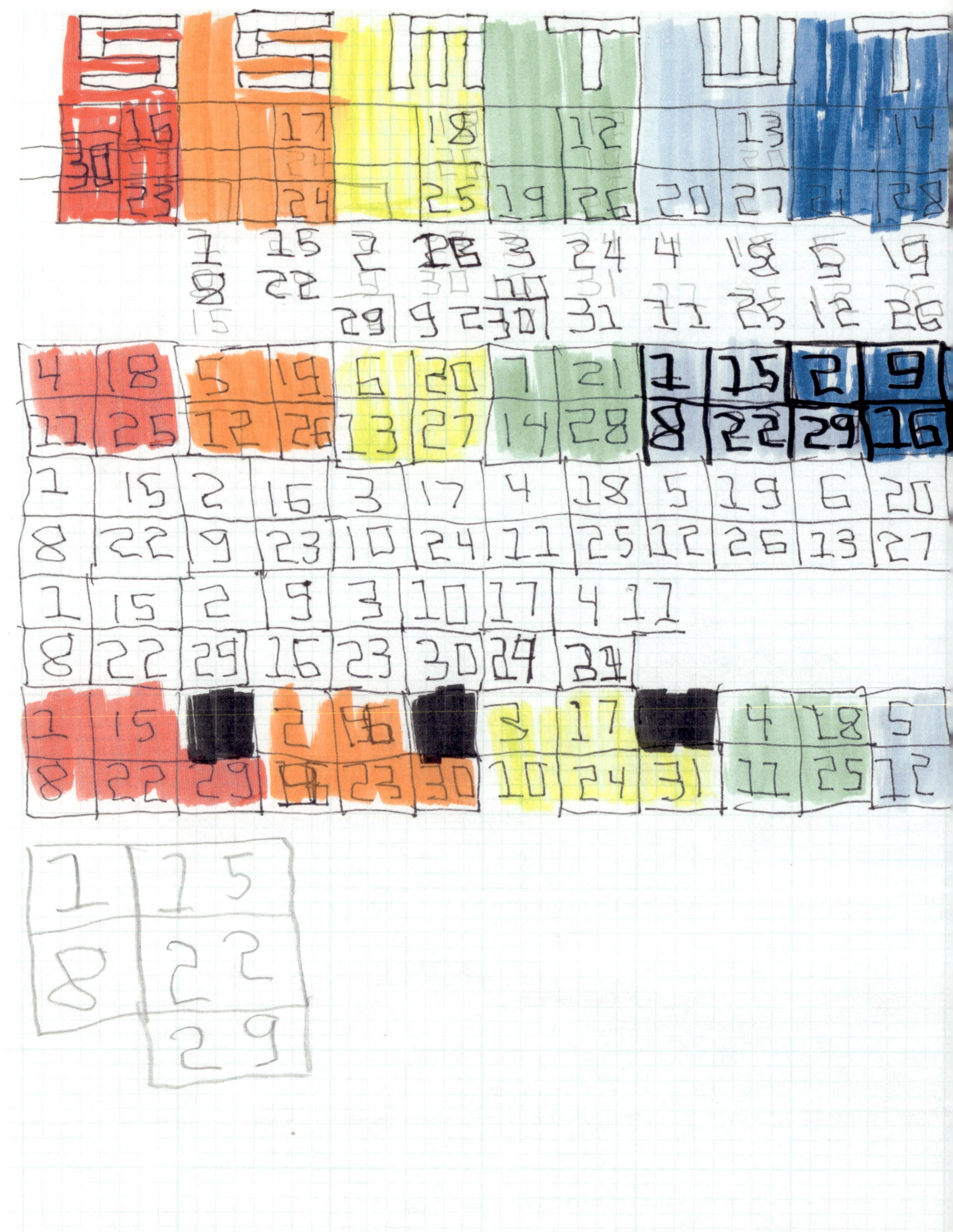
S S M T W T

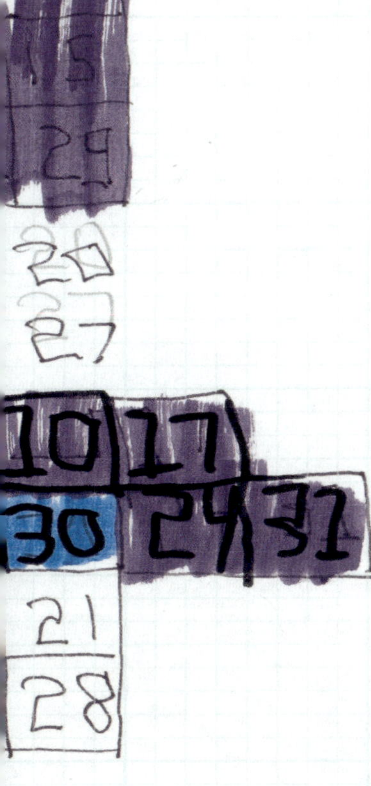
15
29
20
27
10
17
30
24
31
21
28

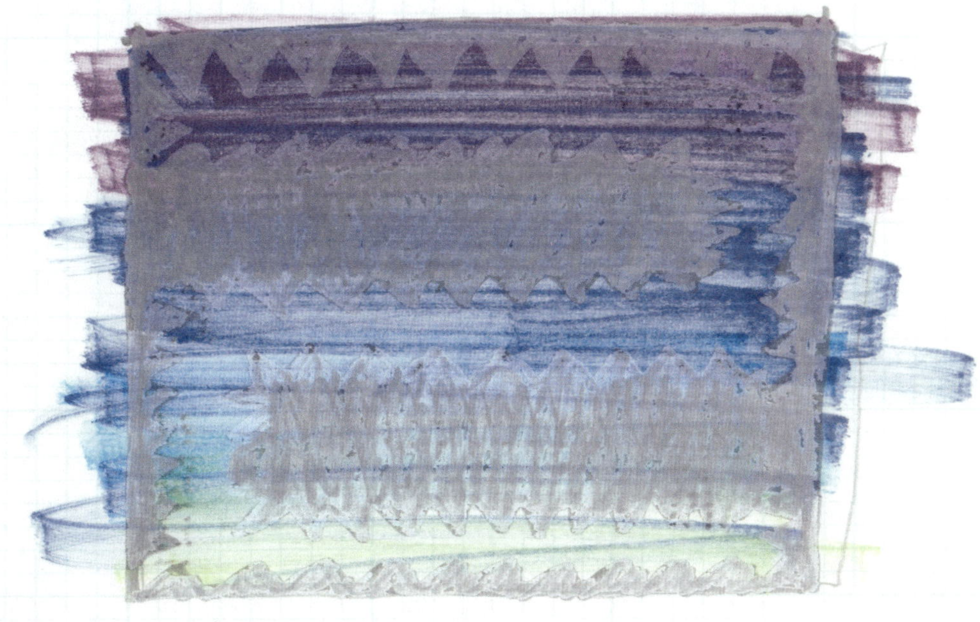

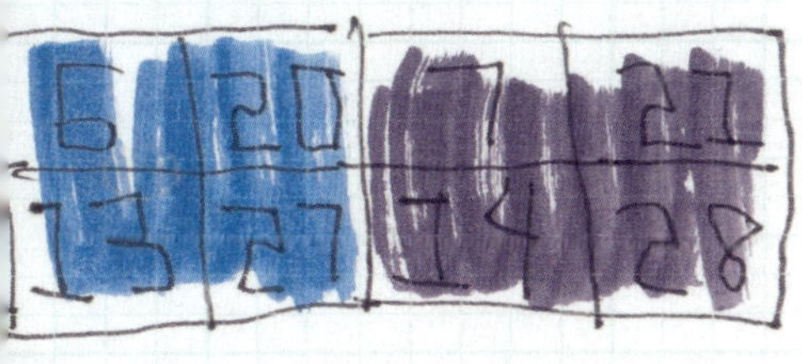
6
20
21
13
27
14
28

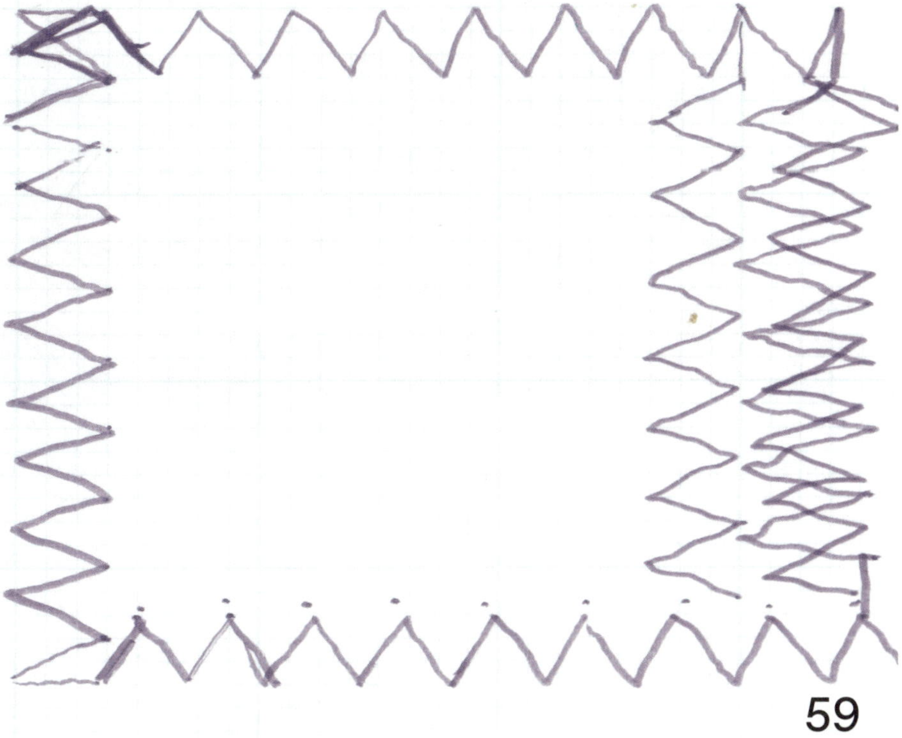

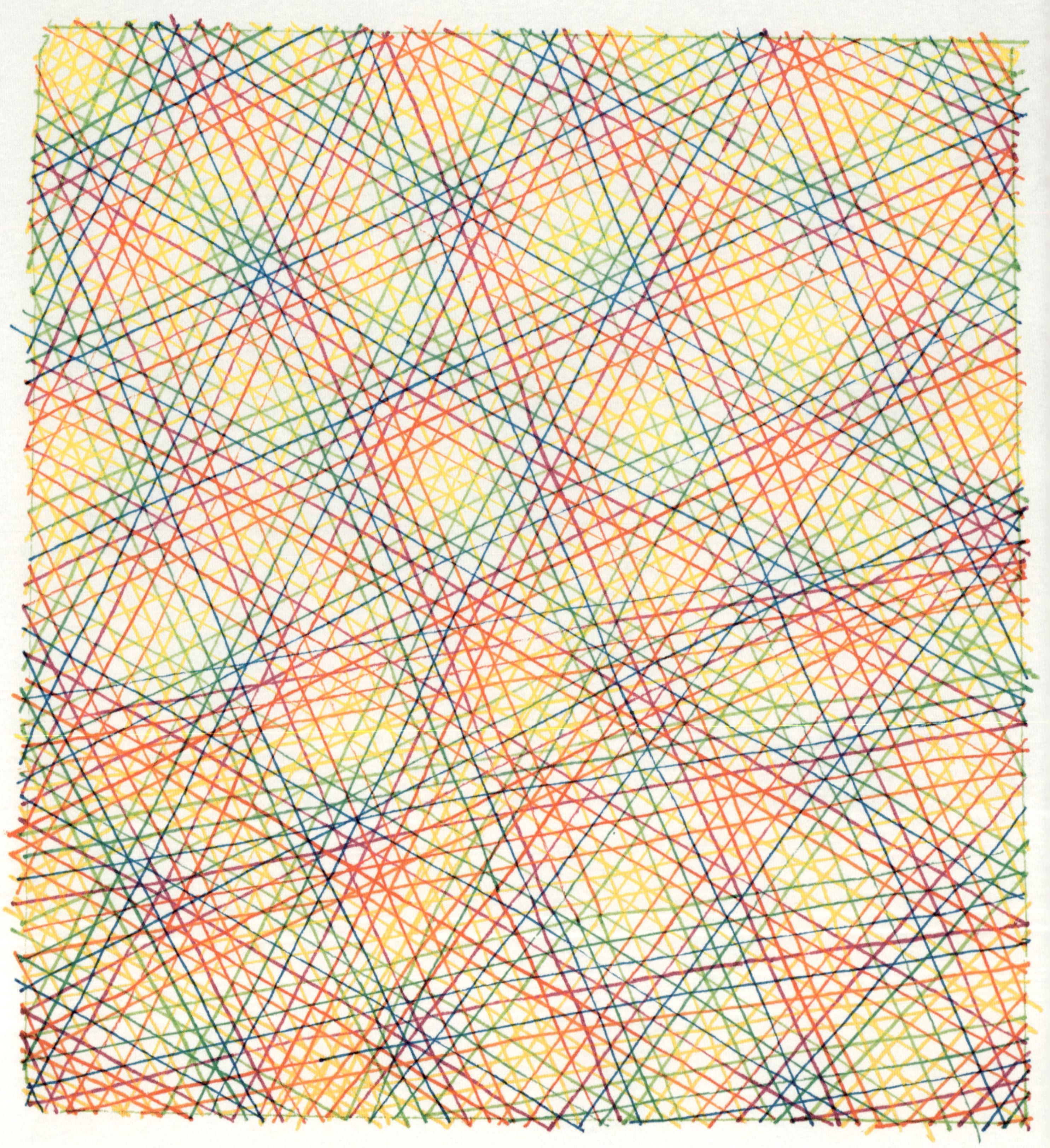

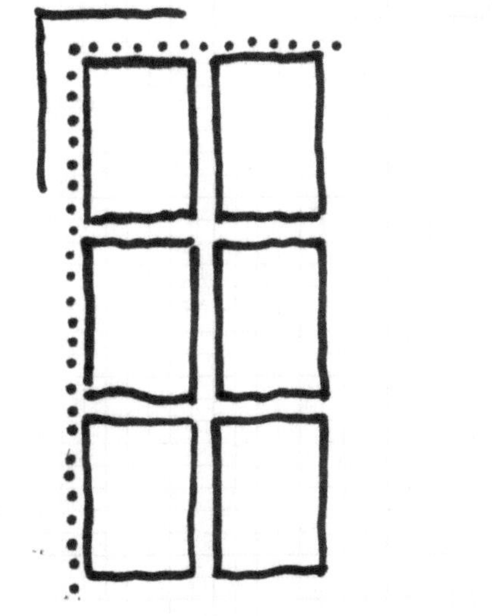

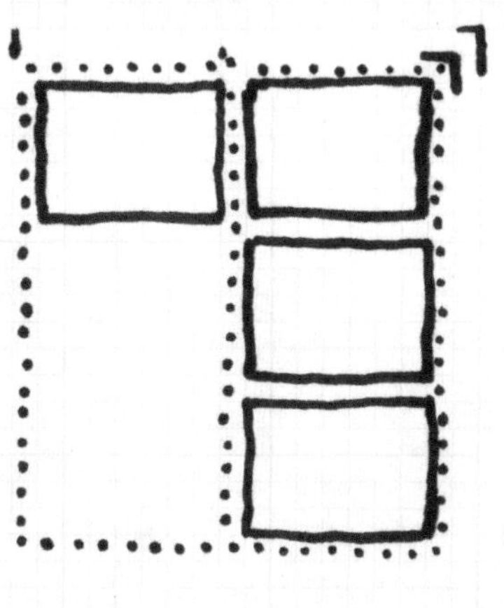

25x13 114 x 202
57 x

138
154

10.6
202

11 00 11	11 11 00	00 00 11	00 11 00	01 00 11	01 11 00	10 00 11	10 11 00
00 11 01	00 00 10	11 11 01	11 00 10	10 11 01	10 00 10	01 11 01	01 00 10
11 01 00	11 10 11	00 01 00	00 10 11	01 01 00	01 10 11	10 01 00	10 10 11
00 10 10	00 01 01	11 10 10	11 01 01	10 10 10	10 01 01	01 10 10	01 01 01
11 01 10	11 10 01	00 01 10	00 10 01	01 01 10	01 10 01	10 01 10	10 10 01
00 10 00	00 01 11	11 10 00	11 01 11	10 10 00	10 01 11	01 10 00	01 01 11
11 00 01	11 11 10	00 00 01	00 11 10	01 00 01	01 11 10	10 00 01	10 11 10
00 11 11	00 00 00	11 11 11	11 00 00	10 11 11	10 00 00	01 11 11	01 00 00

45.5
76

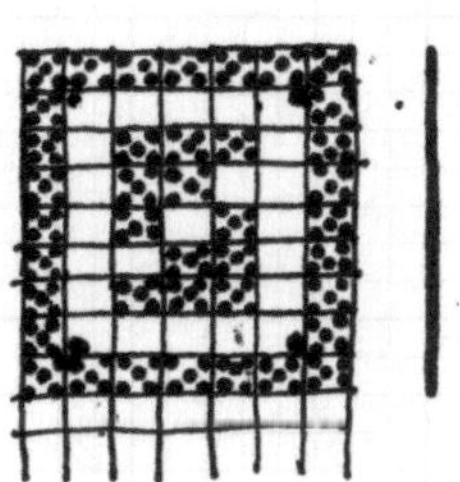

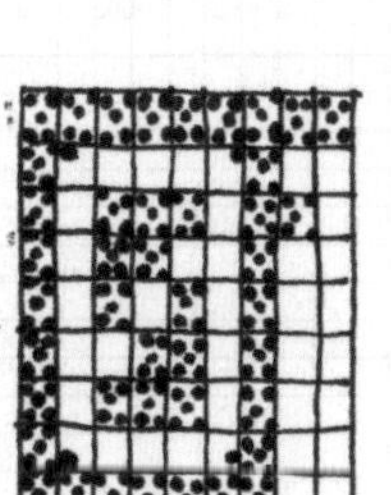

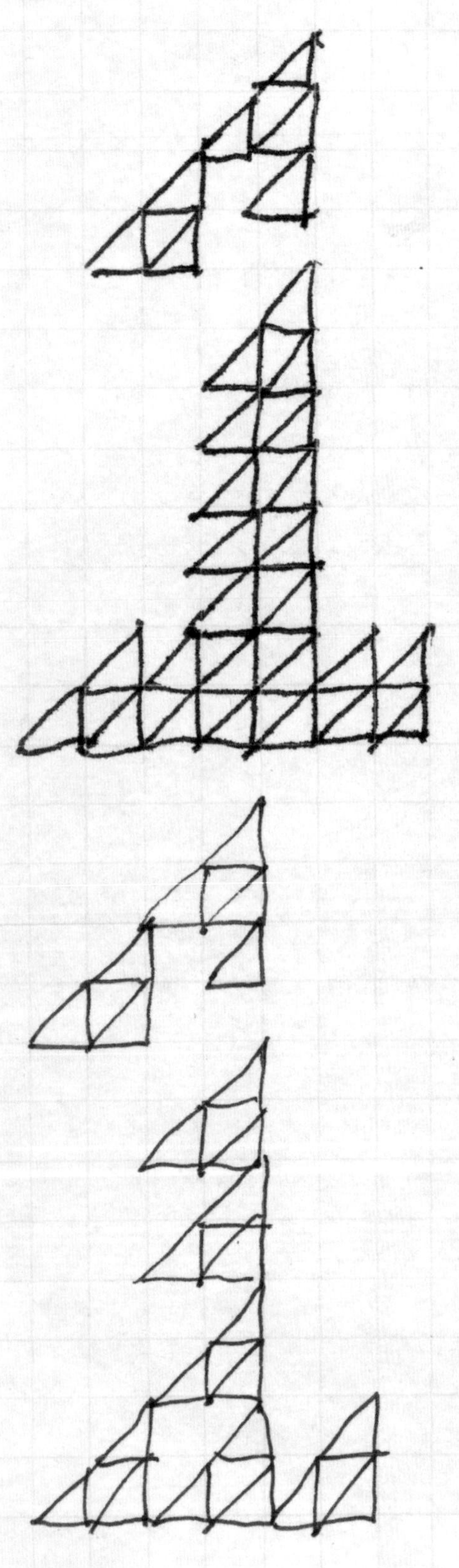

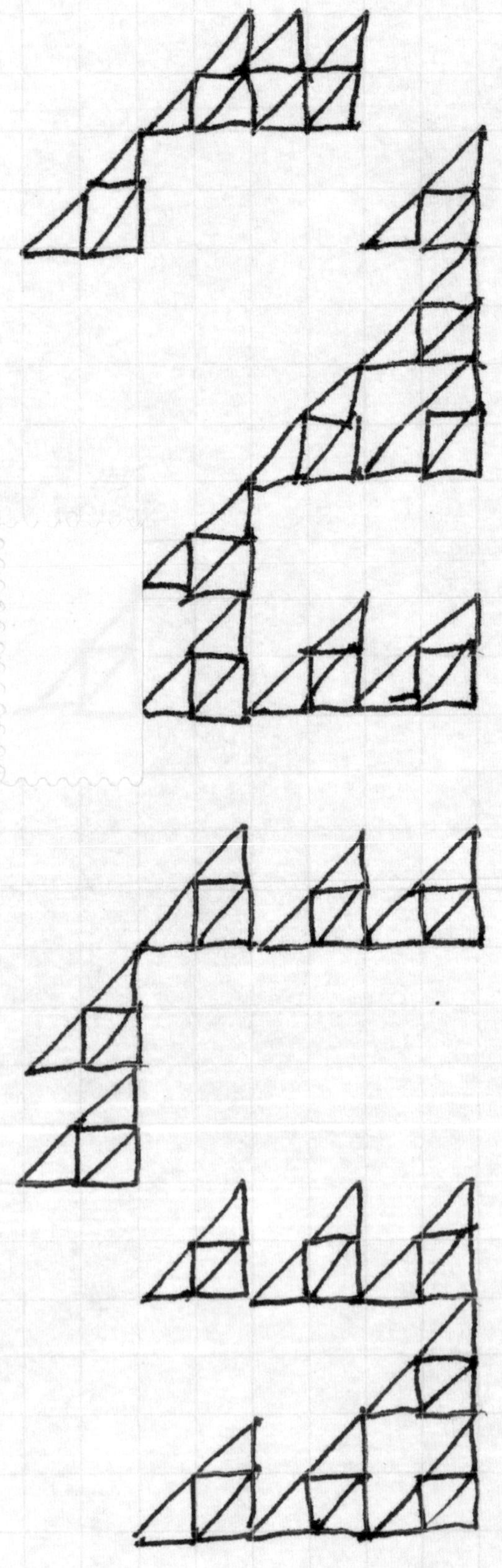

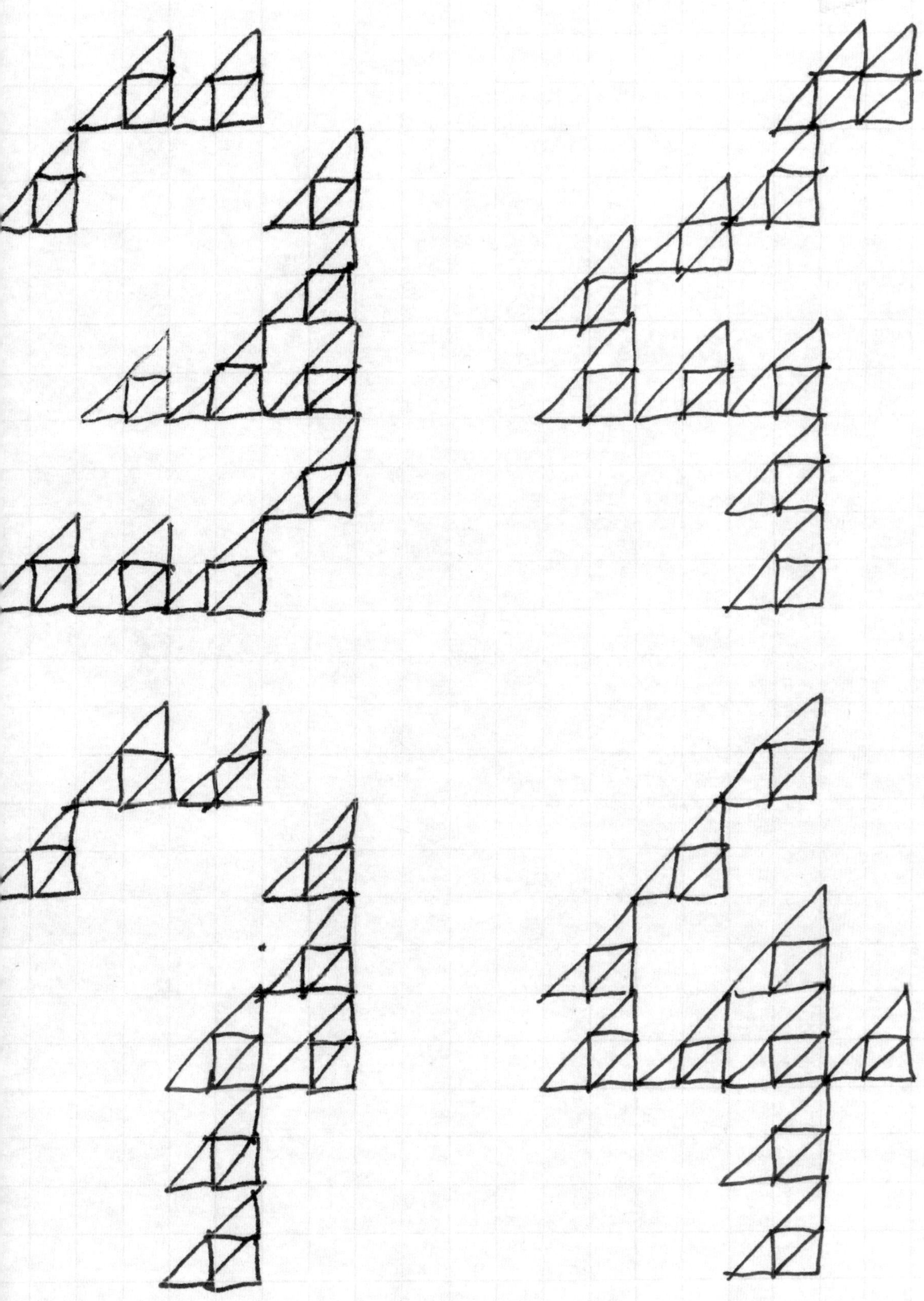

216 : 6192204516665901352286753878632978742693965 12

217 : 10019197373256043094732062378984339333024812 97

218 : 16211401889921944447018816257617318075718778 09

219 : 26230599263177987541750878636601657408743591 06

220 : 42442001153099993198876969489421897548446236 915

221 : 68672600416277919530520573530820632893205960 21

222 : 11111460156937785151929026842503960837766832936

223 : 17978720198565577104981084195586024127087428957

224 : 29090180355503362256910111038089984964854261893

225 : 47068900554068939361891195233676009091941690850

226 : 76159080909572301618801306271765994056795952743

227 : 123227981463641240980692501505442003148737643593

228 : 199387062373213542599493807777207997205533596336

229 : 322615043836854783580186309282650000354271239929

230 : 522002106210068326179680117059857997559804836265

231 : 844617150046923109759866426342507997914076076194

232 : 1366619256256991435939546543402365995473880912459

233 : 2211236406303914545699412969744873993387956988653

234 : 3577855662560905981638959513147239988861837901112

235 : 5789092068864820527338372482892113982249794889765

236 : 9366947731425726508977331996039353971111632790877

237 : 15156039800290547036315704478931467953361427680642

238 : 24522987531716273545293036474970821924473060471519

239 : 39679027332006820581608740953902289877834488152161

240 : 64202014863723094126901777428873111802307548623680

241 : 103881042195729914708510518382775401680142036775841

242 : 168083057059453008835412295811648513482449585399521

243 : 271964099255182923543922814194423915162591622175362

244 : 440047156314635932379335110006072428645041207574883

245 : 712011255569818855923257924200496343807632829750245

246 : 1152058411884454788302593034206568772452674037325128

247 : 1864069667454273644225850958407065116260306867075373

248 : 3016128079338728432528443992613633888712980904400501

249 : 4880197746793002076754294951020699004973287771475874

250 : 7896325826131730509282738943634332893686268675876375

251 : 12776523572924732586037033894655031898659556447352249

252 : 20672849399056463095319772838289364792345825123228624

253 : 33449372971981195681356806732944396691005381570580873

254 : 54122222371037658776676579571233761483351206693809497

255 : 87571595343018854458033386304178158174356588264390370

256 : 141693817714056513234709965875411919657707794958199867

257 : 229265413057075367692743352179590077832064383222590237

258 : 370959230771131880927453318055001997489772178180790104

259 : 600224643828207248620196670234592075321836561403380341

260 : 971183874599339129547649988289594072811608739584170445

261 : 1571408518427546378167846658524186148133445300987550786

262 : 2542592393026885507715496646813780220945054040571721231

263 : 4114000911454431885883343305337966369078499341559272017

264 : 6656593304481317393598839952151746590023553382130993248

265 : 10770594215935749279482183257489712959102052723690265265

266 : 17427187520417066673081023209641459549125606105821258513

267 : 28197781736352815952563206467131172508227658829511523778

268 : 45624969256769882625644229676772632057353264935332782291

269 : 73822750993122698578207436143903804565580923764844306069

270 : 119447720249892581203851665820676436622934188700177088360

271 : 193270471243015279782059101964580241188515112465021394429

272 : 312718191492907860985910767785256677811449301165198482789

273 : 505988662735923140767969869749836918999964413630219877218

274 : 818706854228831001753880637535093596811413714795418360007

275 : 1[illegible]5516964754142521850507284930515811378128425638237225

276 : [illegible]2371193585144275731144820024112622791843221056597232

277 : [illegible]7888158339286797581652104954628434169971646694834457

278 : [illegible]0259351924431073312796924978741056961814867751431689

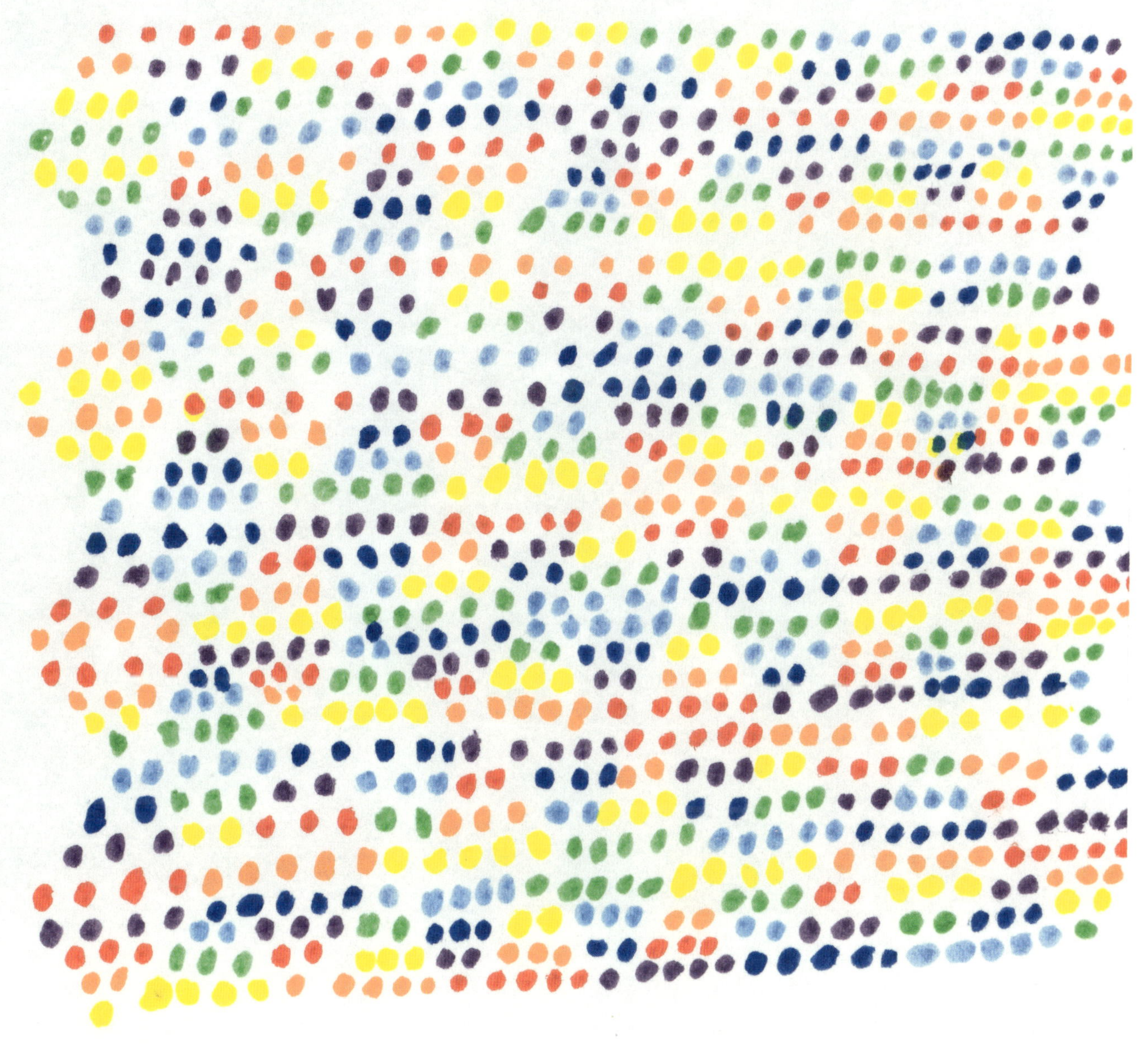

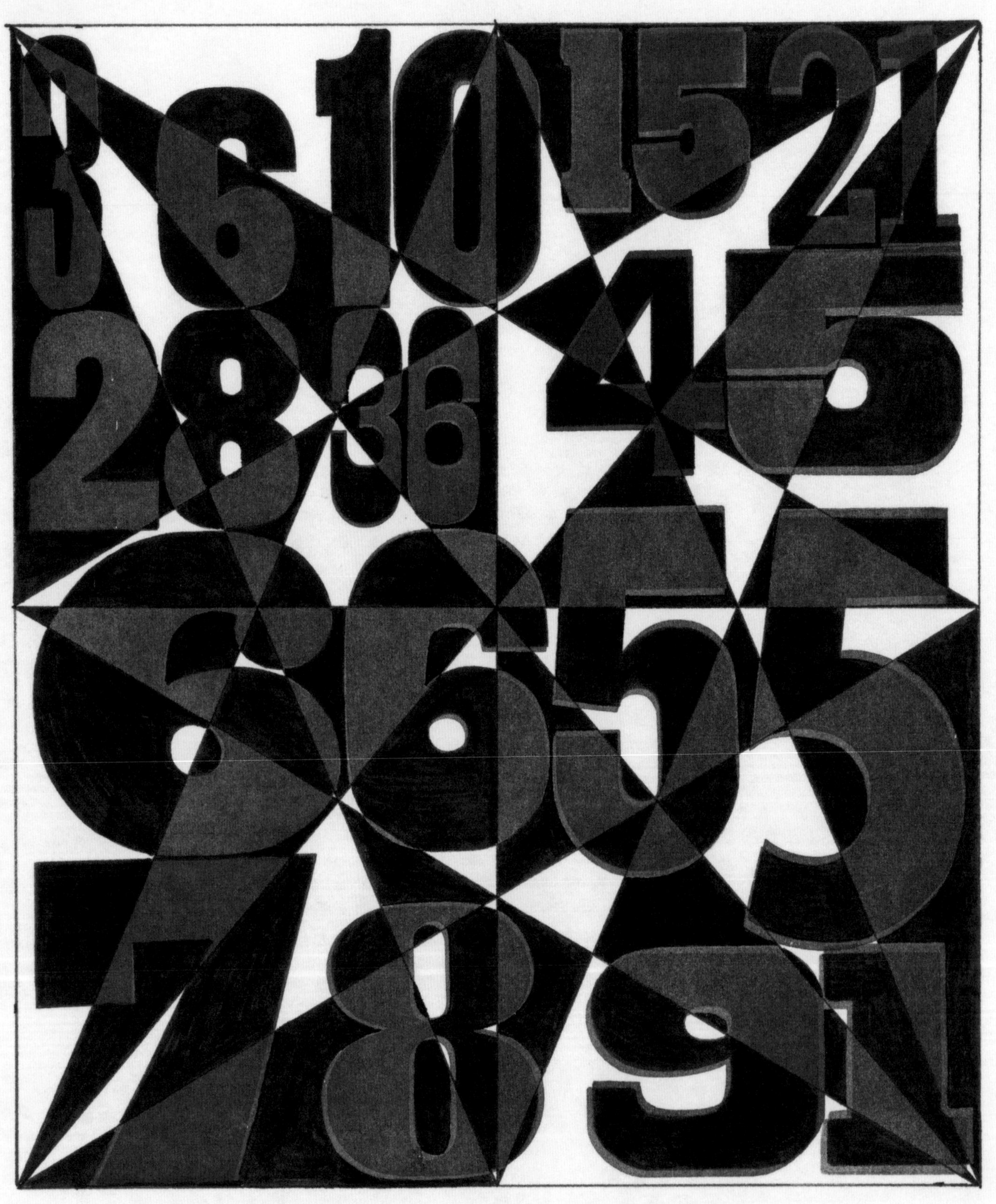

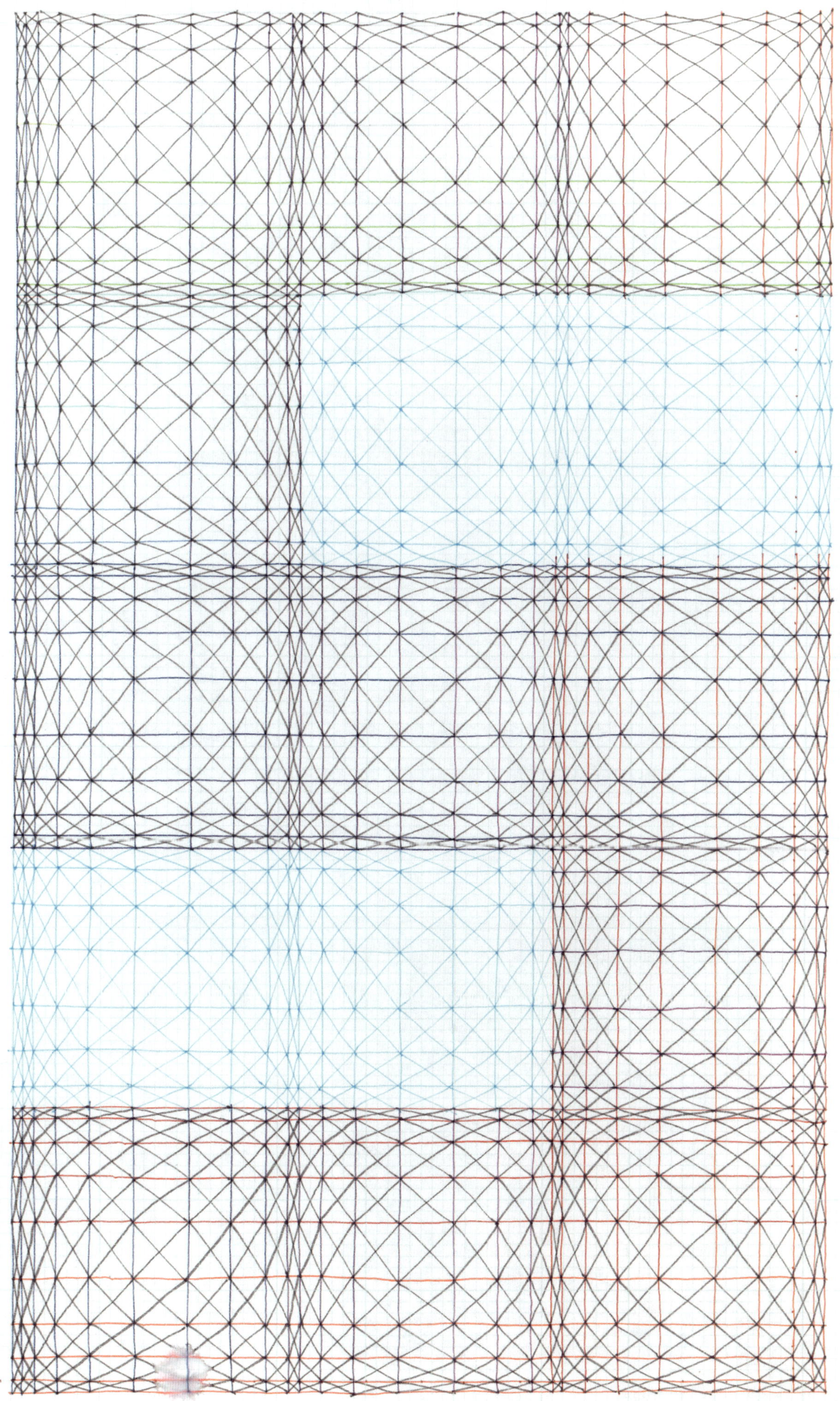

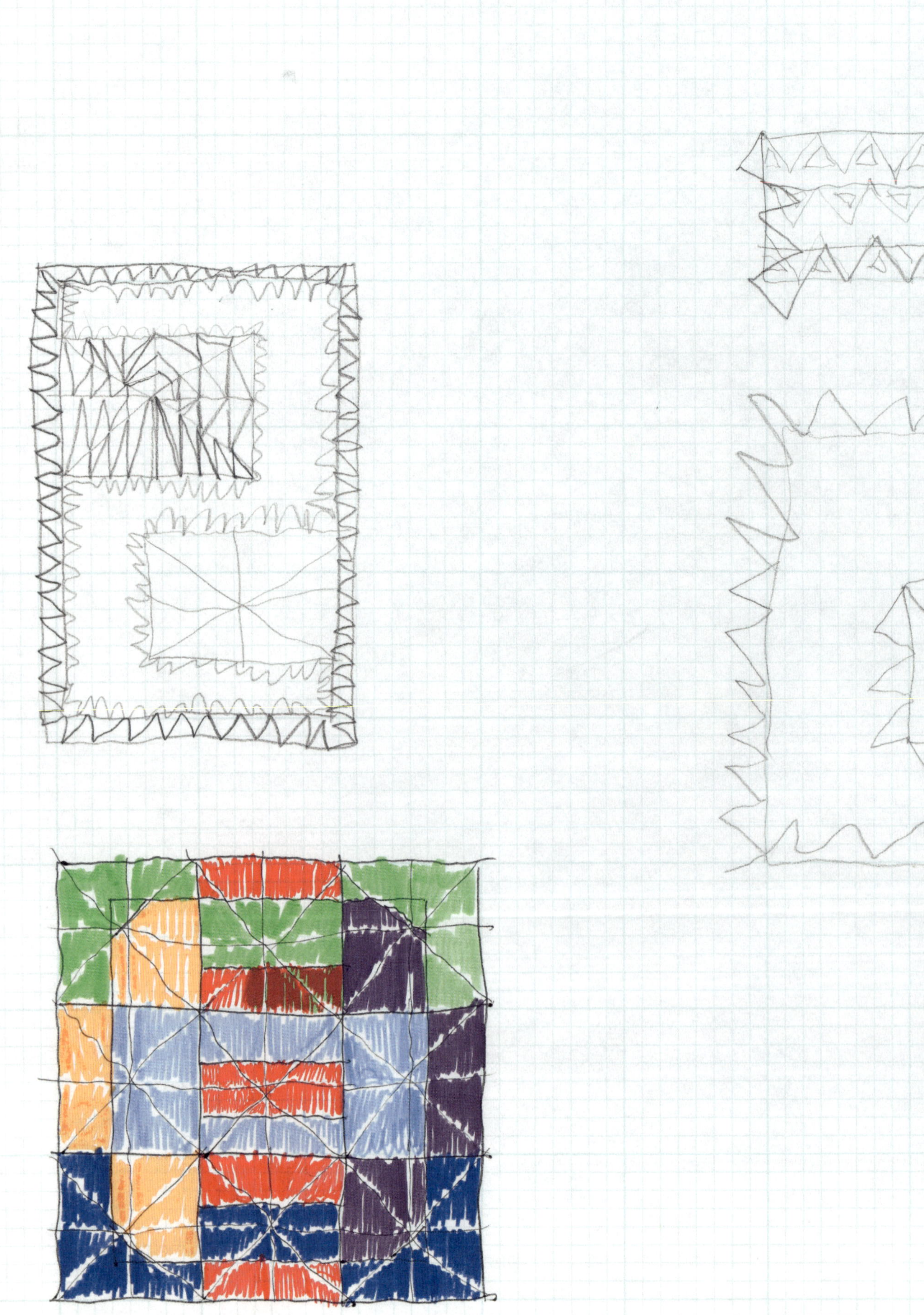

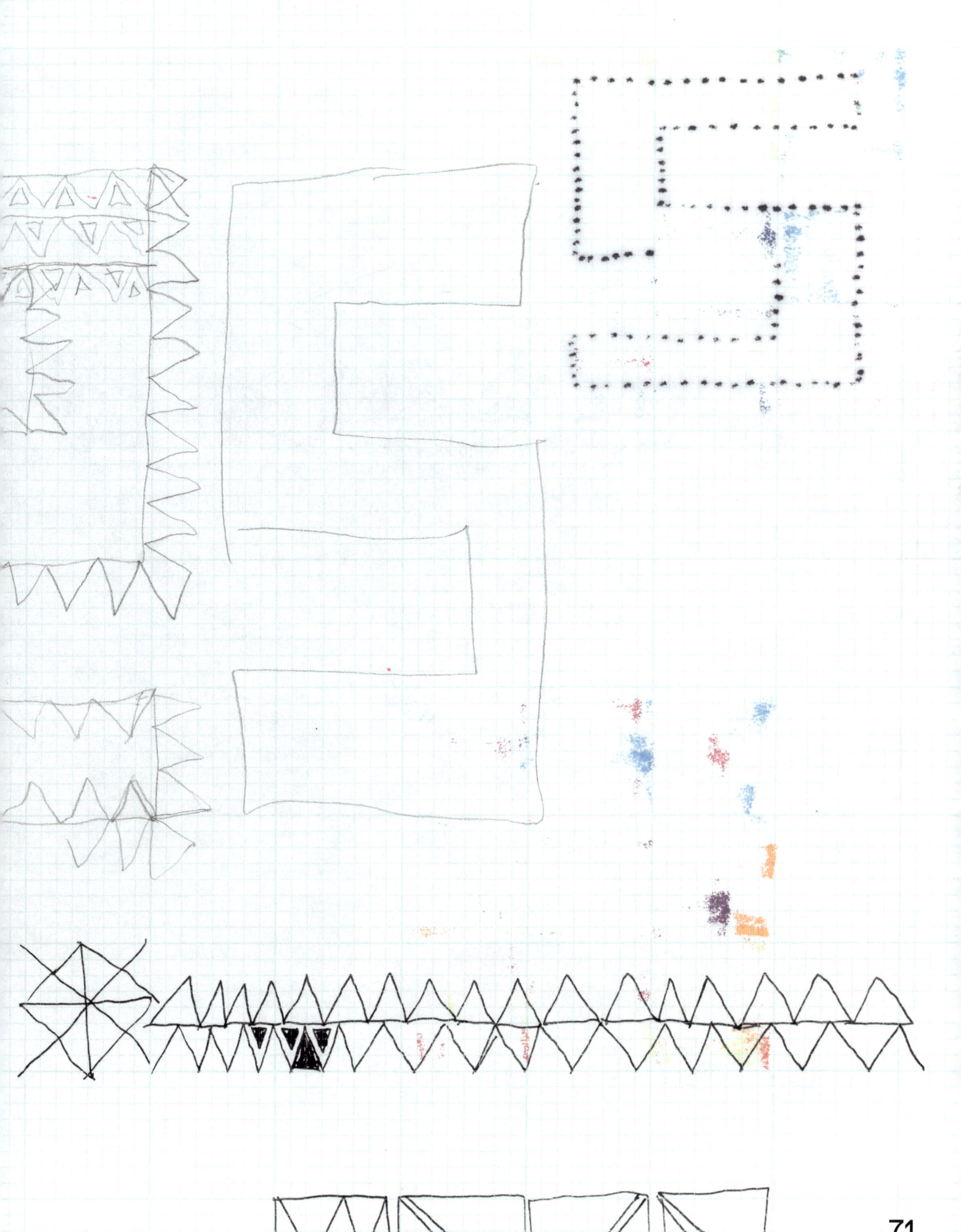

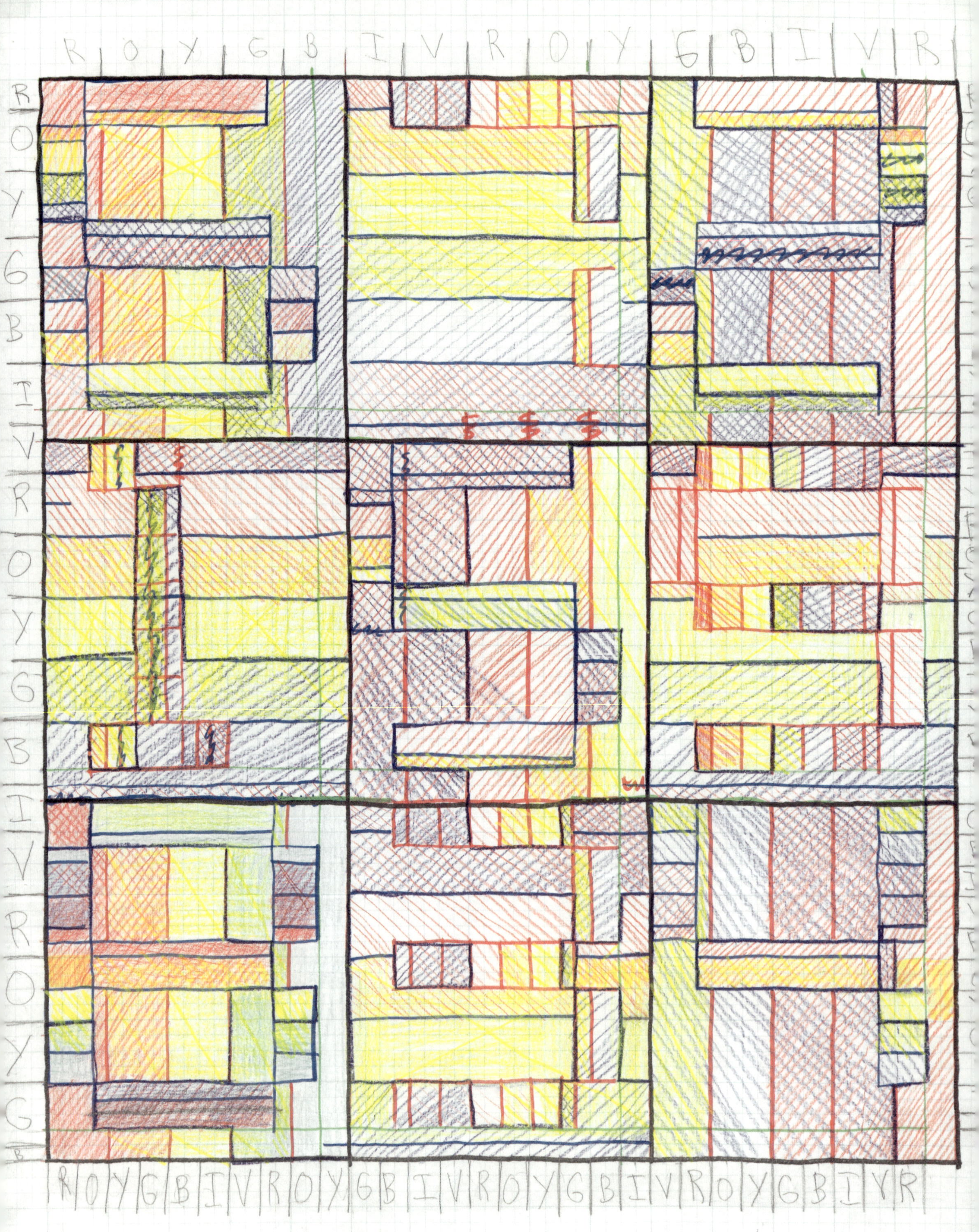

R O Y G B I V R O Y G B I V R
R O Y G B I V R O Y G B I V R O Y G B
R O Y G B I V R O Y G B I V R O Y G B I V R O Y G B I V R

CANADA
55 CHRYSTIE STREET NEW YORK 10002
CANADANEWYORK.COM
T: 212-925-4631

23

55
66
171
595
666 .. 36
3003 .. 77
5995 .. 109
8778 .. 132
15051
66066
617716
828828
1269621
1680861
3544453
5073705
5676765
6295926
35133153
61477416

30103
30203
30403
30703
30803
31033
31513
32323
32423
33533
34543
34843
35053
35153
35353
35753
36263
36563
37273
37573
38083
38183
38783
39293

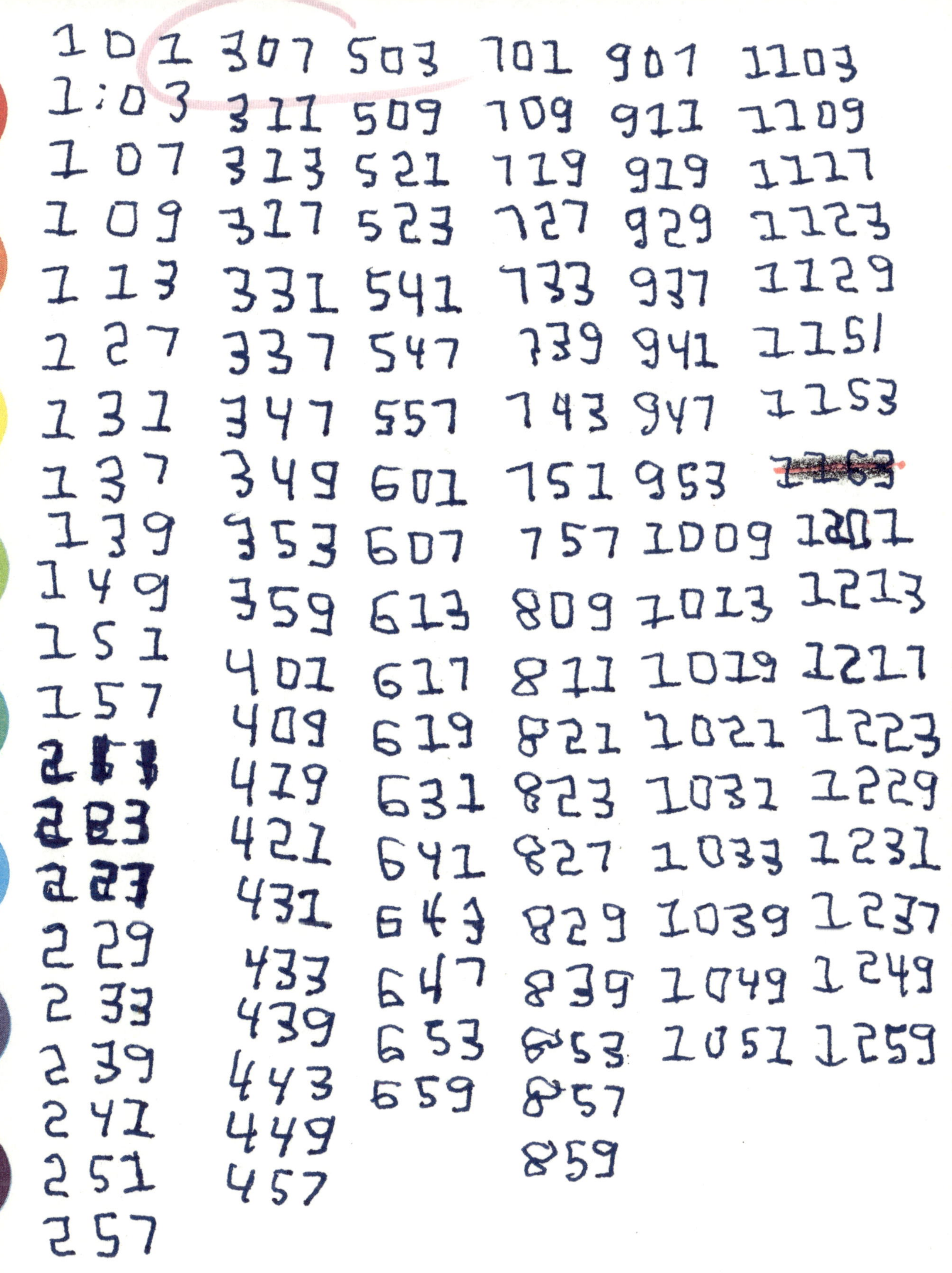

101
103
107
109
113
127
131
137
139
149
151
157
211
223
227
229
233
239
241
251
257
307
311
313
317
331
337
347
349
353
359
401
409
419
421
431
433
439
443
449
457
503
509
521
523
541
547
557
601
607
613
617
619
631
641
643
647
653
659
701
709
719
727
733
739
743
751
757
809
811
821
823
827
829
839
853
857
859
901
911
919
929
937
941
947
953
1009
1013
1019
1021
1031
1033
1039
1049
1051
1103
1109
1117
1123
1129
1151
1153
~~1163~~
1201
1213
1217
1223
1229
1231
1237
1249
1259

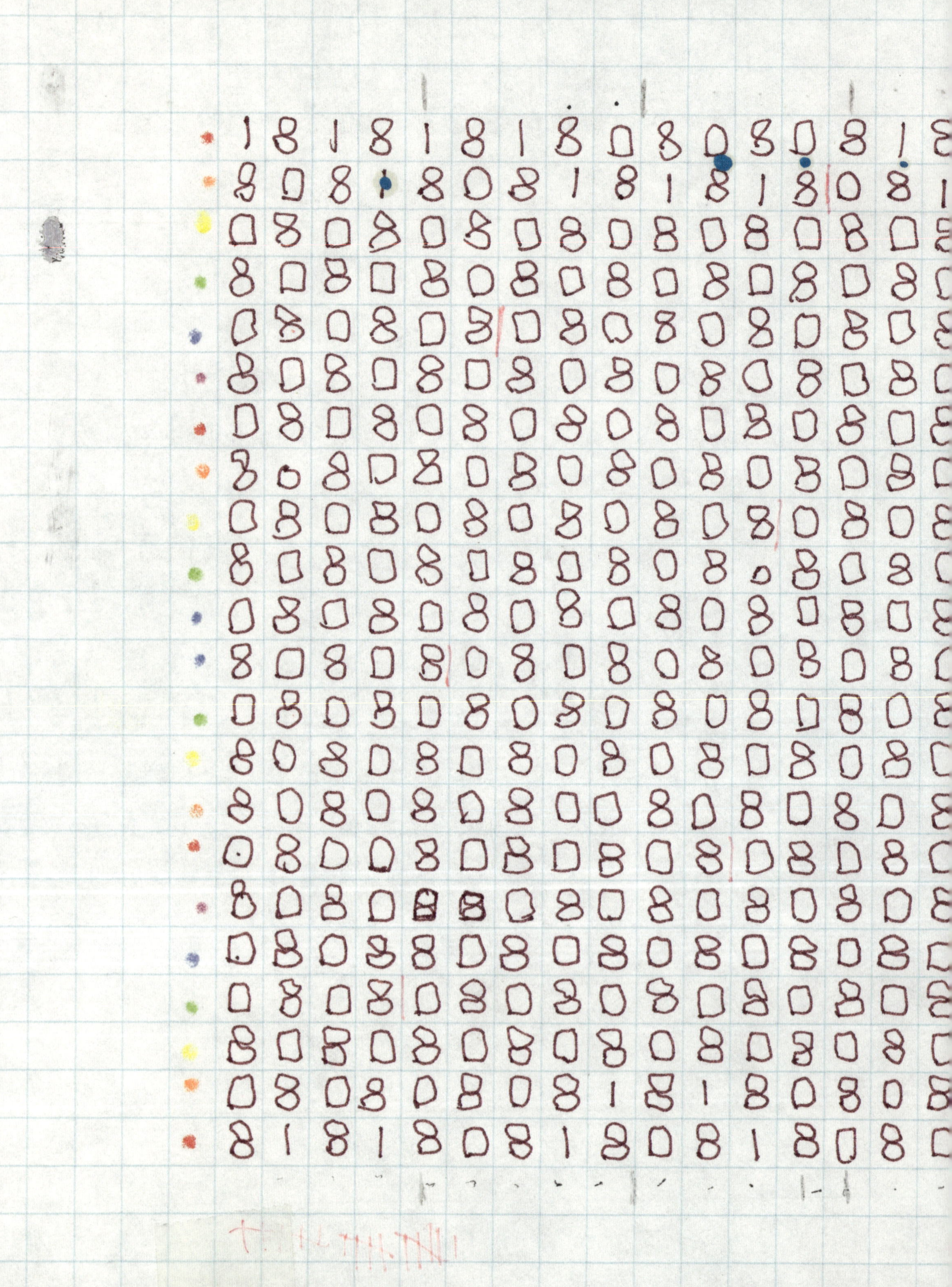

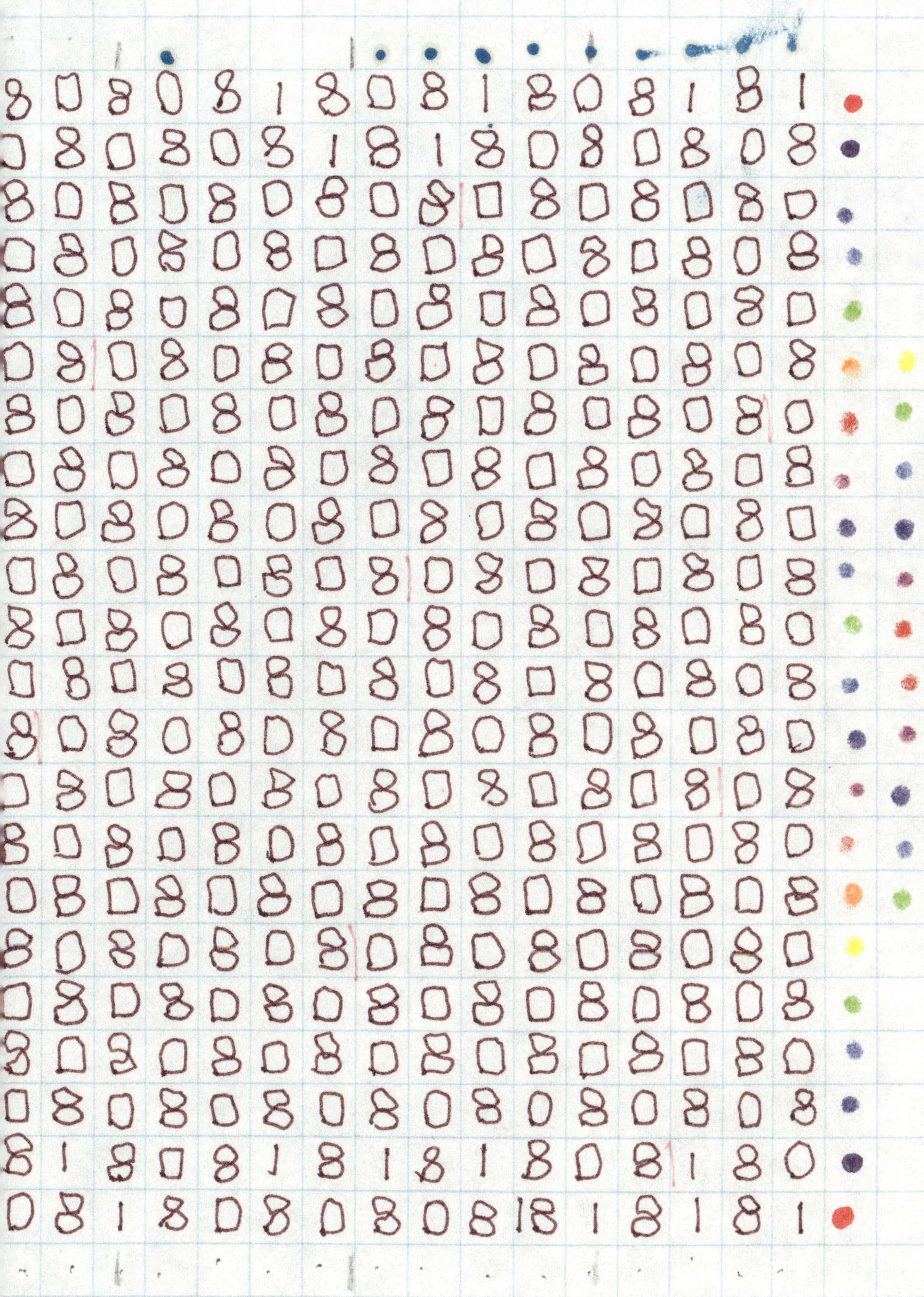

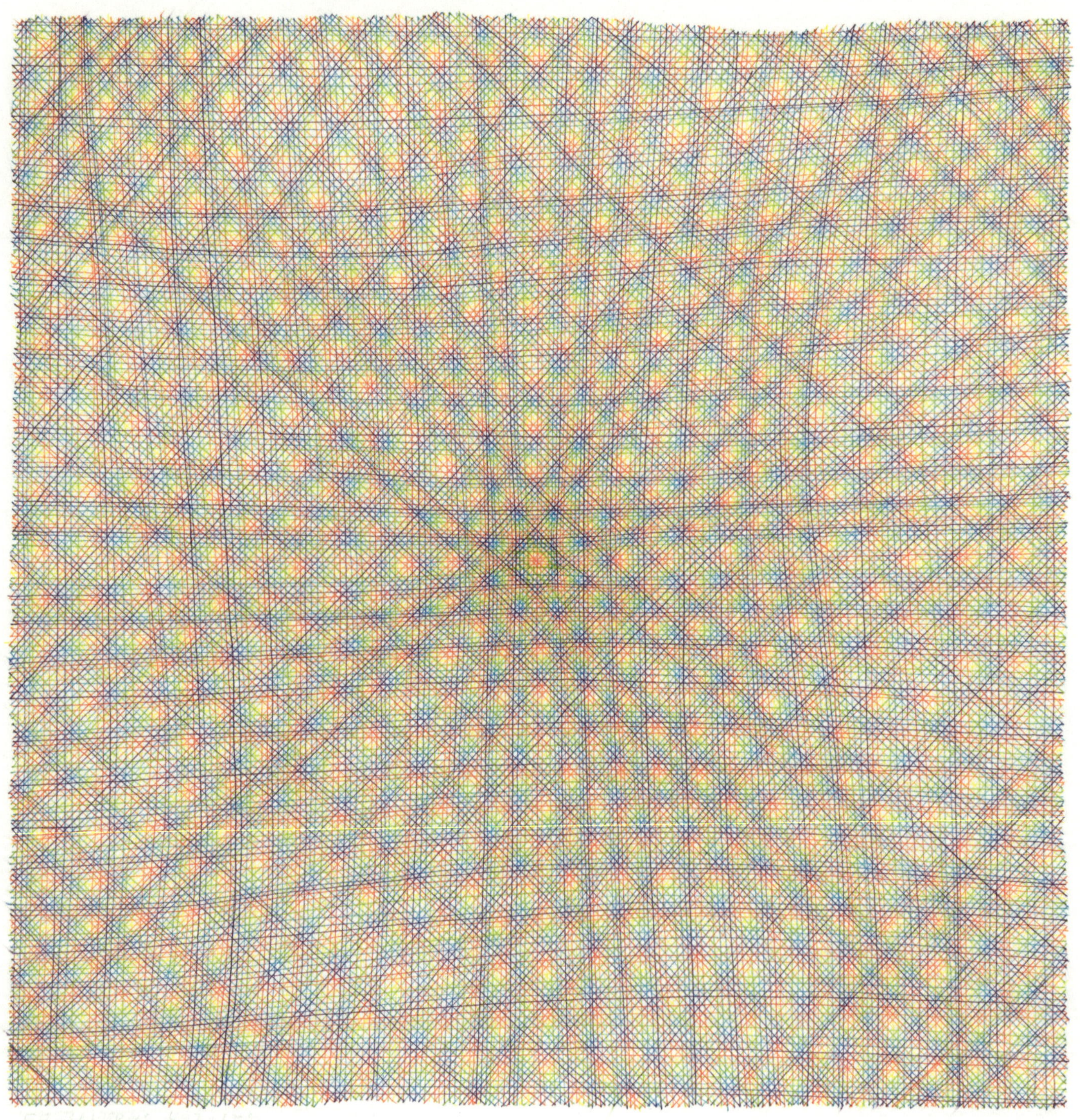

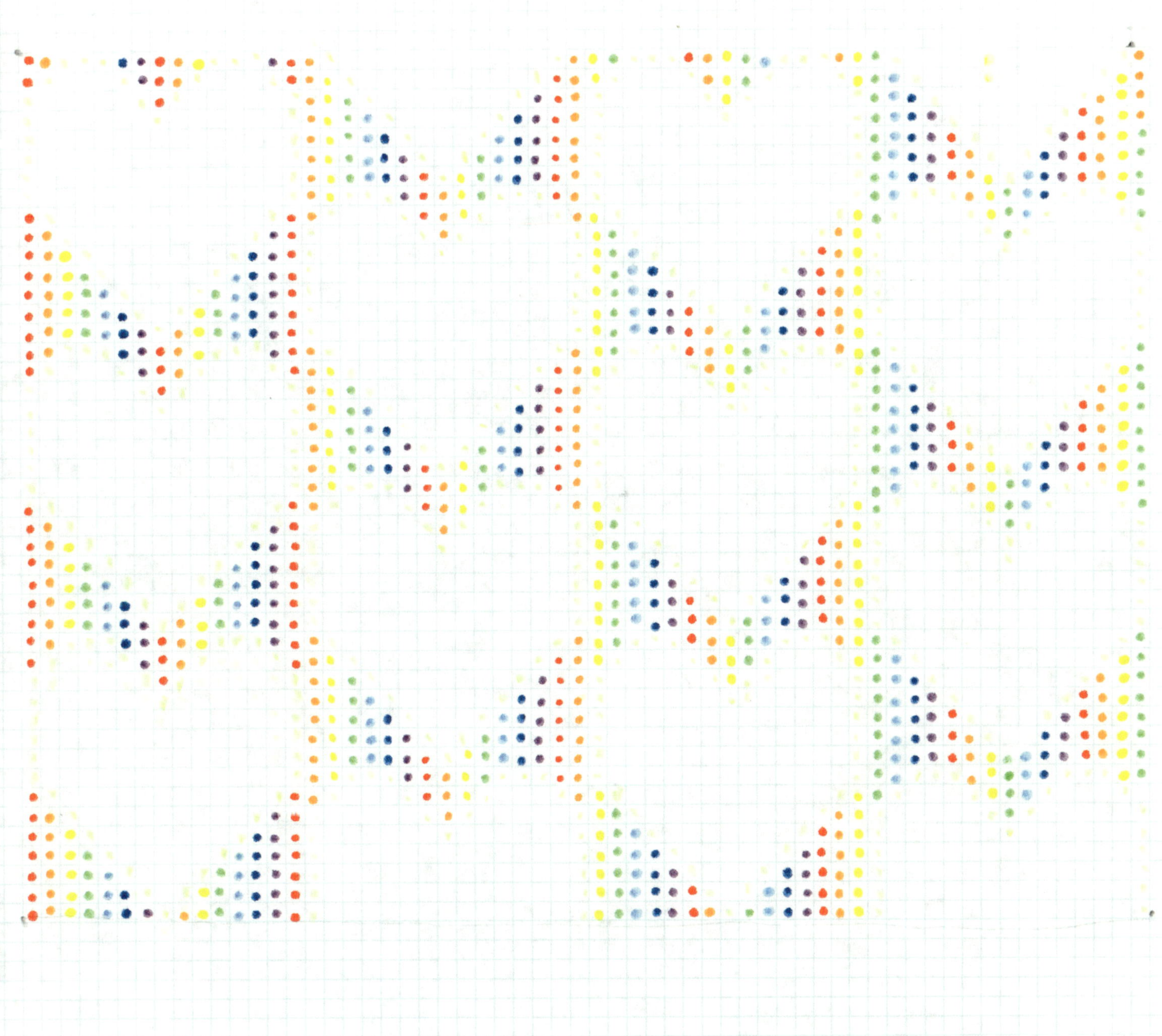

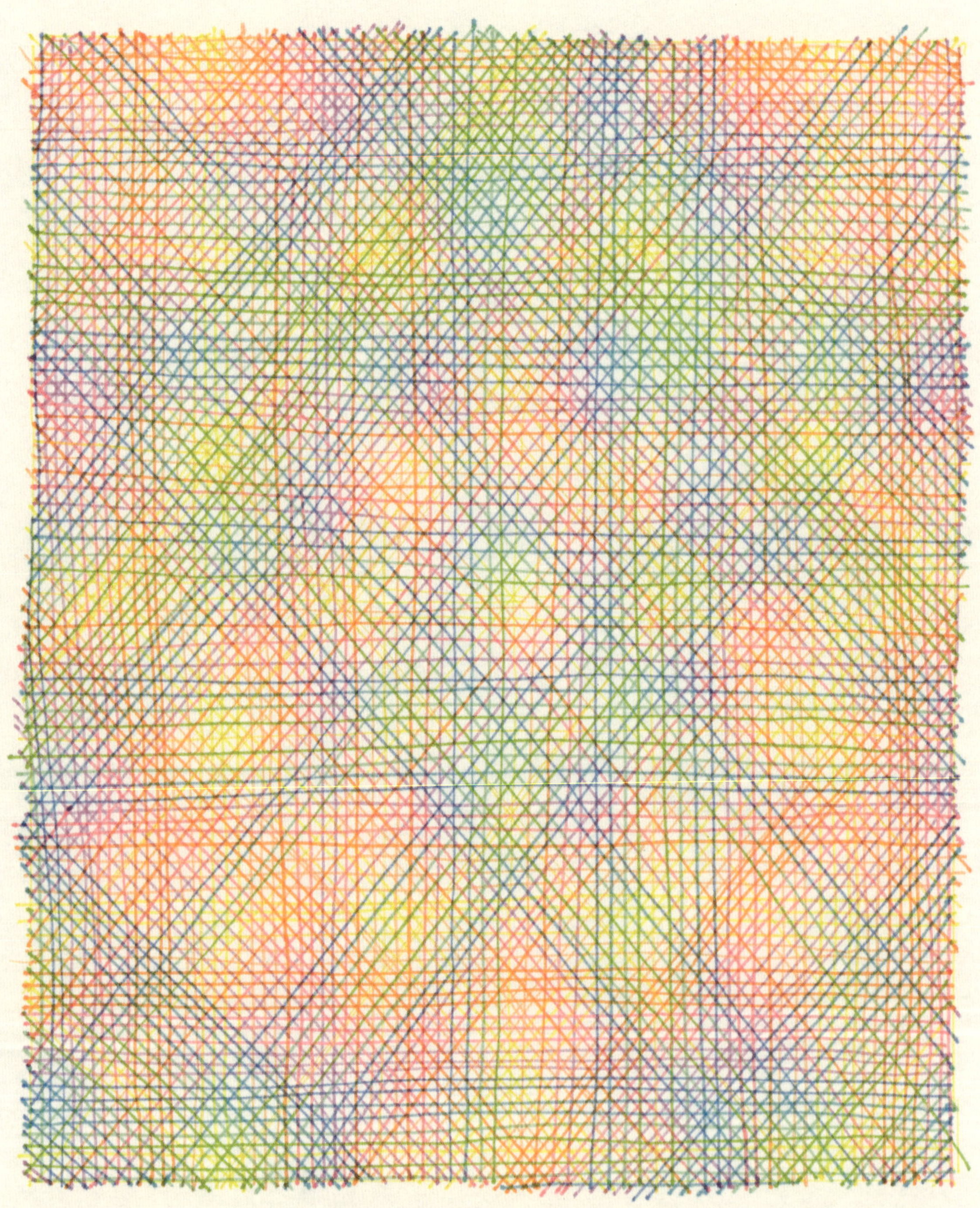

1261. ||||5|5||||

1264. ||||777||||

1265. ||||599||||

1292. ← |||4|4|4|||

1303. |||5|||5|||

1307. |||55555||| ← |||88888|||

1341. |||99|99||| ← ||4|444|4|

1592.

1702. ||5|||||5||

2132. |88|8|88||

2250. ||59||||59||

2258. ||555|999511

2404. |2|2|2|2|2|2|

2525. ← |2222|2222|

3502. |3|||3|||3|

3508. |333|||333| ← |3||3|3||3| 3530. |3|3||[illegible]31

3923.

4538. |4||||||||4|

4564. |4|4|4|4|4|4| ← |7777|7777|

8532

8916 |8||||||||8|

8924 |8||888||8|

9648 |88|8|8|88|

10043 |9|99999|9|

9030

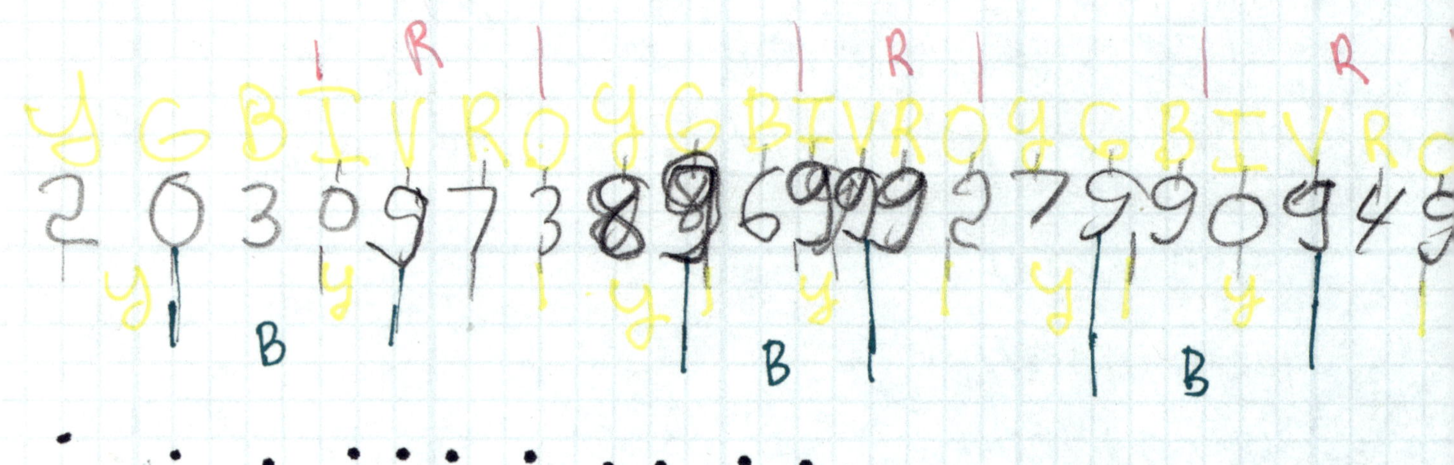

369738969992799094977977157372 7

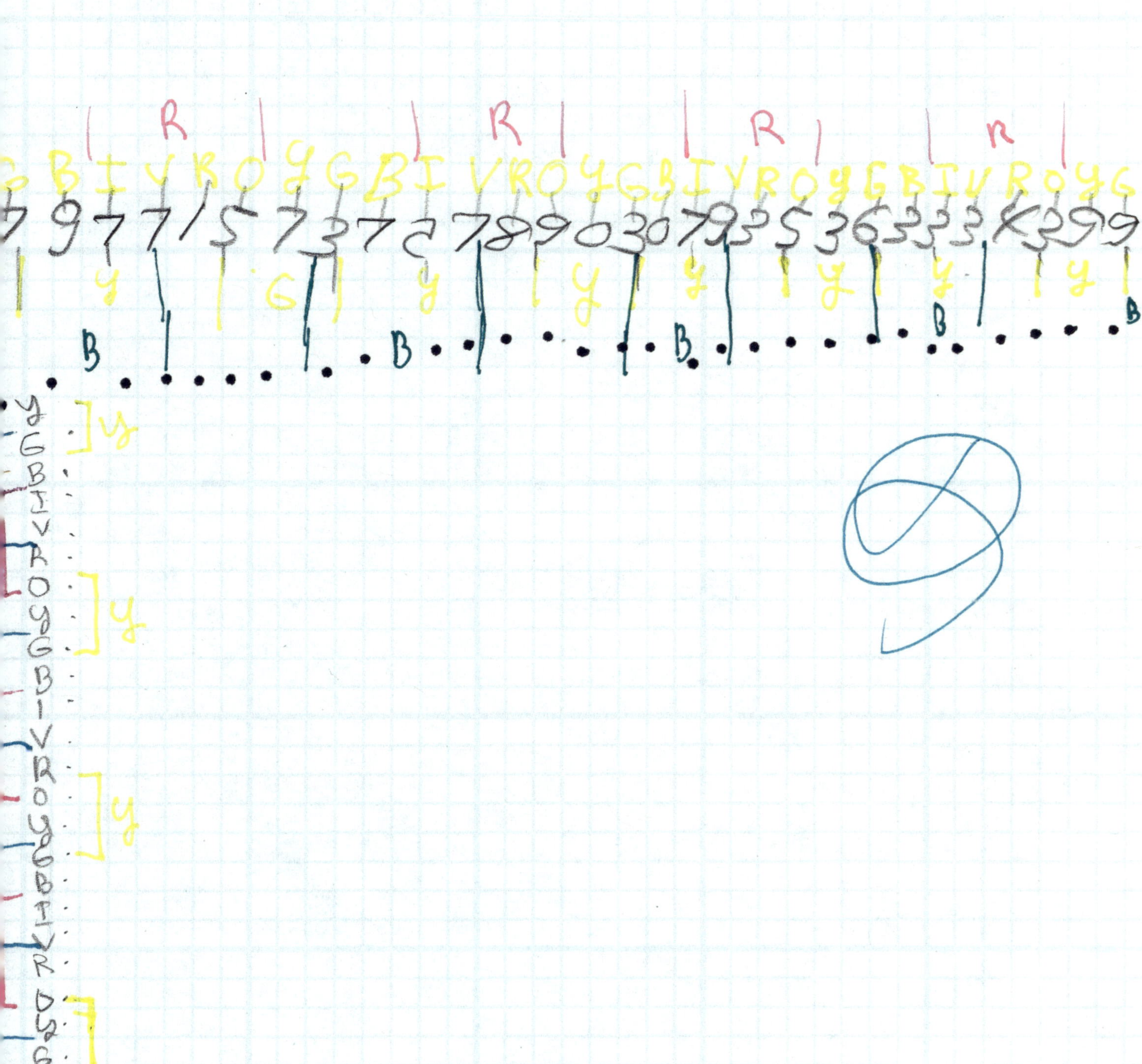

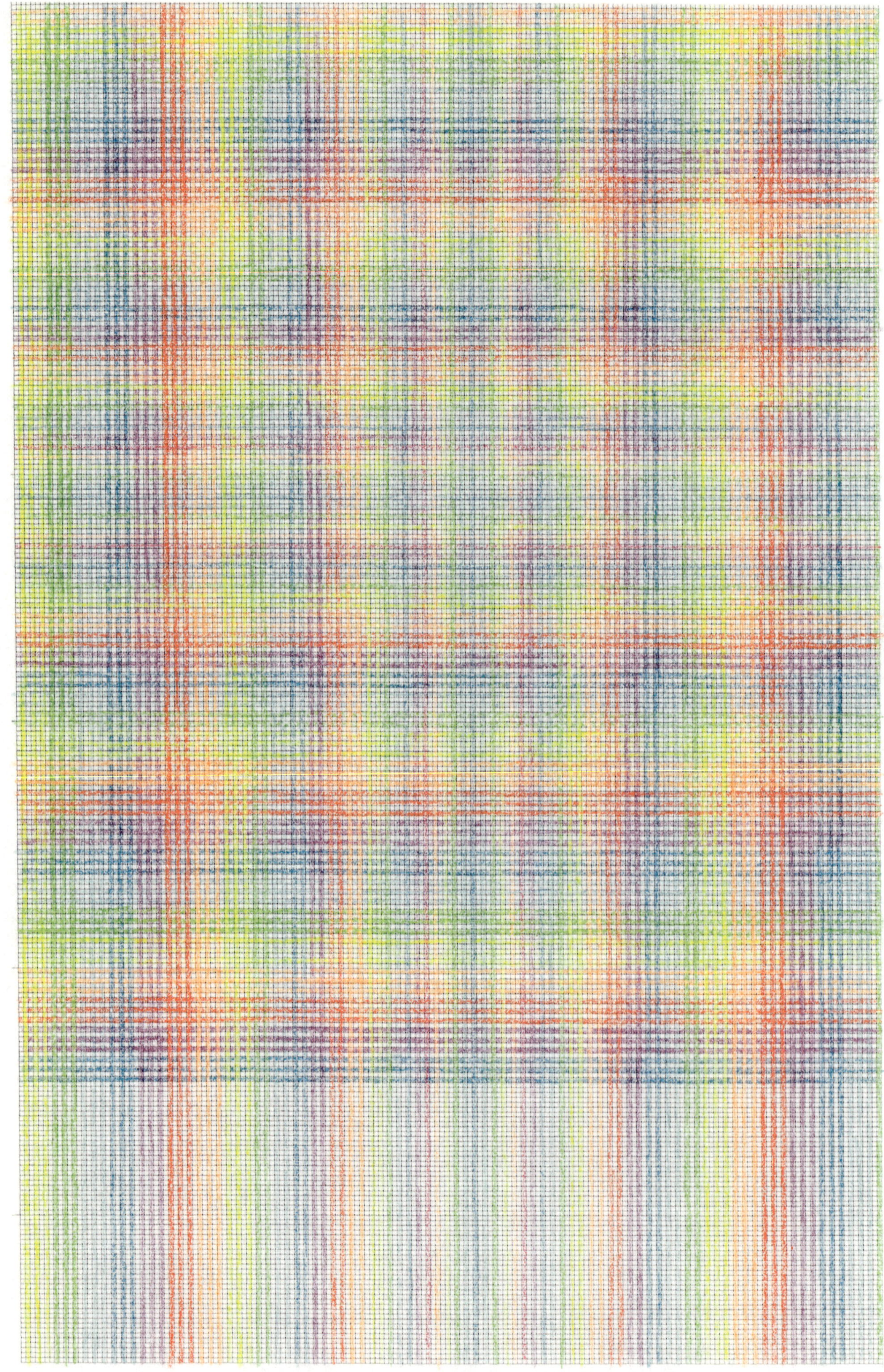

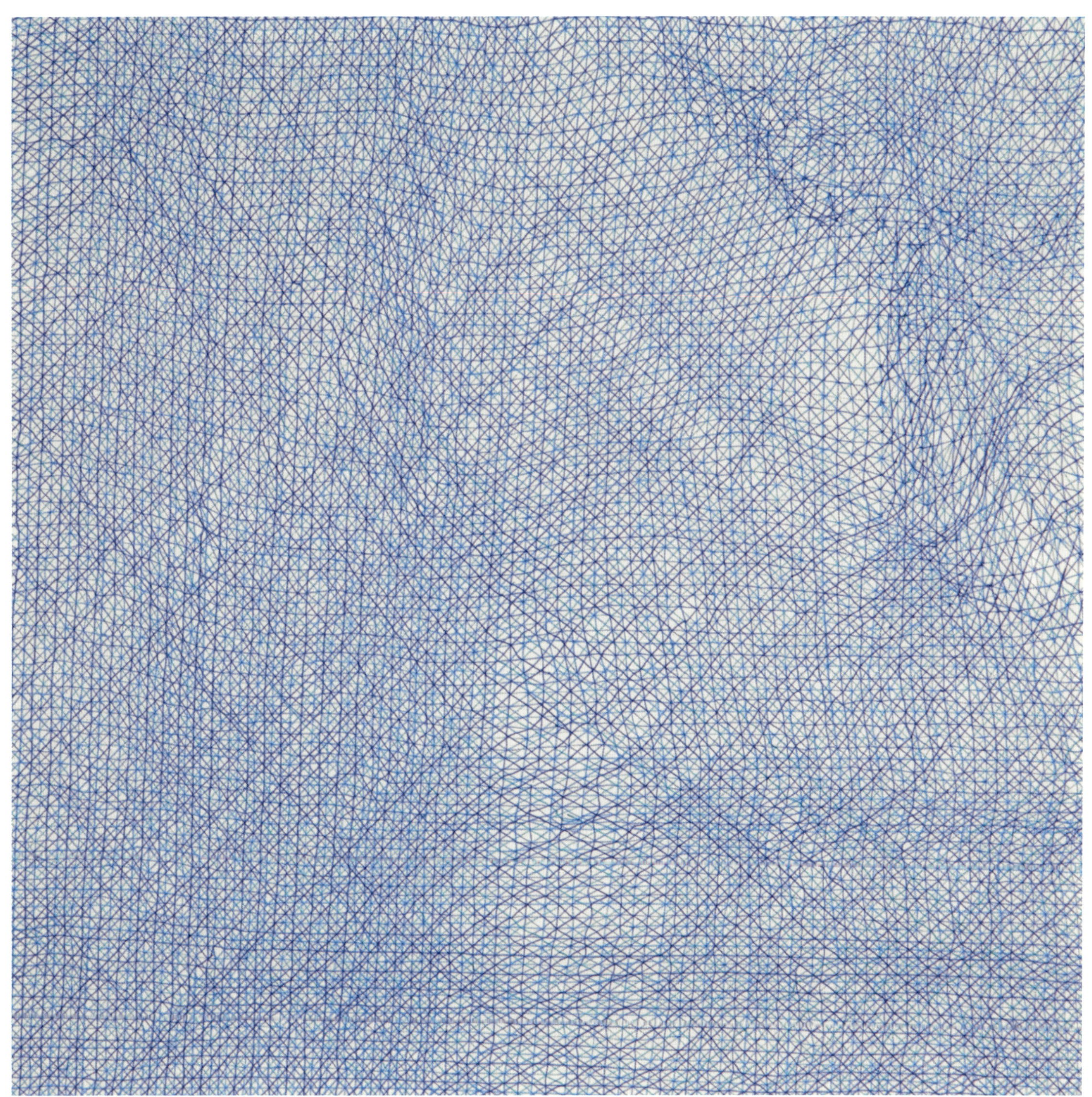

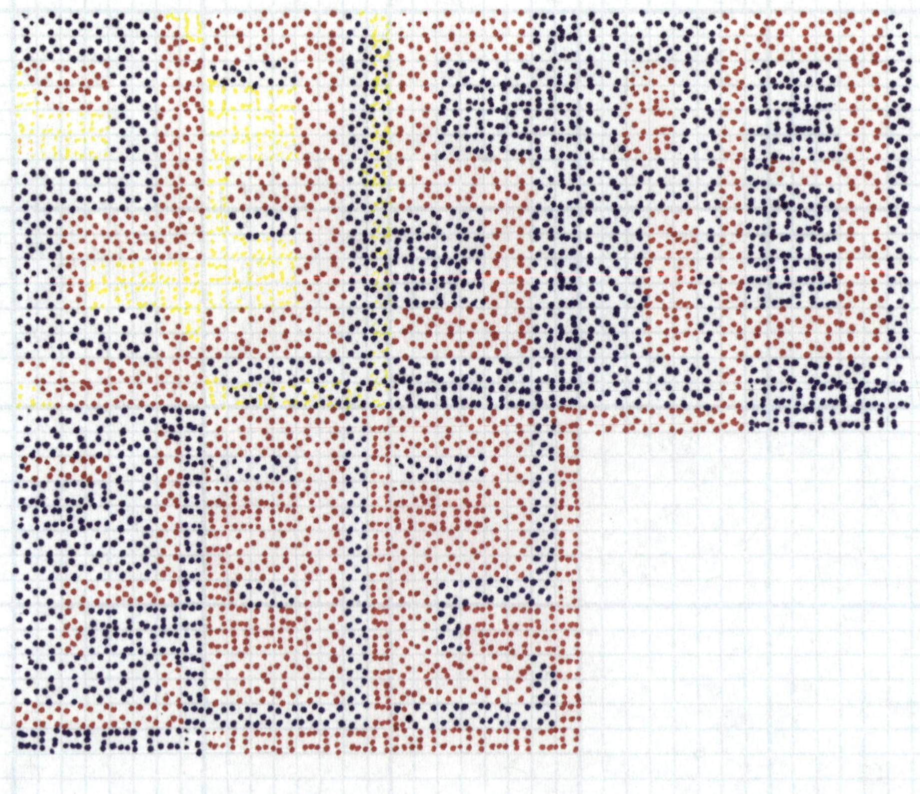

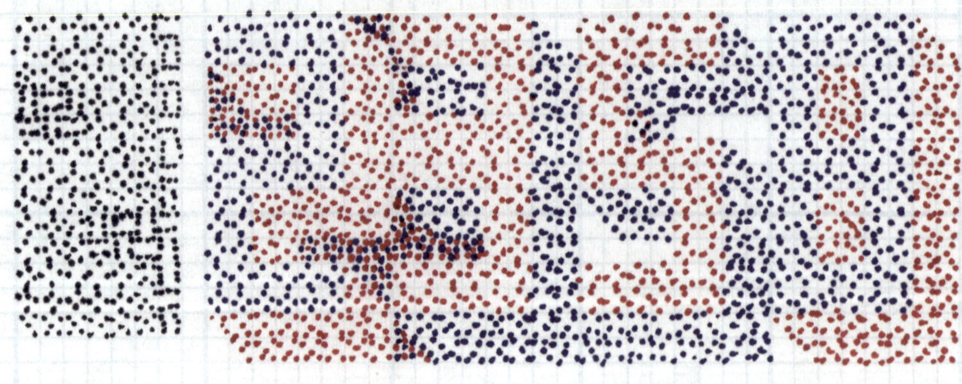

Figure 1: **A palindromic prime pyramid of step size two**

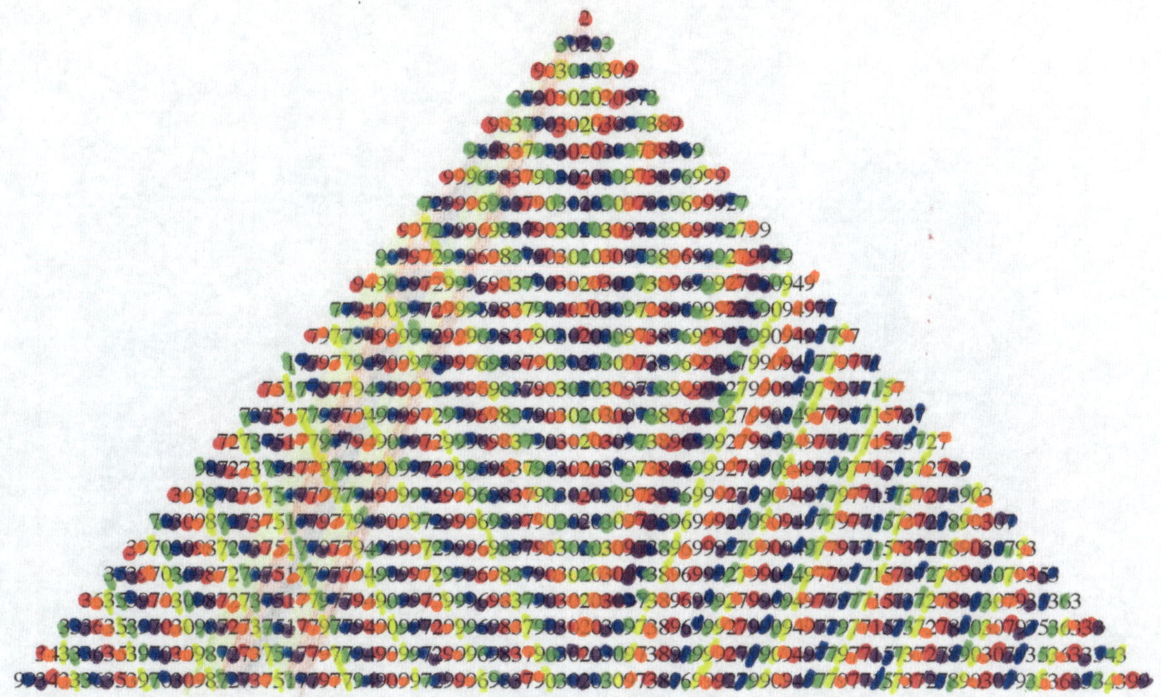

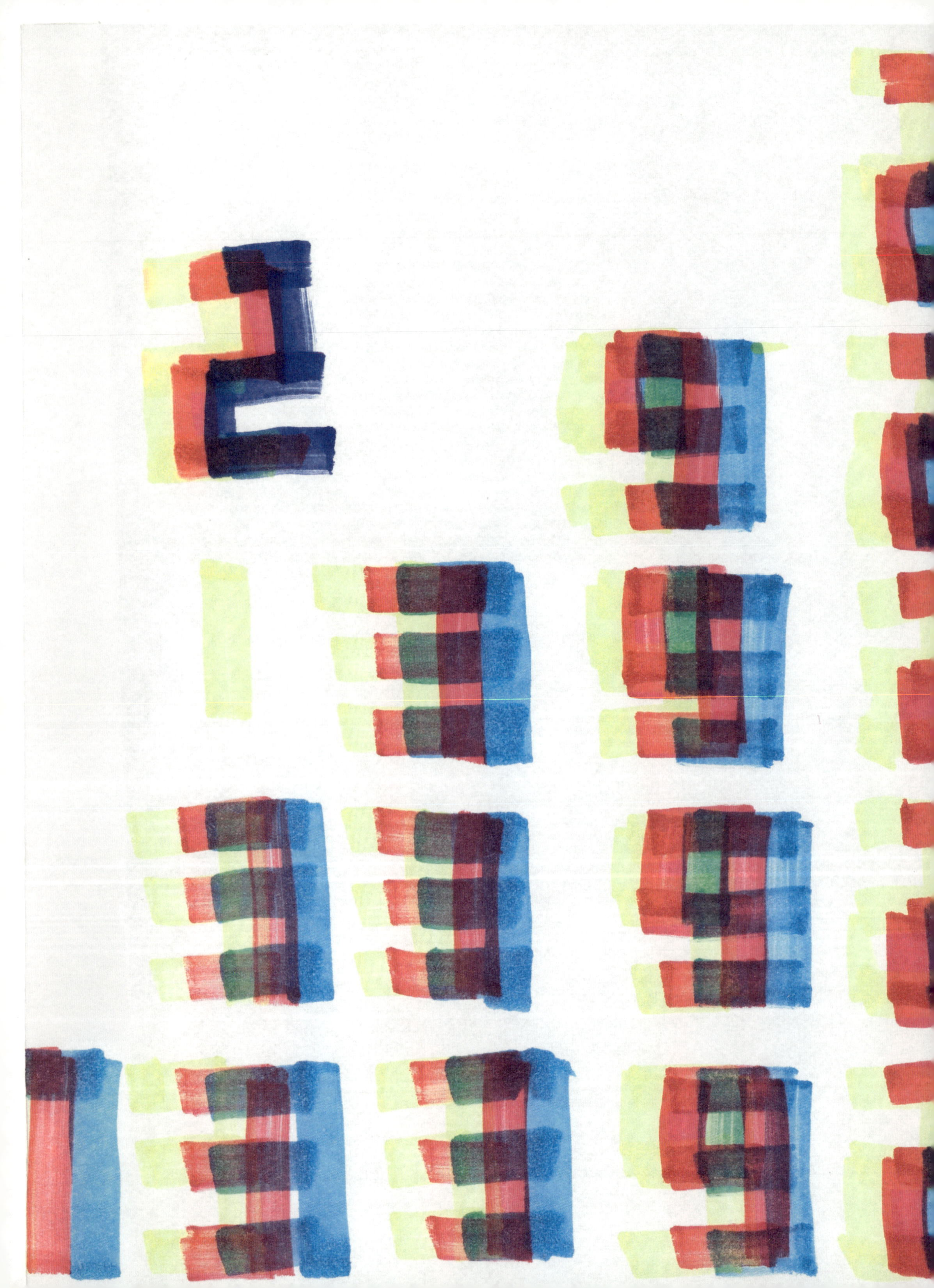

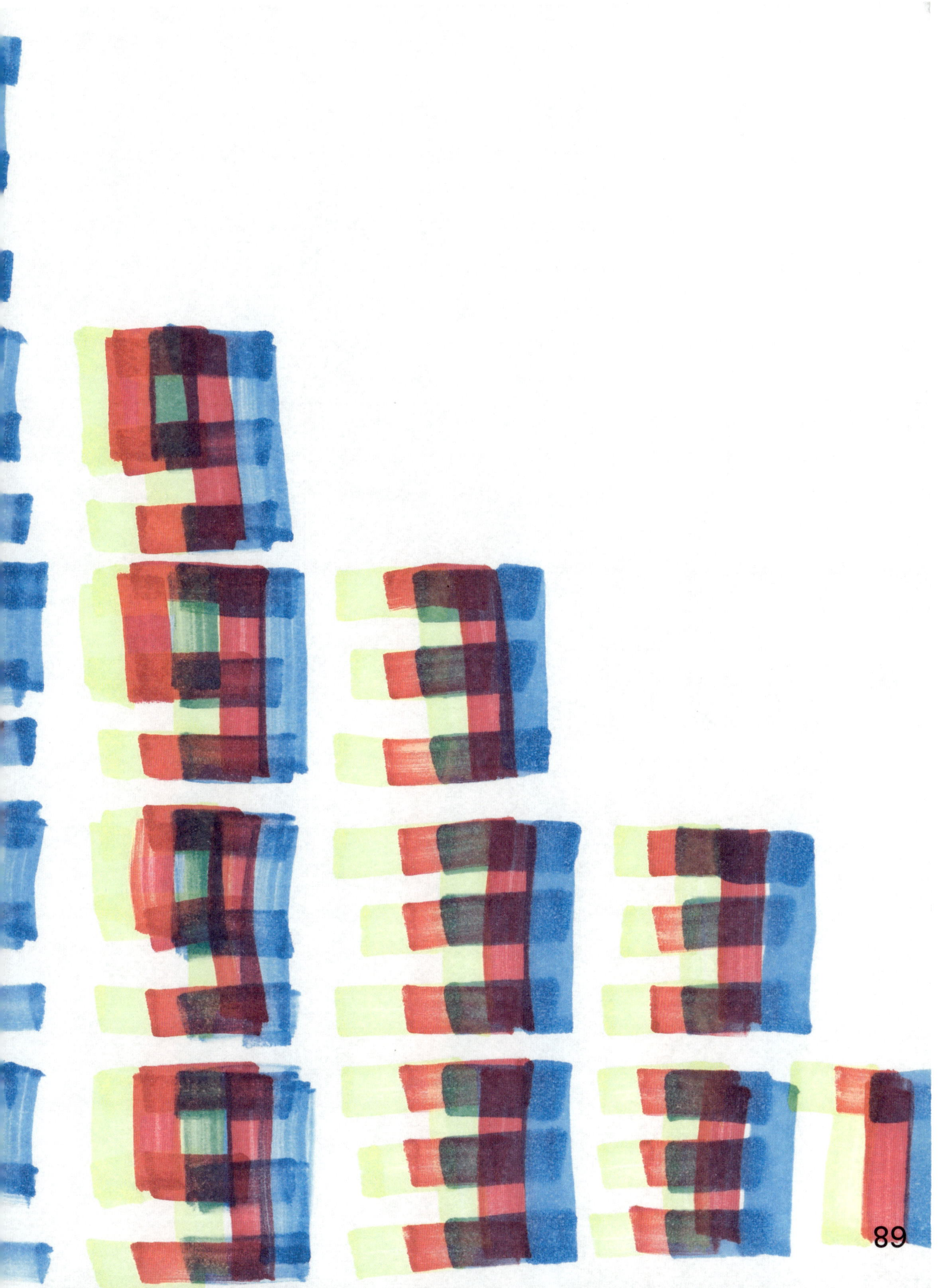

2
3
5
10
14
16
23
25
32
41
43
52
56
61
65
104
113
115
124
131
133
142
146
155
166
203
205
212
214
221
241
245
254
256
302
304
313
322
326
335
344
346
362
364
401
403
421
436
443
445
452
461
463
506
515
524
533
535
544
551
553
566
616
623
625
632
652
661
1004
1006
1013
1022
1033
1042
1051
1055
1064
1105
1112
1123
1136
1141
1154
1156
1165
1202
1211
1222
1226
1231
1235
1253
1264
1301
1312
1316
1325
1343
1345
1402
1411
1424
1433
1442
1444
1453
1466
1505
1514
1516
1525
1534
1541
1543
1561
1604
1606
1613
1622
1631
1633
1651
1655
1664
2005
2021
2032
2045
2056
2065
2104
2111
2122
2131
2135

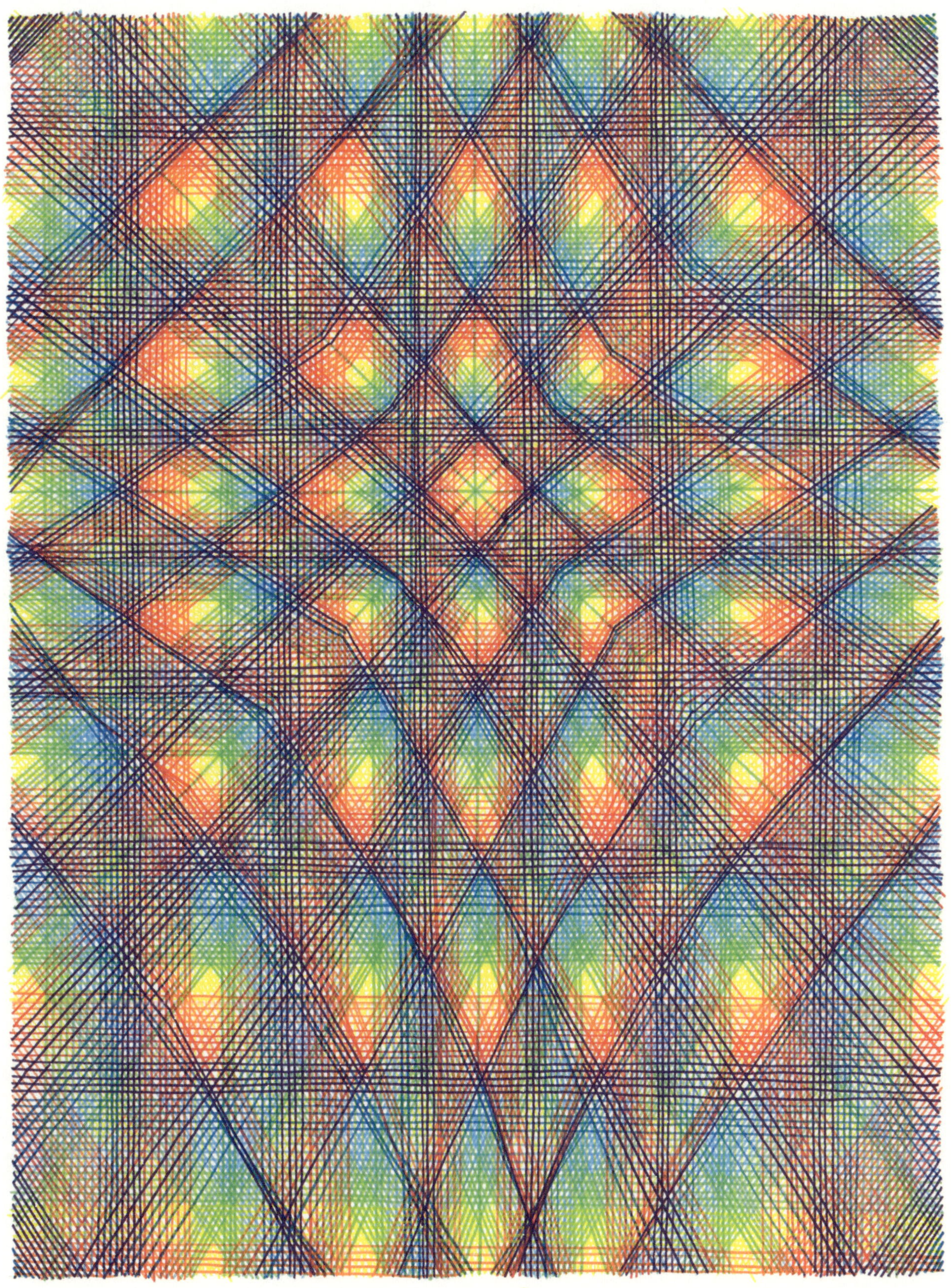

79997

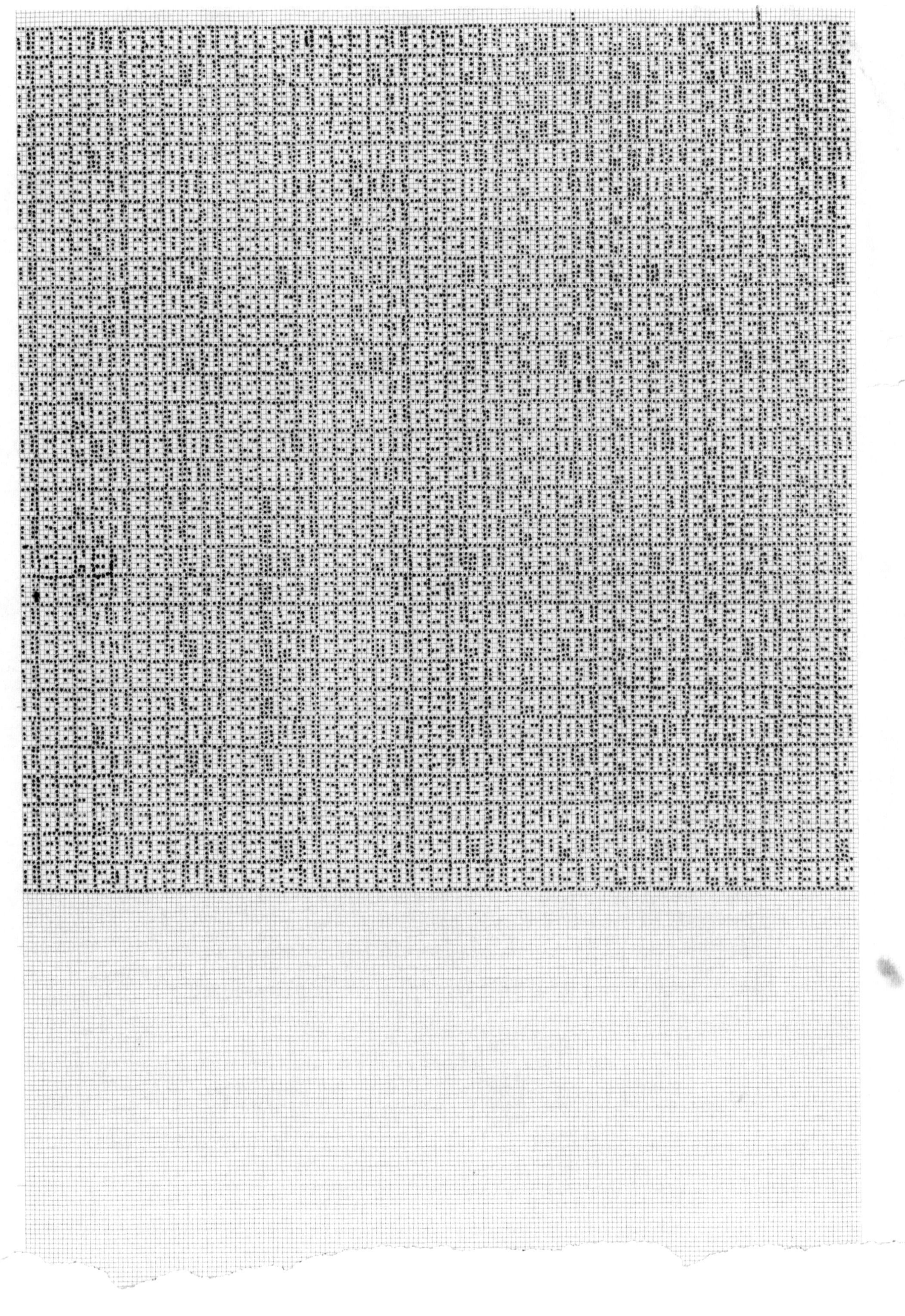

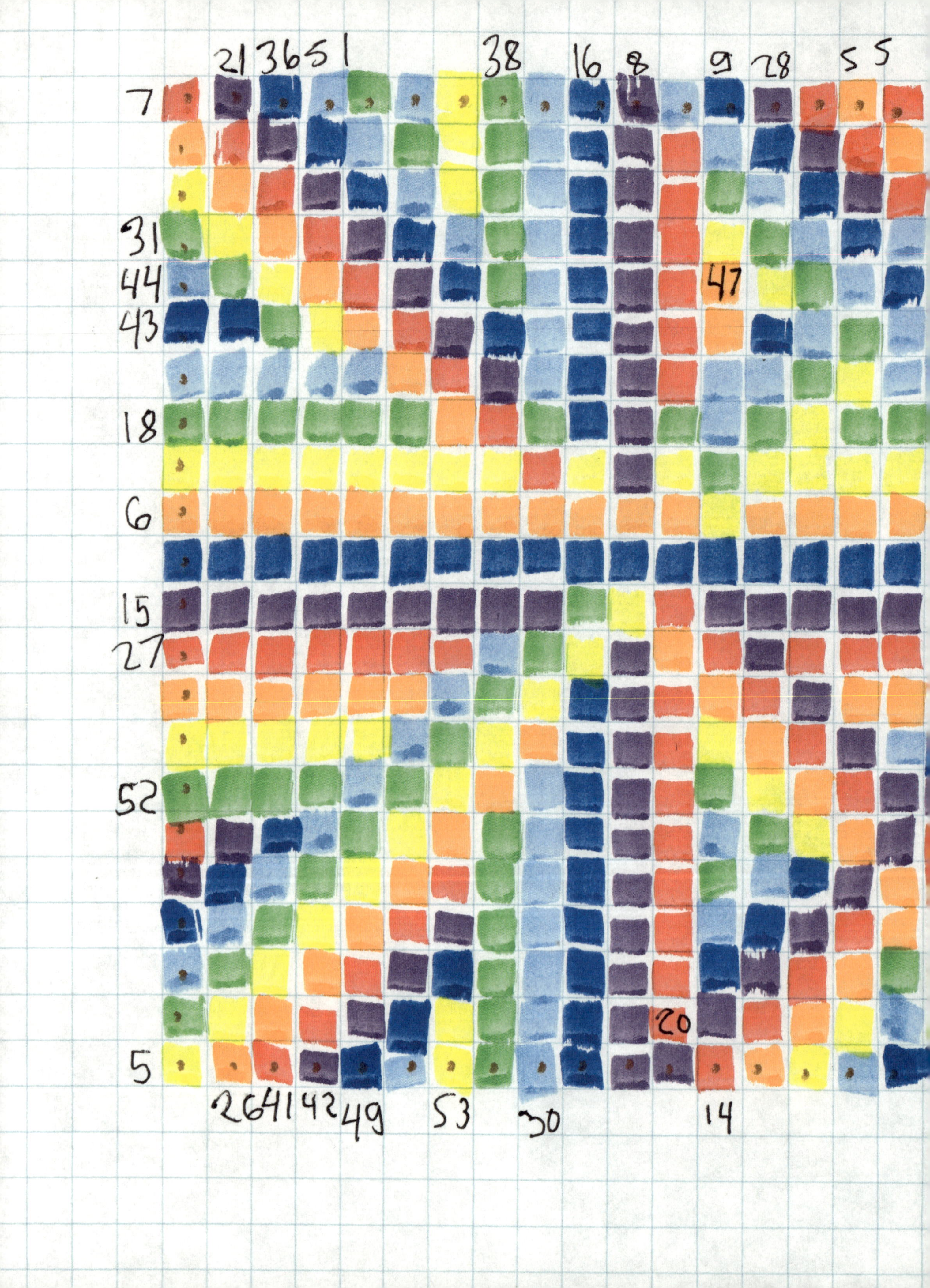
21 36 51 38 16 8 9 28 55
7
31
44
47
43
18
6
15
27
52
20
5
26 41 42 49 53 30 14

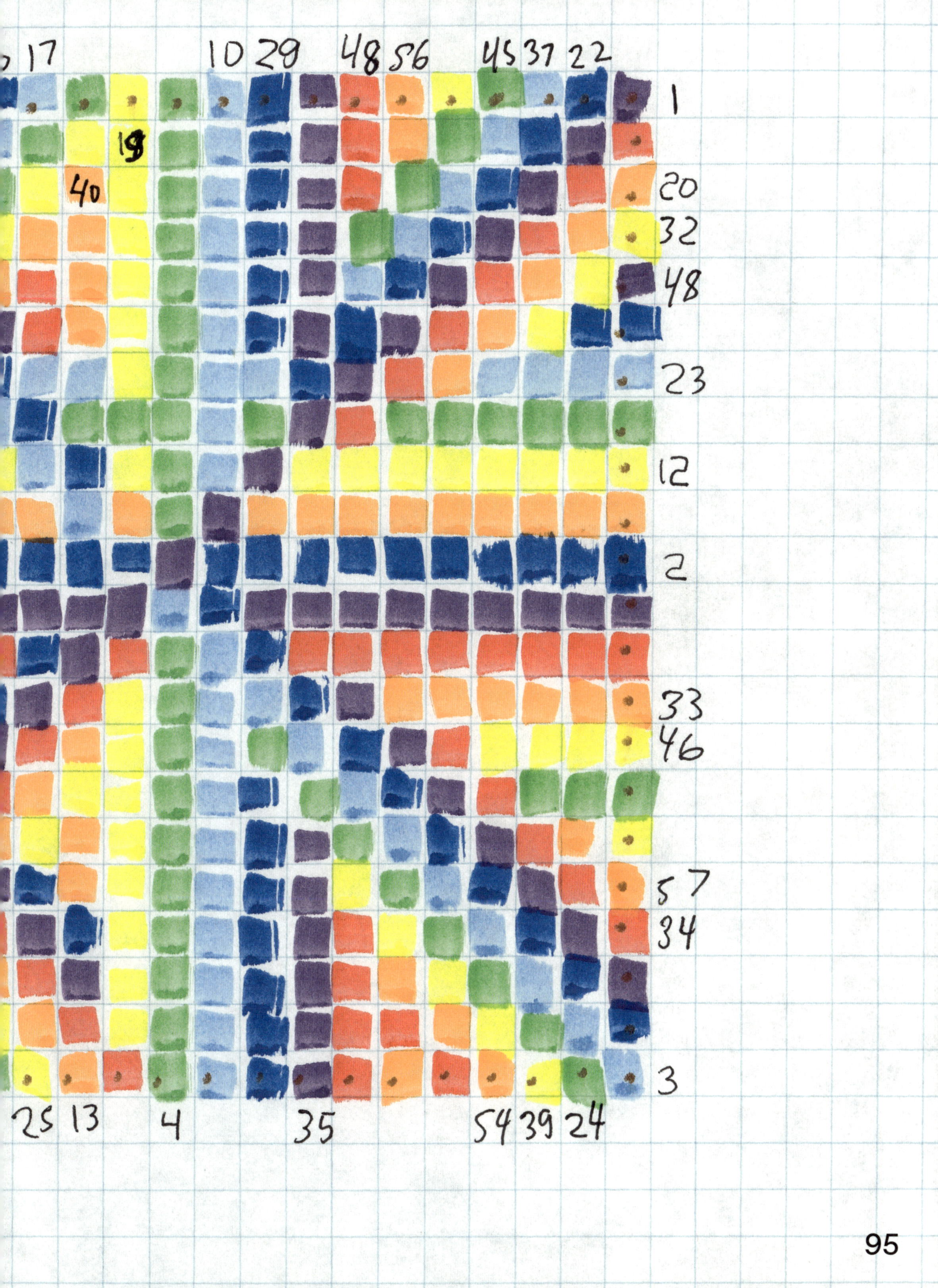
17 10 29 48 56 45 37 22
1
19
40
20
32
48
23
12
2
33
46
57
34
3
25 13 4 35 54 39 24

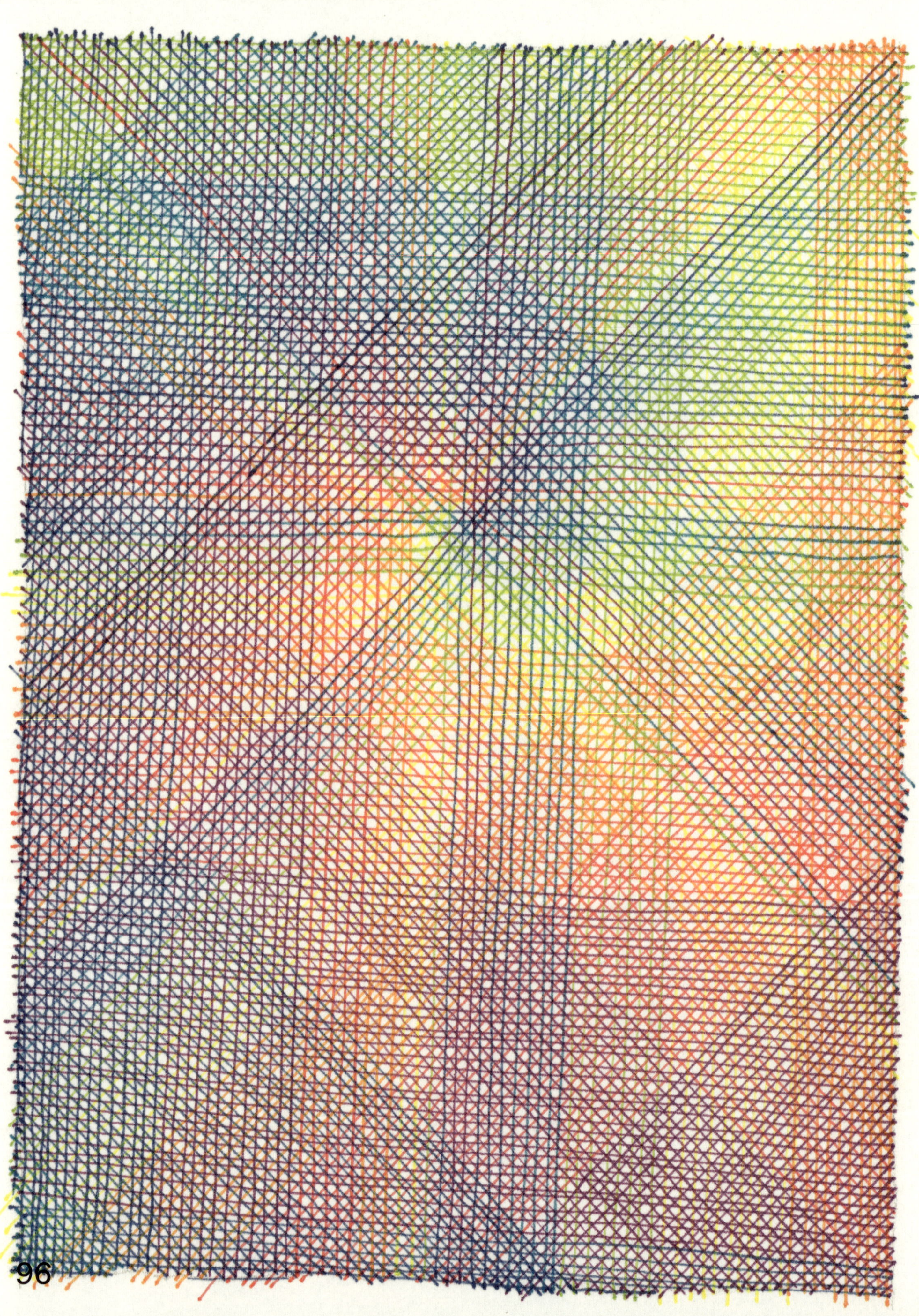

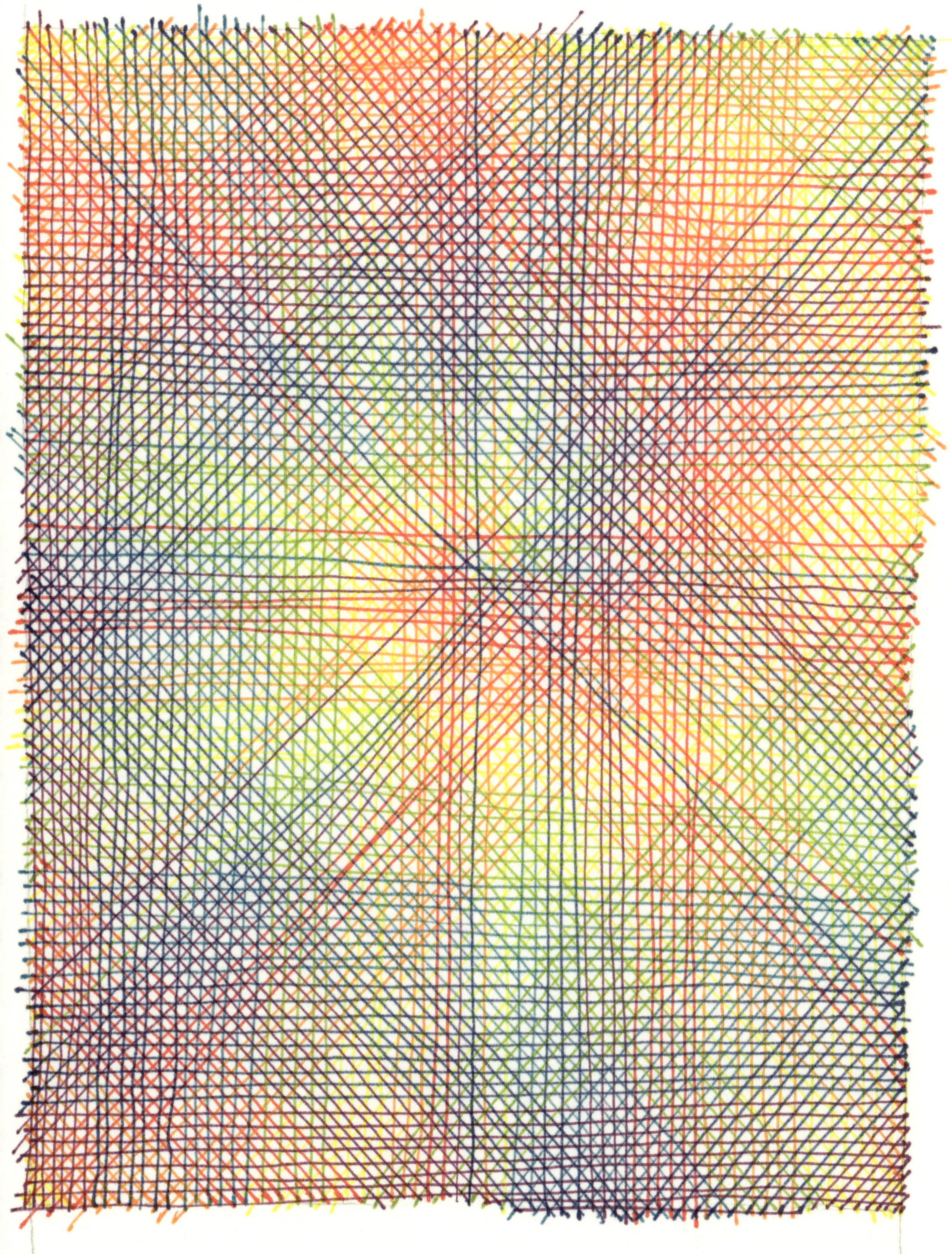

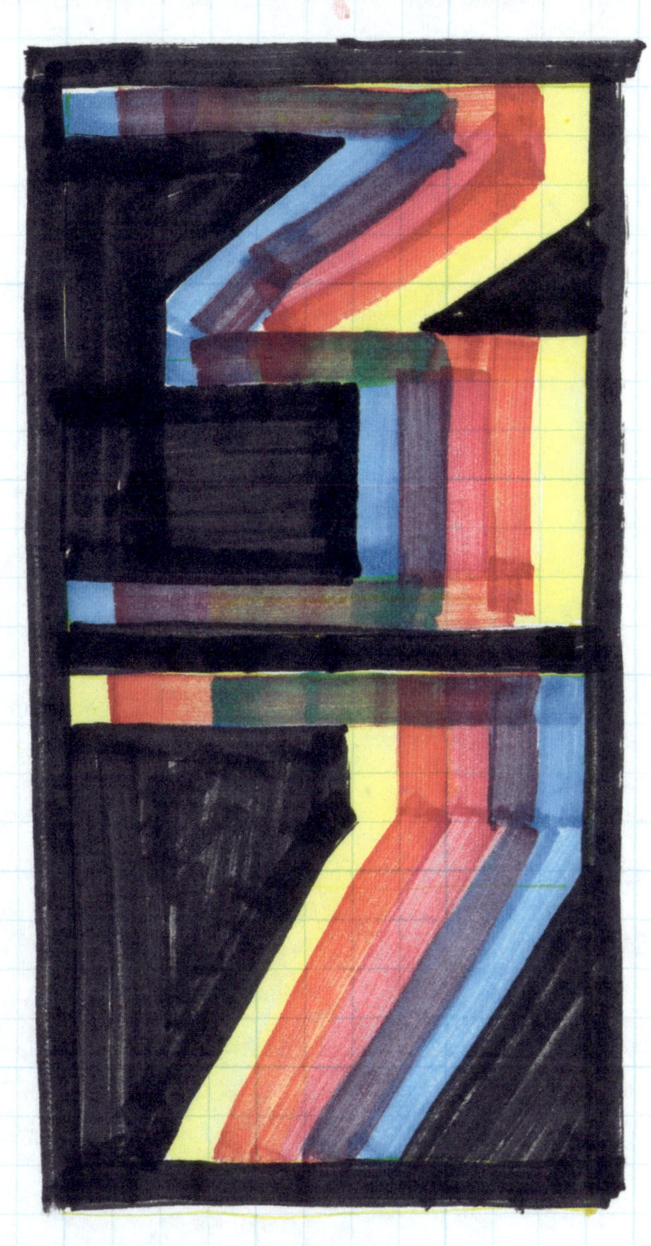

· 10000500001 10042324001
· 10000900001 10041514001
· 10001610001 10039293001
· 10002220001 10037773001
· 10002520001 10037473001
· 10003630001 10037173001
· 10006560001 10036563001
· 10008180001 10035553001
· 10009290001 10034743001
· 10013031001 10033833001
· 10013131001 10033533001
· 10014741001 10029892001
· 10016961001 10029792001
· 10021512001 10027972001
· 10021912001 10027572001
· 10022722001 10027272001
· 10022922001 10027072001
· 10023232001 10025652001
· 10023732001 10024542001
· 10023832001 10024042001

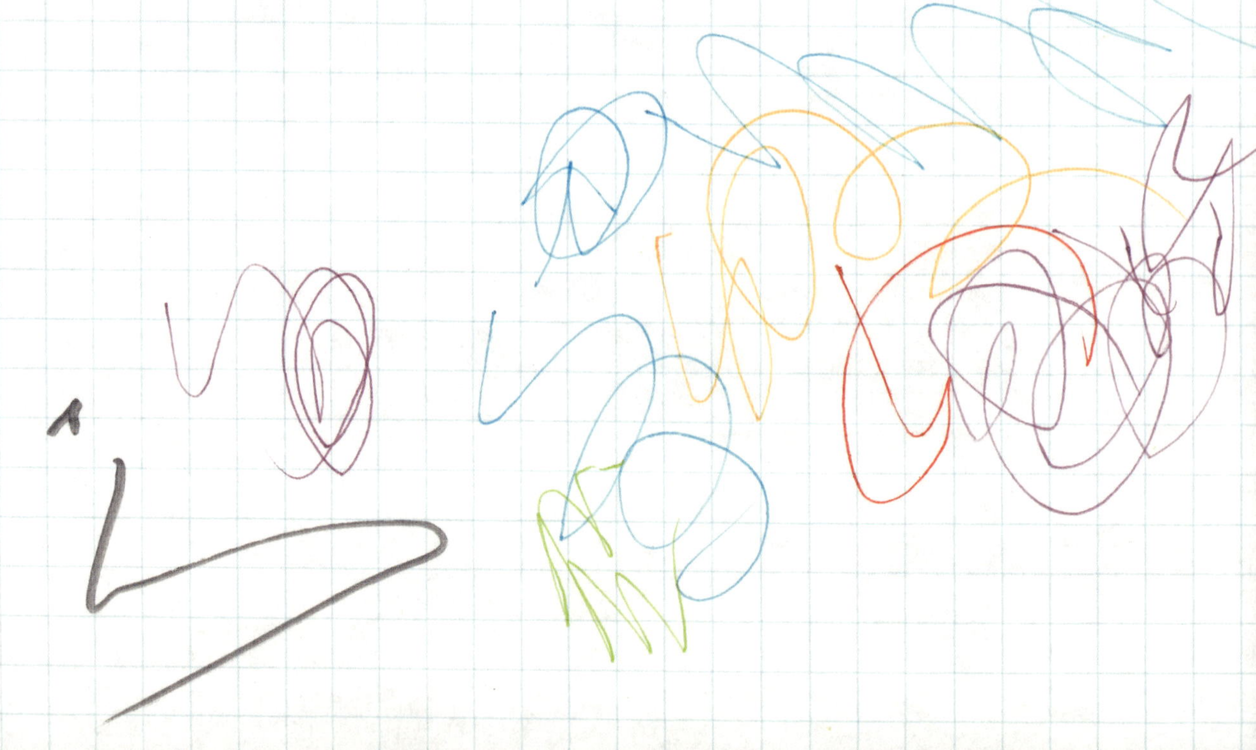

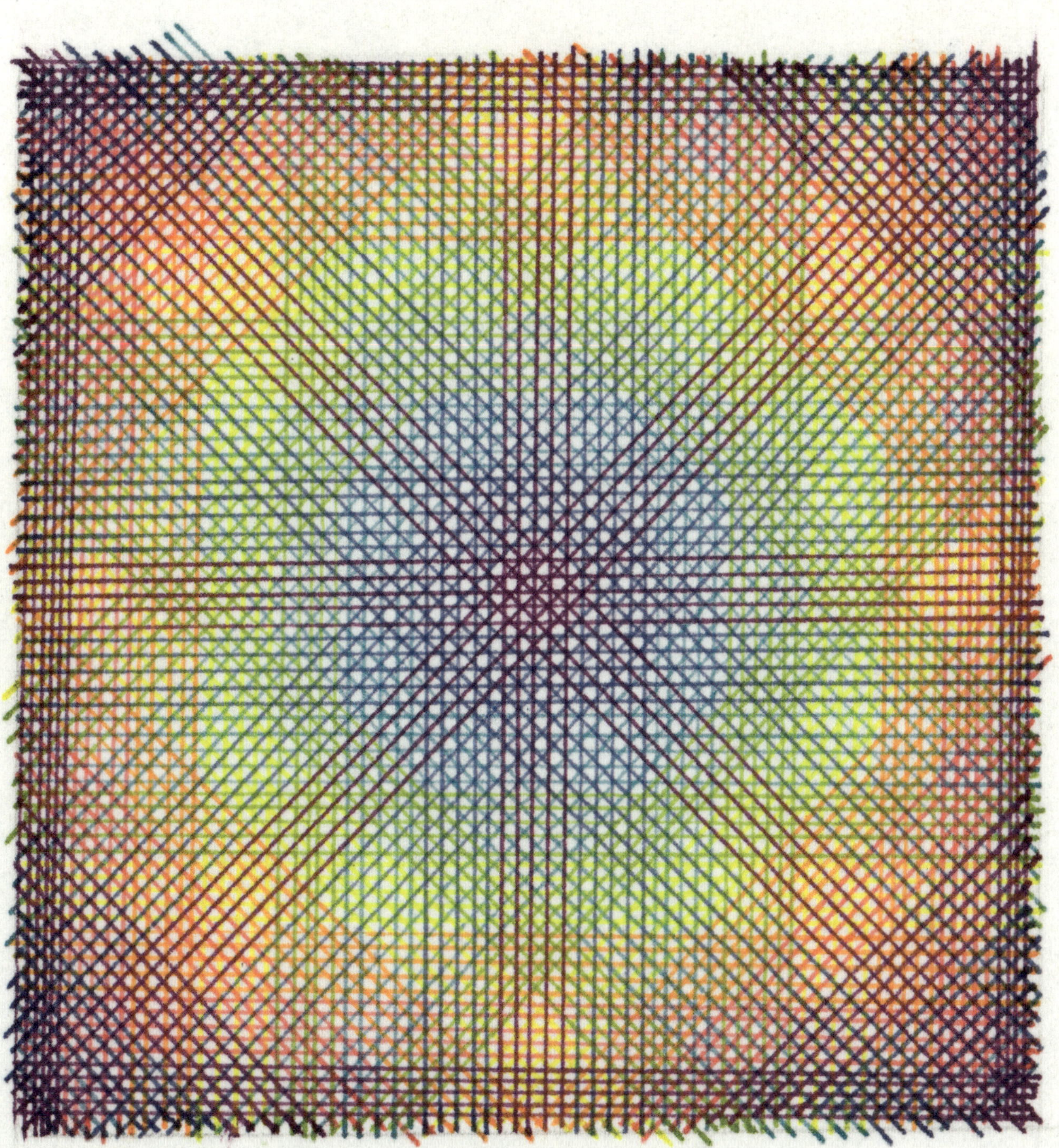

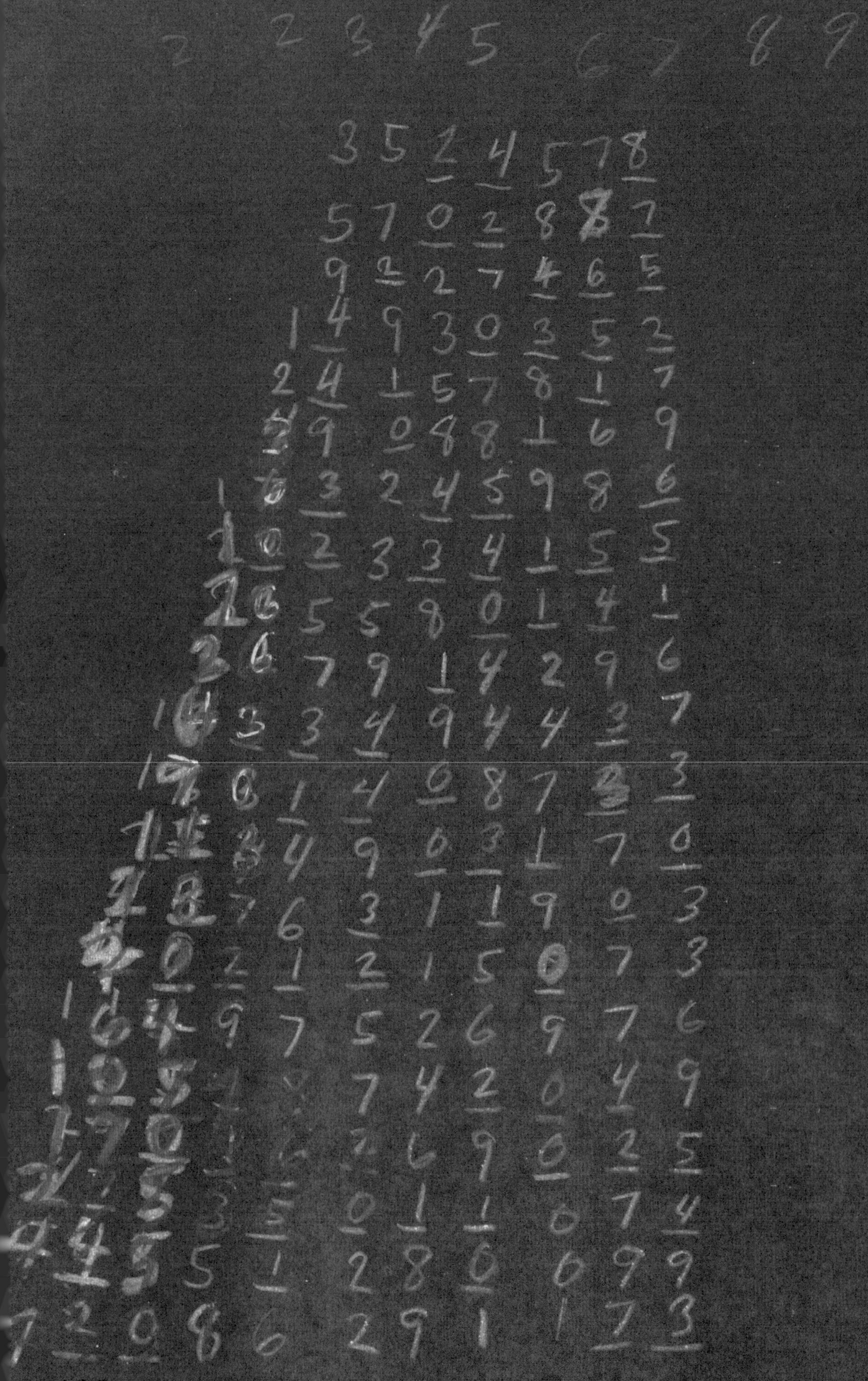

Fibonacci numbers, from 301-th to 500-th

Unless a number is explicitly marked "Prime", it is composite, but its factorization is not given here.
Produced by Maple

301 : 35957932520658356096176566517218909905236721430926723225558980 1
302 : 58181156983600400649150555863409906625903415340576699724656940 1
303 : 94139089504258756745327122380628816531140136771503422950215920 2
304 : 152320246487859157394477678244038723157043552112080122674872860 3
305 : 246459335992117914139804800624667539688183688835835456250887805
306 : 398779582479977071534282478868706262845227240995663668299616408
307 : 645238918472094985674087279493373802533410929879247213925050421 3
308 : 104401850095207205720836975836208006537863817087491088222501206 21
309 : 168925741942416704288245703785545386791204910075415809615006248 34
310 : 273327592037623910009082679621753393329068727162906897837507454 55
311 : 442253333980040614297328383407298780120273637238322707452513702 89
312 : 715580926017664524306411063029052173449342364401229605290021157 44
313 : 115783425999770513860373944643635095356961600163955231274253486033
314 : 187341518601536966291015050946540312701895836604078191803255601777
315 : 303124944601307480151388995590175408058857436768033423077509087810
316 : 490466463202844446442404046536715720760753273372111614880764689587
317 : 793591407804151926593793042126891128819610710140145037958273777397
318 : 1284057871006996373036197088663606849580363983512256652839038466984
319 : 2077649278811148299629990130790497978399974693652401690797312244381
320 : 3361707149818144672666187219454104827980338677164658343636350711365
321 : 5439356428629292972296177350244602806380313370817060034433662955746
322 : 8801063578447437644962364569698707634360652047981718378070013667111
323 : 14240420007076730617258541919943310440740965418798778412503676622857
324 : 23041483585524168262220906489642018075101617466780496790573690289968
325 : 37281903592600898887947944840958532851584258288557927520307736691282 5
326 : 60323387178125067141700354899227346590944200352359771993651057202793
327 : 97605290770725966021179803308812675106786783237939047196728424115618
328 : 157928677948851033162880158208040021697730983590298819190379481318411
329 : 255533968719576999184059961516852696804517766828237866387107905434029
330 : 413462646668428032346940119724892718502248750418536685577487386752440
331 : 668996615388005031531000081241745415306766517246774551964595292186469
332 : 1082459262056433063877940200966638133809015267665311237542082678938909
333 : 1751455877444438095408940282208383549115781784912085789506677971125378
334 : 2833915139500871159286880483175021682924797052577397027048760650064287
335 : 4585371016945309254695820765383405232040578837489482816555438621189665
336 : 7419286156446180413982701248558426914965375890066879843604199271253952
337 : 12004657173391489668678522013941832147005954727556362660159637892443617
338 : 19423943329837670082661223262500259061971330617623242503763837163697569
339 : 31428600503229159751339745276442091208977285345179605163923475056141186
340 : 50852543833066829834000968538942350270948615962802847667687312219838755
341 : 82281144336295989585340713815384441479925901307982452831610787275979941
342 : 133133688169362819419341682354326791750874517270785300499298099495818696
343 : 215414832505658809004682396169711233230800418578767753330908886771798637
344 : 348548520675021628424024078524038024981674935849553053830206986267617333
345 : 563963353180680437428706474693749258212475354428320807161115873039415970
346 : 912511873855702065852730553217787283194150290277873860991322859307033303
347 : 1476475227036382503281437027911536541406625644706194668152438732346449273
348 : 2388987100892084569134167581129323824600775934984068529143761591653482576
349 : 3865462327928467072415604609040860366007401579690263197296200323999931849
350 : 6254449428820551641549772190170184190608177514674331726439961915653414425
351 : 10119911756749018713965376799211044556615579094364594923736162239653346274

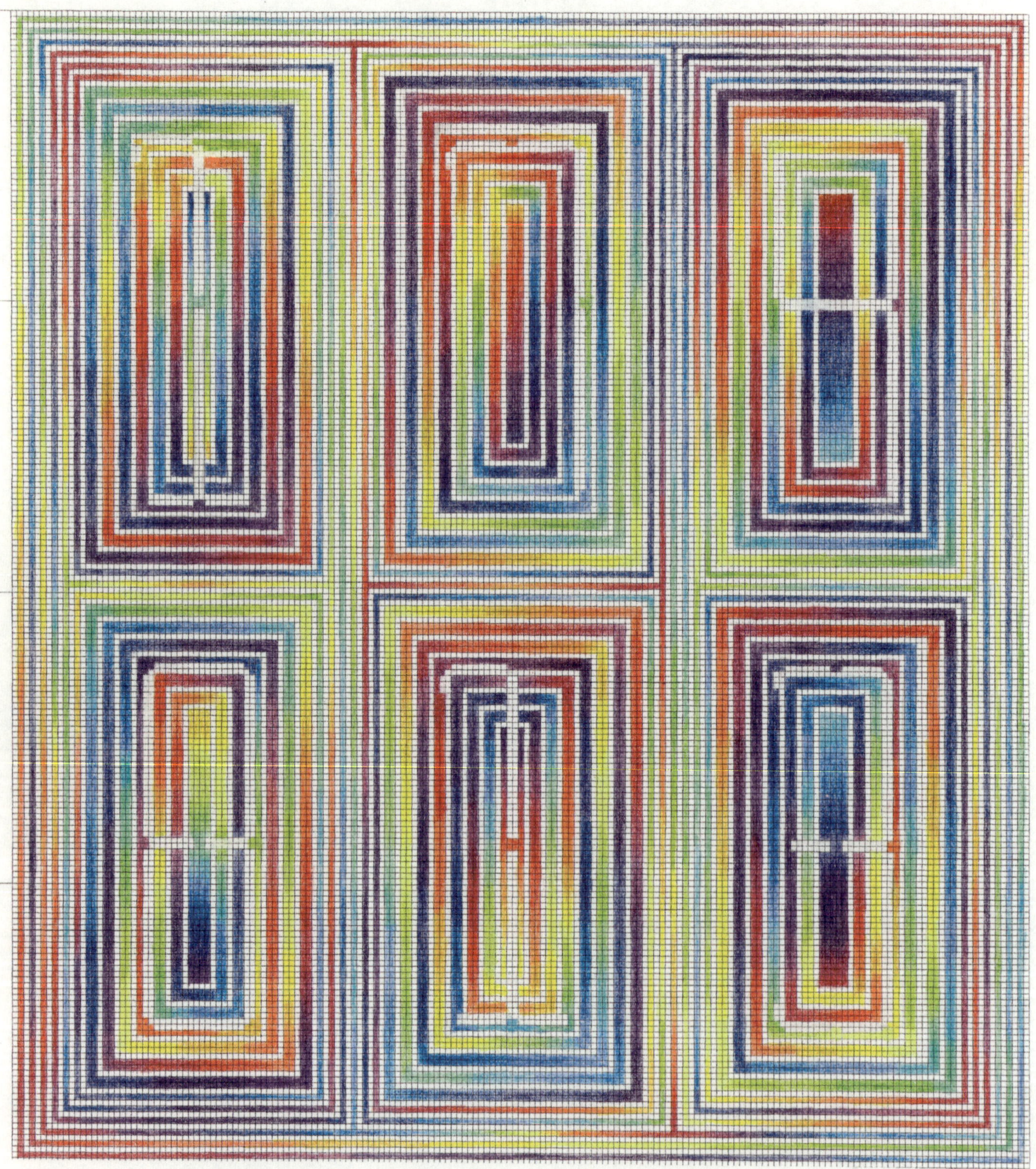

P=18181818080808180808081808180818180818081818180818080808181
8080808080808080808080808080808080808080808080808080808080808
0808080808080808080808080808080808080808080808080808080808080
8080808080808080808080808080808080808080808080808080808080808
0808080808080808080808080808080808080808080808080808080808080
8080808080808080808080808080808080808080808080808080808080808
0808080808080808080808080808080808080808080808080808080808080
8080808080808080808080808080808080808080808080808080808080808
0808080808080808080808080808080808080808080808080808080808080
8080808080808080808080808080808080808080808080808080808080808
0808080808080808080808080808080808080808080808080808080808081
8180808081808181818081808181808180818080808180808081818181

Q=36363636161616361616163616361636361636163636361636161616363
6161616161616161616161616161616161616161616161616161616161616
1616161616161616161616161616161616161616161616161616161616161
6161616161616161616161616161616161616161616161616161616161616
1616161616161616161616161616161616161616161616161616161616161
6161616161616161616161616161616161616161616161616161616161616
1616161616161616161616161616161616161616161616161616161616161
6161616161616161616161616161616161616161616161616161616161616
1616161616161616161616161616161616161616161616161616161616161
6161616161616161616161616161616161616161616161616161616161616
1616161616161616161616161616161616161616161616161616161616163
6361616163616363636163616363616361636161616361616163636363

R =
727272723232327232323272327232727232723272727272327232323232727 23
232323232323232323232323232323232323232323232323232323232323232
323232323232323232323232323232323232323232323232323232323232323
232323232323232323232323232323232323232323232323232323232323232
323232323232323232323232323232323232323232323232323232323232323
232323232323232323232323232323232323232323232323232323232323232
323232323232323232323232323232323232323232323232323232323232323
232323232323232323232323232323232323232323232323232323232323232
323232323232323232323232323232323232323232323232323232323232323
232323232323232323232323232323232323232323232323232323232323232
323232323232323232323232323232323232323232323232323232323232727
23232327232727272327232727232723272323232723232327272727

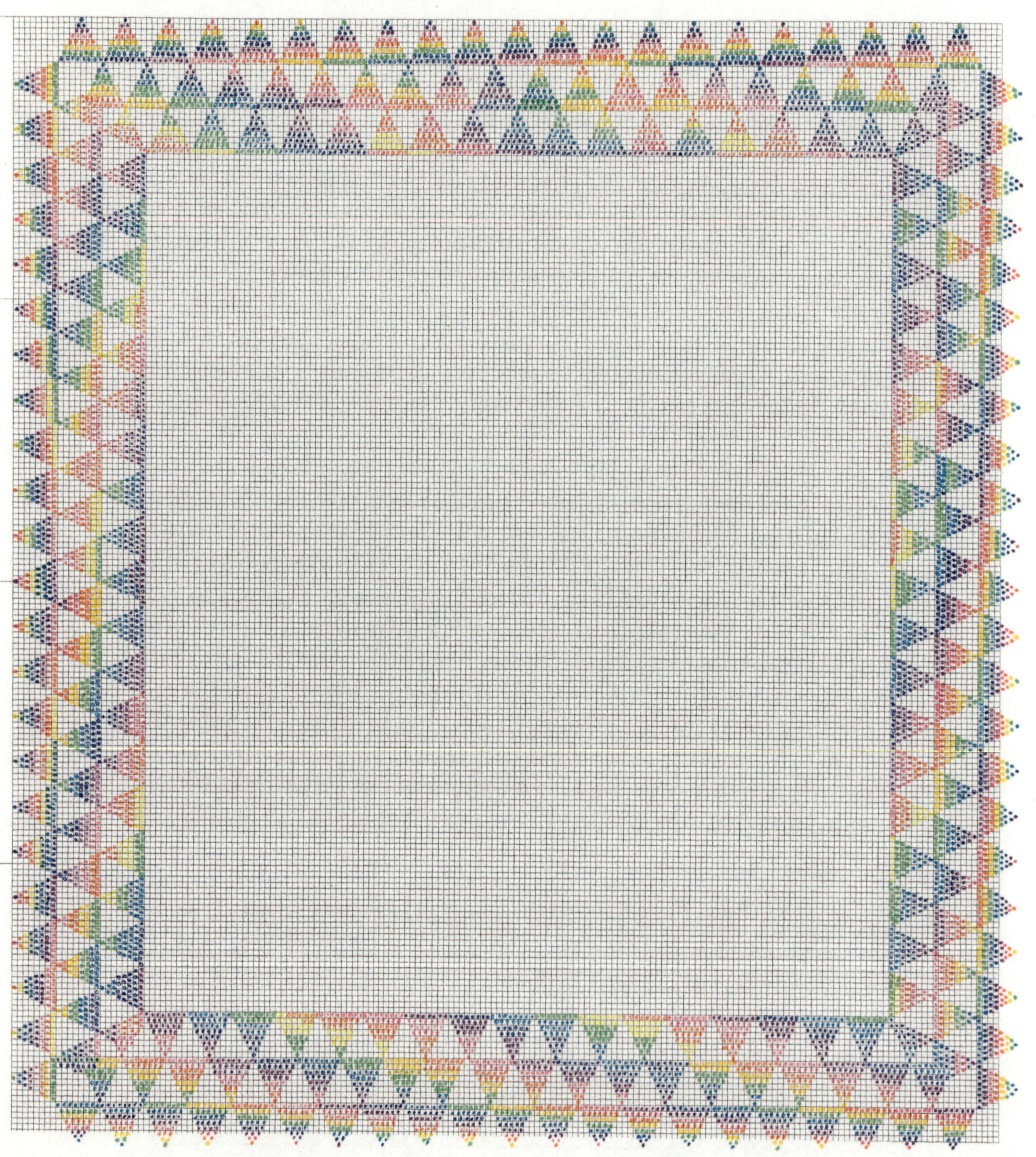

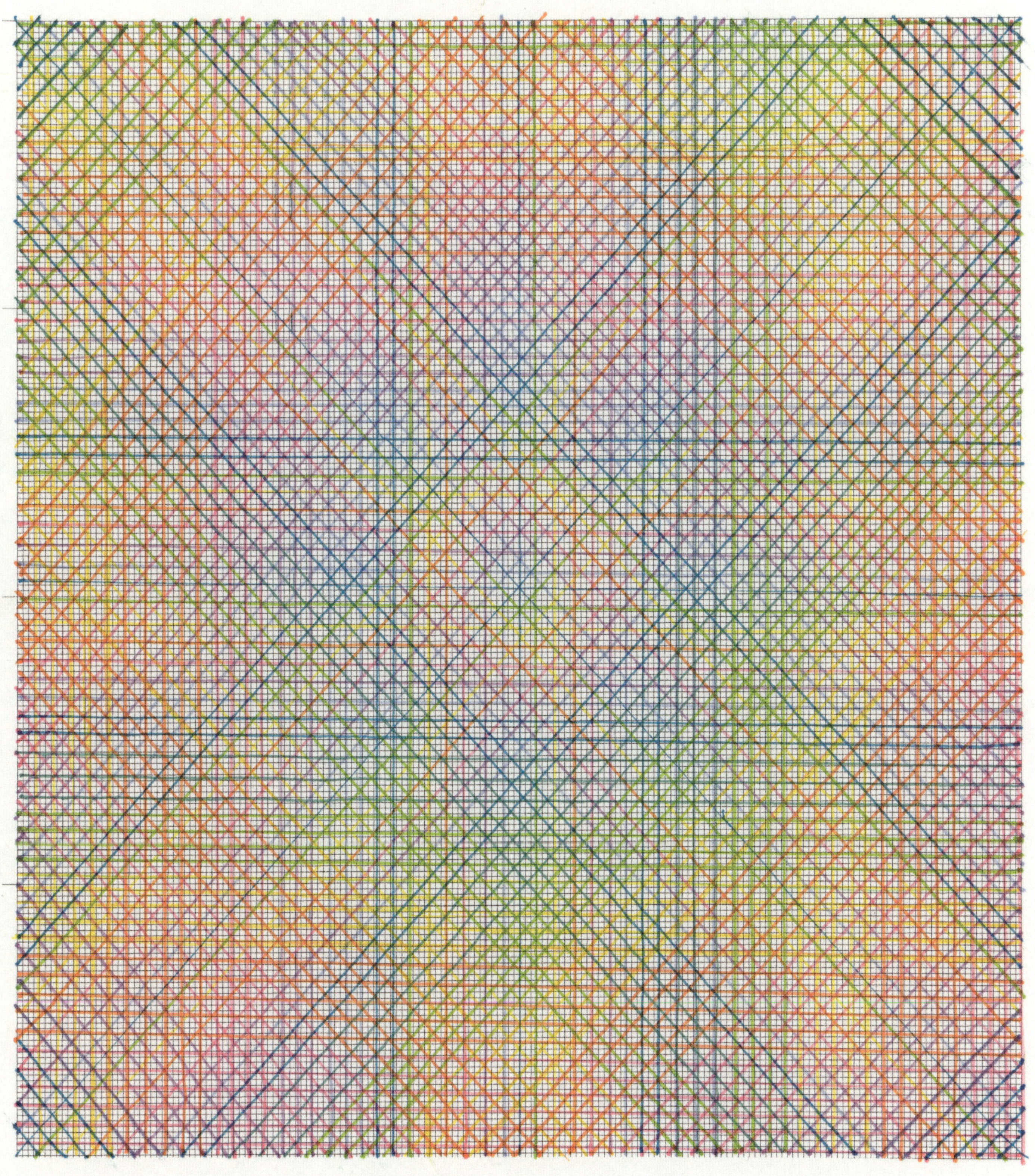

10002220001
10002520001
10003630001
10006560001
10008180001
10009290001
10013031001
10013131001
10014741001
10016961001
10021512001
10021912001
10022722001
10022922001
10023232001
10023732001
10023832001
10024042001
10024542001
10025652001
10027072001
10027272001
10027572001
10027872001
10025792001
10029892001
10033533001
10033833001
10034743001
10035553001
10036563001
10037173001
10037473001
10037773001
10039293001
10041514001
10042324001
10044744001
10045654001
10046364001

10050505001
10051815001
10052125001
10052625001
10053435001
10053535001
10054345001
10055055001
10055155001
10055755001
10056165001
10056265001
10056765001
10057075001
10057275001
10057575001
10058185001
10059495001
10060006001
10060806001
10060906001
10061716001
10061916001
10062826001
10063536001
10064646001
10065456001
10066066001
10066566001
10067376001
10068186001
10069696001
10070307001
10070707001
10071217001
10072227001
10072927001
10073037001
10073737001
10074547001
10075057001
10076967001
10077177001
10078887001
10080408001
10080508001

10084648001
10085658001
10086268001
10086568001
10086768001
10087378001
10087678001
10090009001
10090909001
10094149001
10095259001
10095459001
10097079001
10093779001
10098189001
10098889001
10099599001
10100600101
10101810101
10102220101
10103330101
10104740101
10105250101
10109490101
10110301101
10110501101
10110901101
10113131101
10113431101
10113731101
10114041101
10114641101
10115751101
10116461101
10116761101
10117371101
10117671101
10118481101 (133)

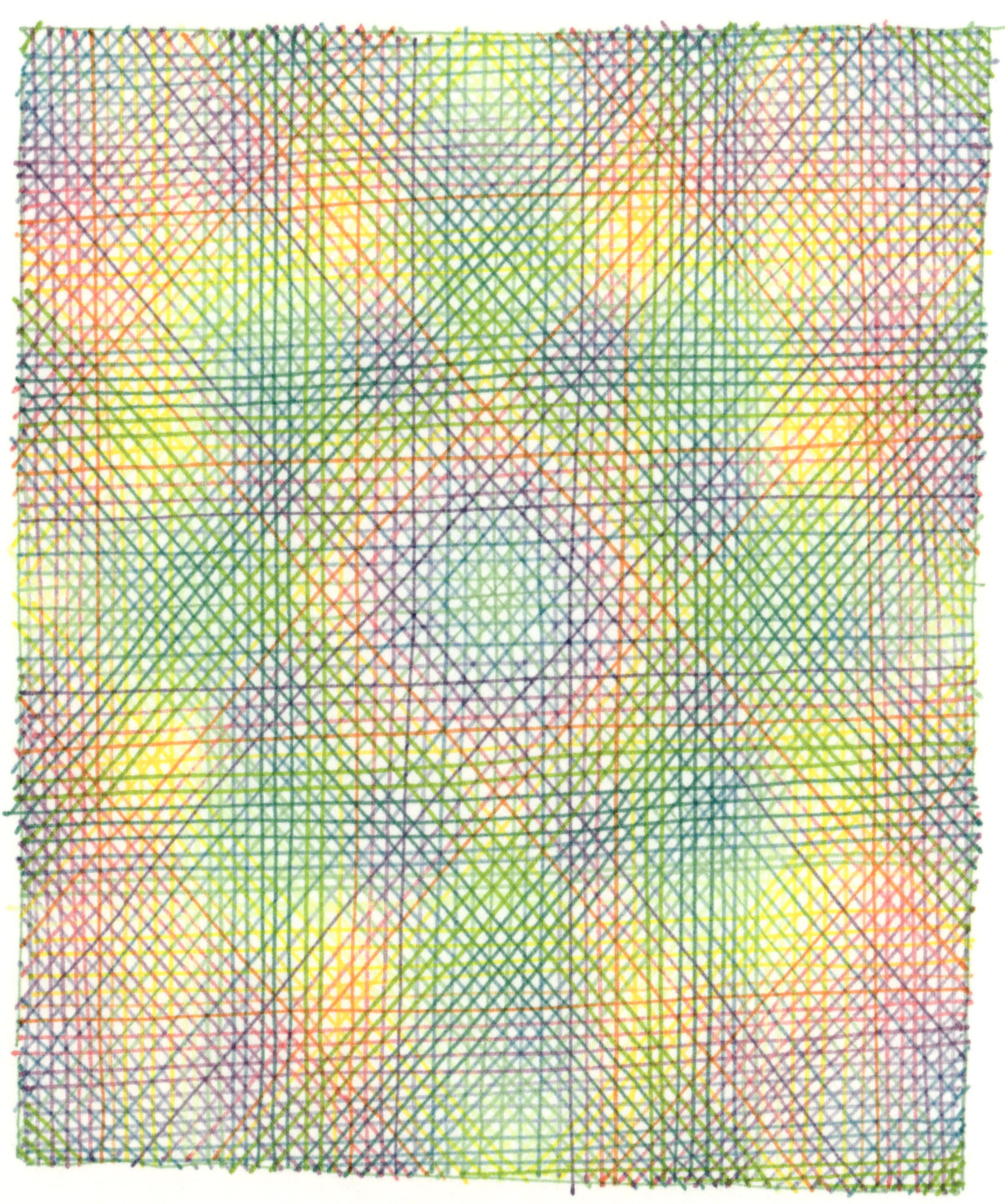

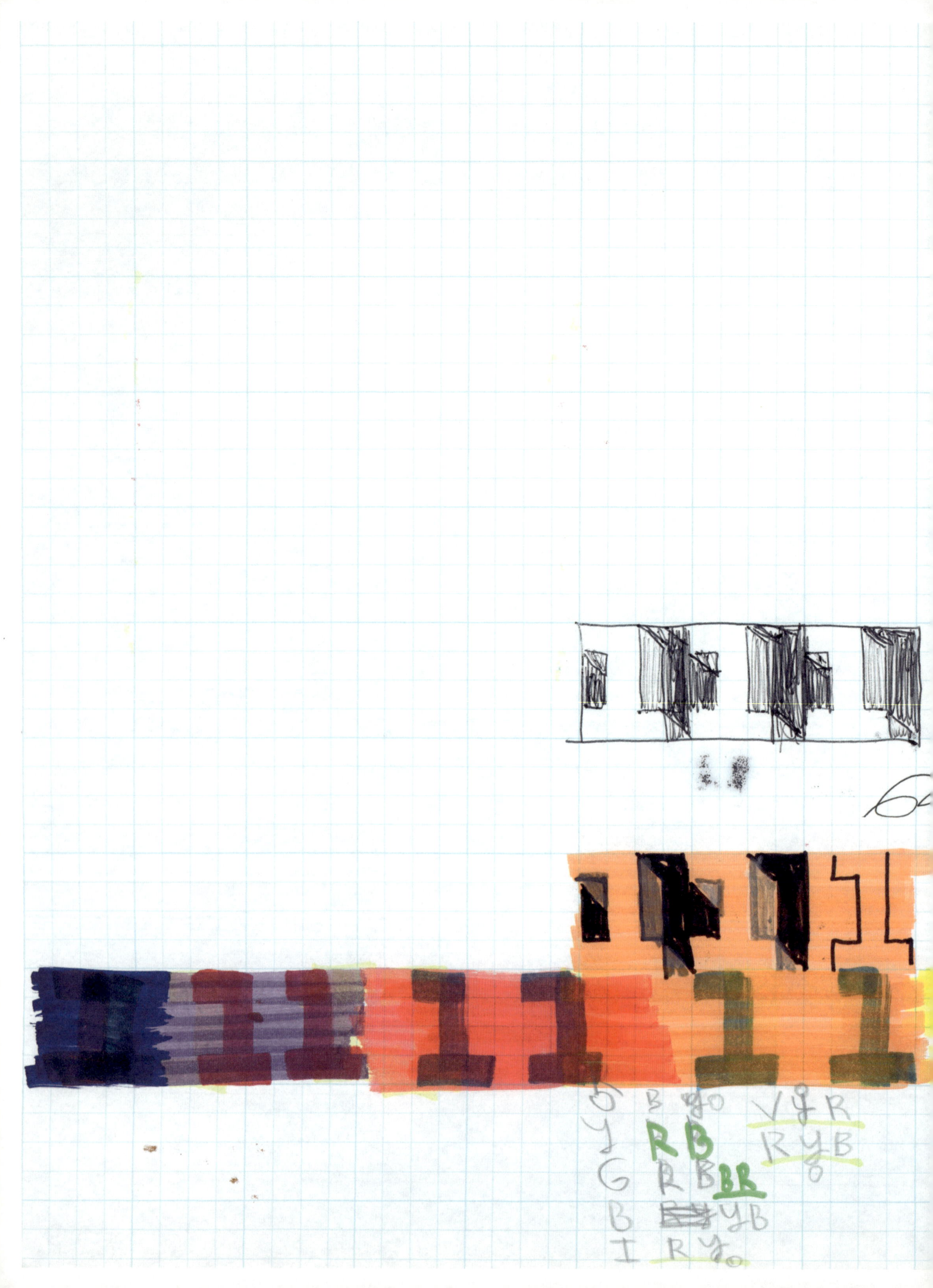

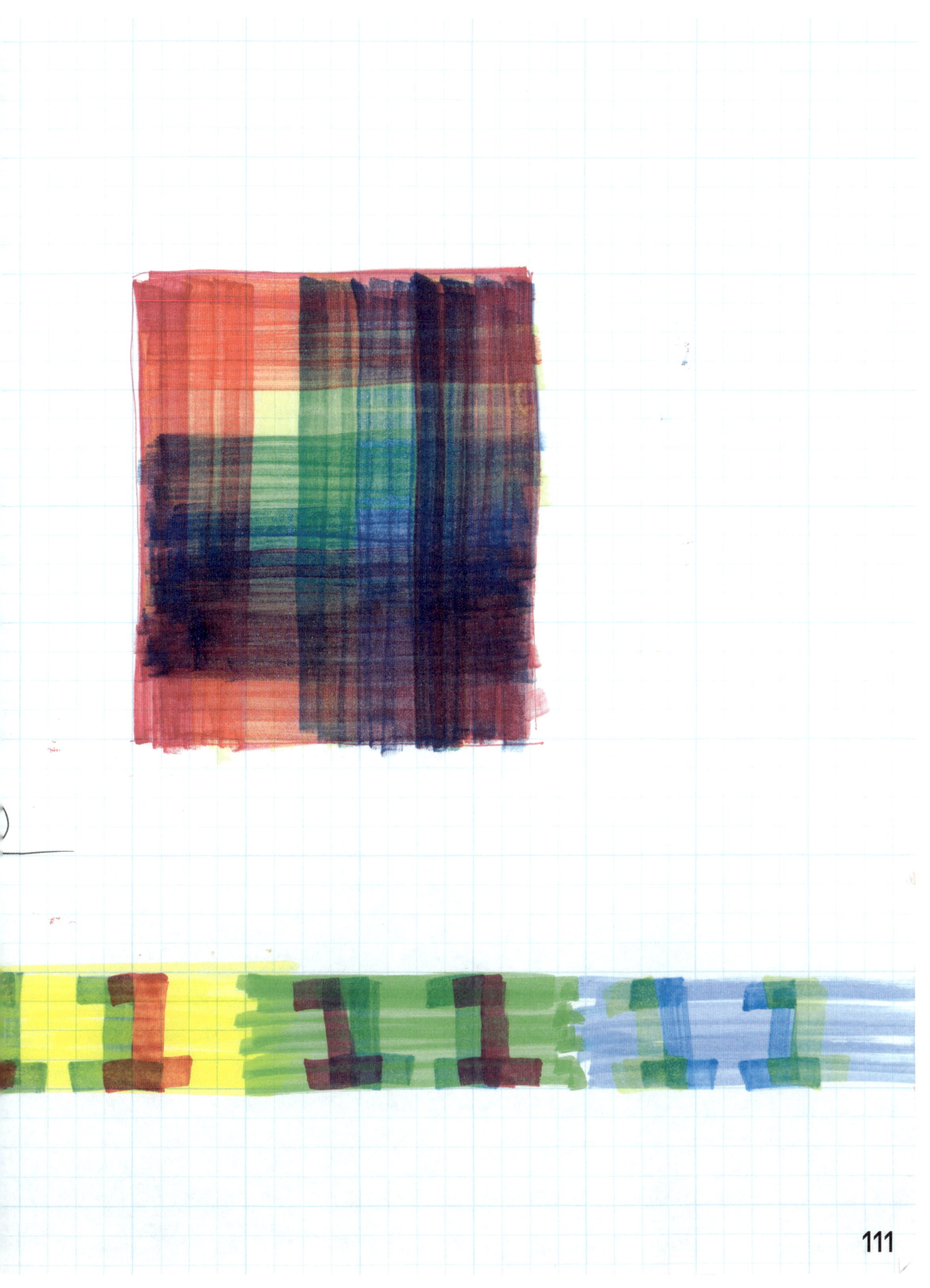

BOUND FOR GLORY

FIVE DOT
3X3 DOT UNIT (9) NR10 GOOD
MAGIC BOX 2BL RNB MACHINE GOOD
BK ON BK NR #1 PRIME TIMES
TWEEN TWIN EVENS 6, 12, 18, 30, 42 NR
RANDOM RECTANGLES TRY AGAIN
9 DOT UNIT (BANK SIGN) 9x5 (7X5) NR 12
HORIZ STAGGER TWICE NOT GOOD
RAINBOW GRAIN 3X3
ROYGBIV BROKEN ON THE X · QUAD
XRAY/SKELETON OF EXISTING PTG OK PRINCESS
PYTHAGOREAN TRIANGLE W/6 PT. STAR AT CTR
NR#11 DOT 1-9 COUNTING ON A SPIRAL IN ROYGBIV GOOD ON TEST
H/V STAGGER TRY AGAIN
NR9 DO UNRULED WHEREIN DOT NUMBER IS SAME, DOT SIZE ADAPTS
JUSTIFYING SCALE
SHADOW TRY AGAIN
CLEFT(S)
STRUCK BY A SHARP PAIN
RIPPLE
THE POSTURE BEARING THE BURDEN OF A CHRONIC DULL ACHE
RANDOM LINES
RADIATION
ONES ARE SKINNY
TRIED MIXED DOT SYSTEM FOR FIG/GROUND 1-4 4-9
THE WHITE W/COLORED OUTLINES
GATES 3D GOOD
FONT FOR WHITE GROUND FOR OPTICAL BLEED

DISRUPTIONS

NYX HYPNOS NOX REX NIGHT KING INSOMNIA PTGS (28 TOTAL)

BACK RUB/FOOT RUB

MOOD CHART NEXT SHOW

PYTHAGOREAN TRIANGLES AS SIX POINTED STARS PLUS SPIRAL SPOKES IN BTWN

DBLX

FOR SG.

MOOD CHART 66 COLUMNS NAT DIV.

RULED GRID, T27th DIGIT IS ON SIDE WRAP AROUND

MOOD CHART NUMBERNINE 67 COLUMNS

UNRULED GRID DBL SNAKE V+H

NAT DIV DOT NUMBER VARIES

– MOOD CHART 55 RULED AT FIRST ROW OF NUMBER, SQUEEZE IN FINAL DIGIT

NUMBER OF DOTS SAME, DOT SIZE COMPENSATES FOR SIZE VARIETIES

DO AGAIN

WHT GRID INTERSECTIONS W/ WHT DOT

#22 4 WAY SPACE BTWN NUMERALS

SHADOW SHIFTS (SOL LEWIT PHOTOS OF SPHERES)

18181818... DONE W/ALTERNATING SIZED ZEROES

OUTLINED NUMBERS W

DRAWING ON 1mm GRID PAPER USING intersection

FIRST NUMBER IS BIG, LIKE A CAPITALIZED WORD

THE SIXTY REPEAT IN THE ONES COLUMN OF FIBONACCI SEQ.

3D-HOLES ARE GROUND

SYLVESTER SPACE AROUND NUMERAL SHIFTS UP/DOWN L/R

THE 60

PAINTED DOTTED LINE GRID NEG. SPACE OF NUMERAL

DRINKING B/W ON 1177 11 DIGIT PP

3NR 21 1777 " "

1818181... BL/RED 0,8 SWITCH 3D

RAINBOW GRID

SUNNY ONLY

– DRUNK OR DRINKING PTG

– GLASSES OFF

– SNOWING

GATES ON WHITE

Basket weave OSCILLATING O SIZES ON 1818181 WHITE GROUND SIMPLE 3X5 5X7 BOX

1818181 in PRINCESS STYLE

2X ✓ SPACE BTWN ~~[illegible]~~ ROWS/COLUMNS

✓ PYTHAGOREAN W/ 7 BASE

✓ ROYGBIV GRID 5X7 V/H

2X ✓ 60 FROM FIBO SEQ.

✓ GRID EXPANSION

DBL COUNTING

BUBBLE FONT W/ TWO TONE COLOUR

SINGLE RNBW CROSSING ON DIAGONALS ⑧

✓ TRIANGLR # 666, 3003, 5995, 8778

✓ A PATCHWORK DETERMINED BY DAY OF THE WK

FLASH W/ POS & NEG

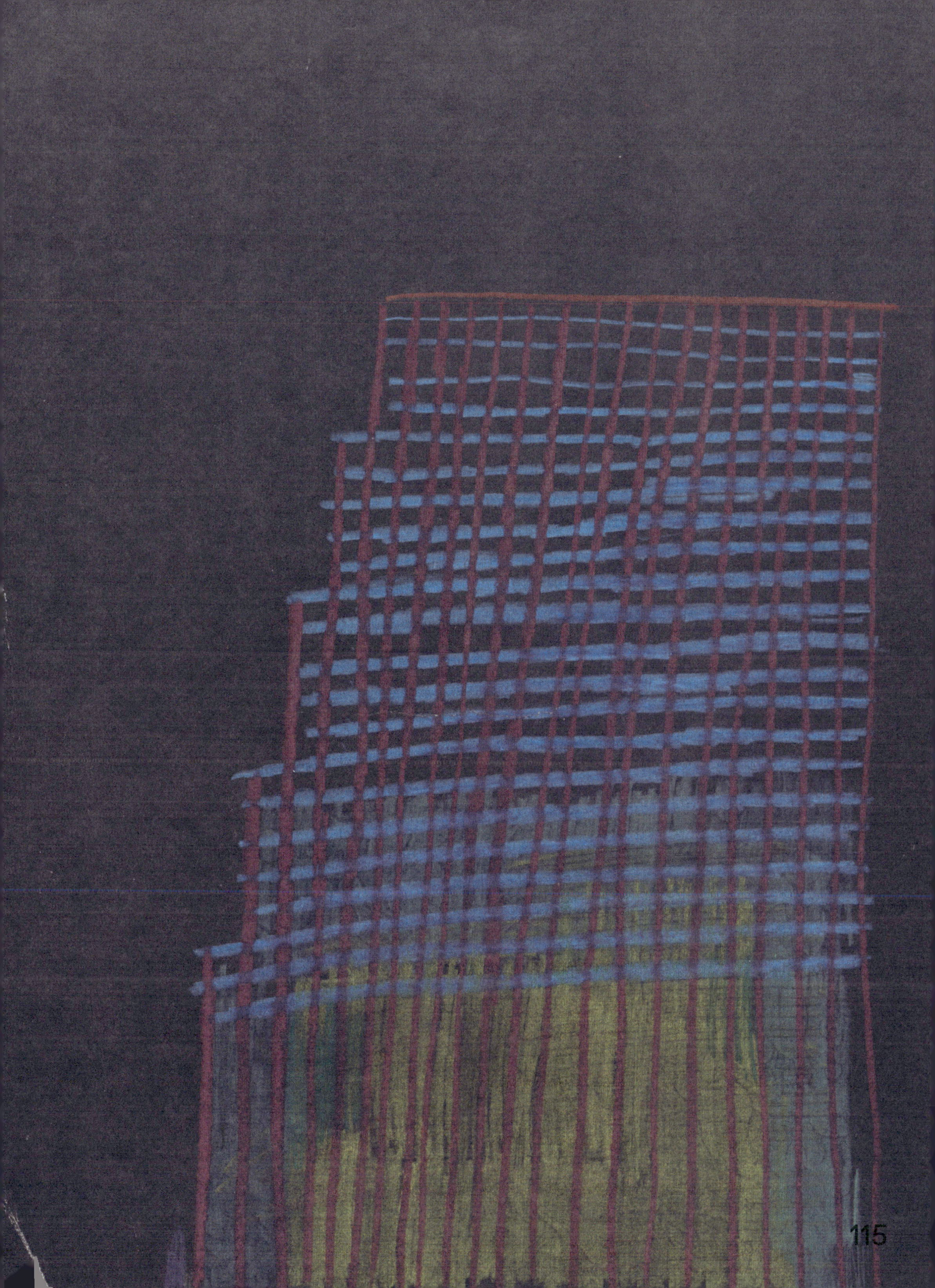

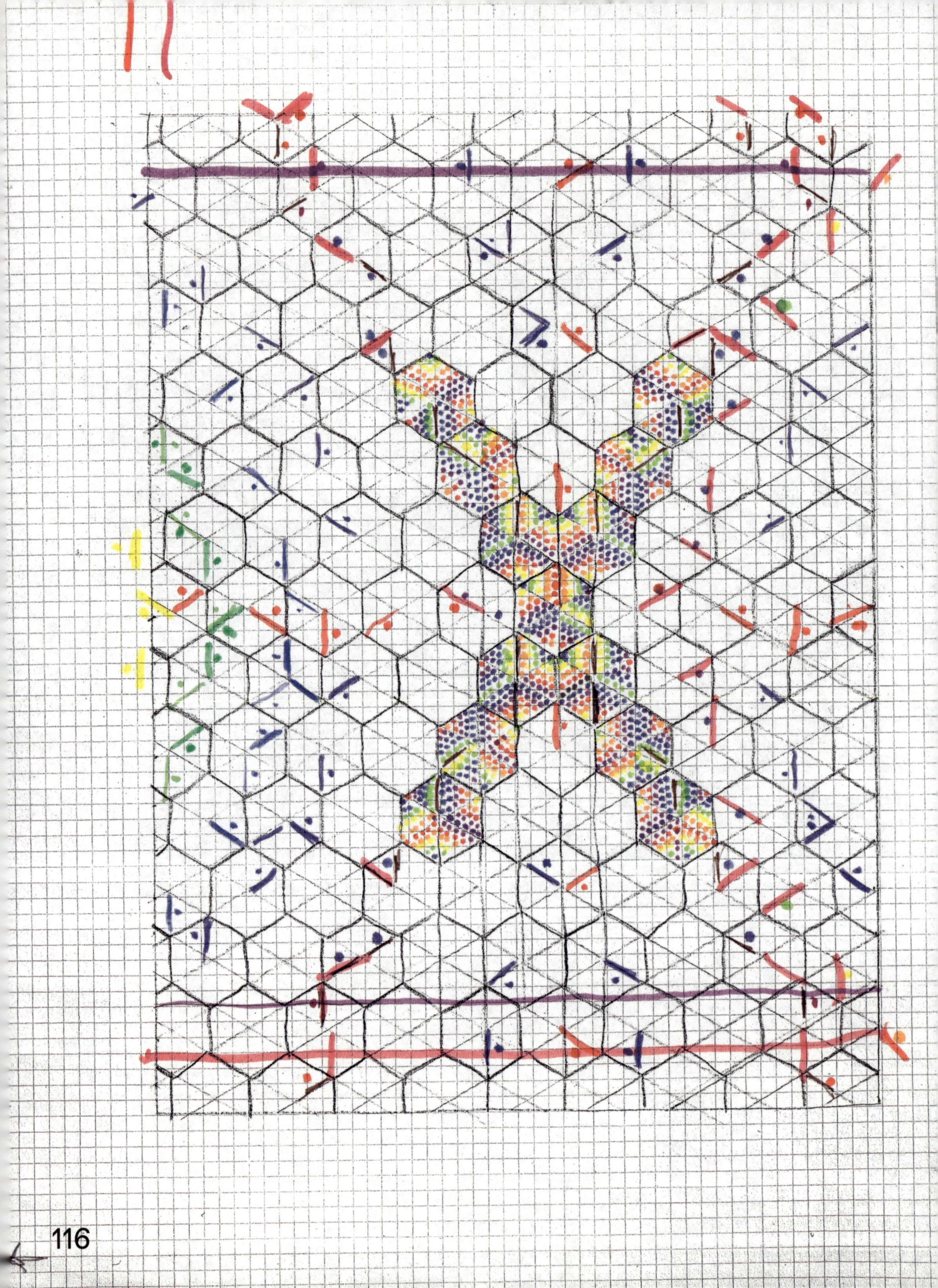

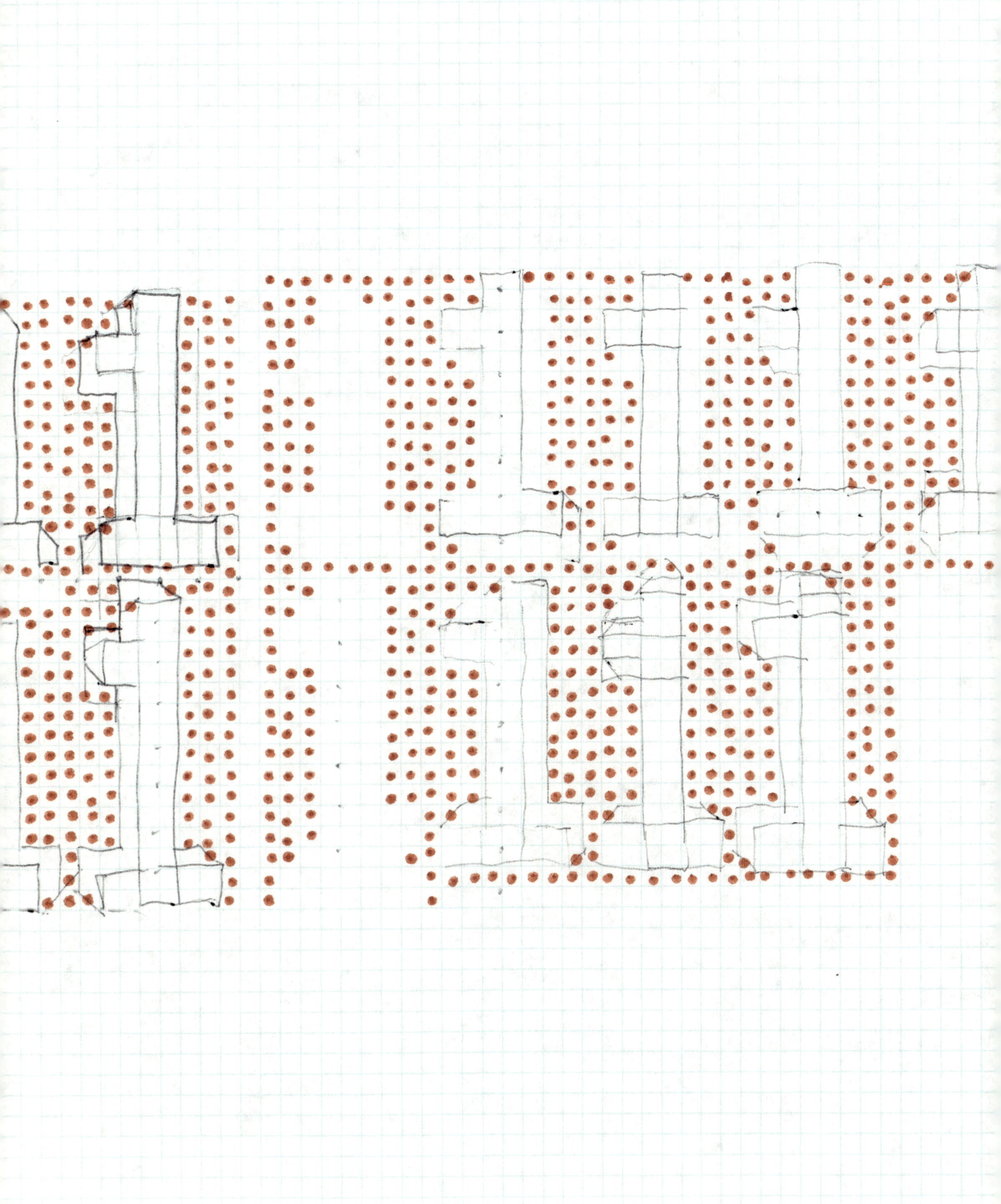

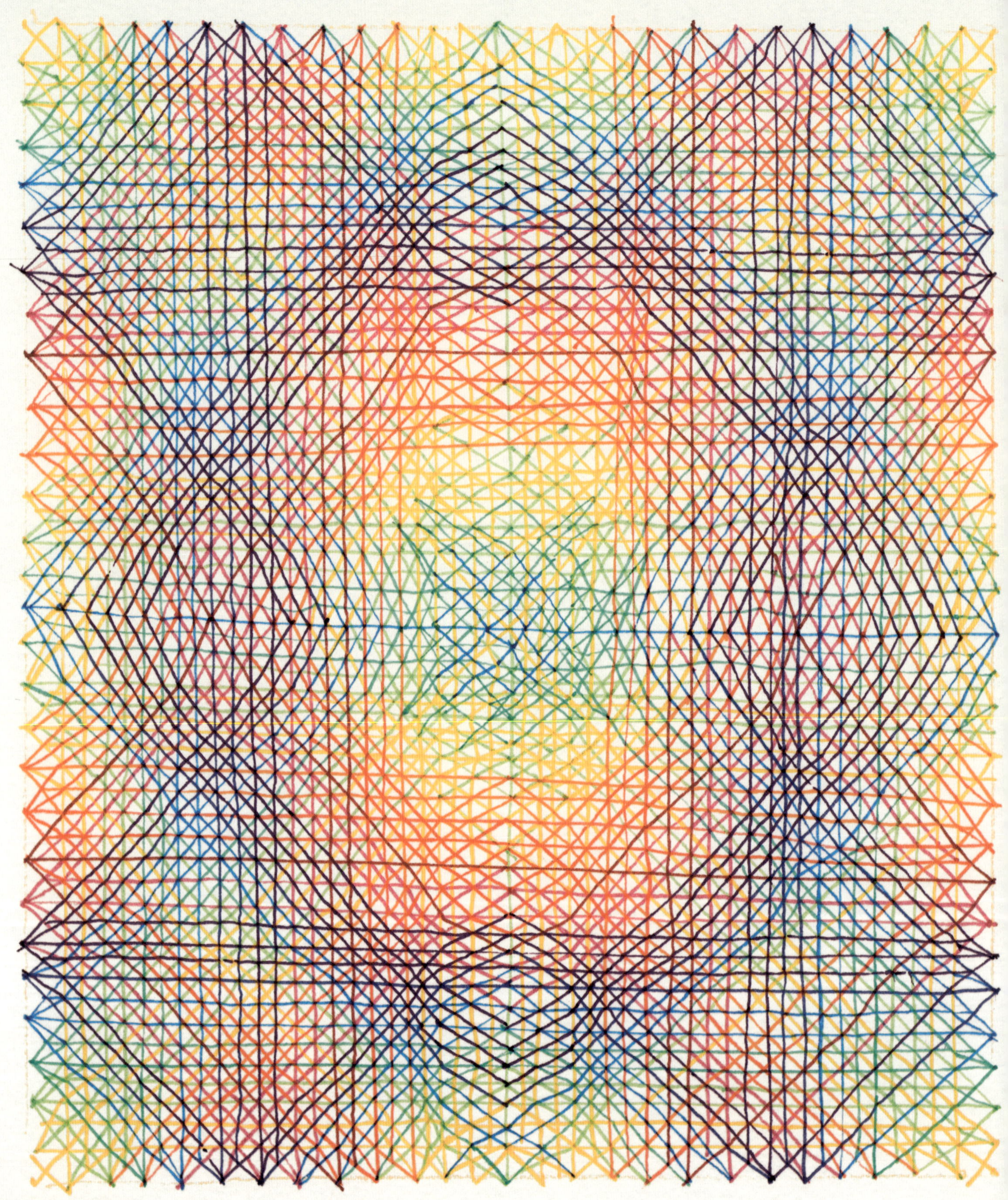

~~1 525 4/4/5768~~

S 3460643 10/27 4762 3812183 4/21 5725 S H 3814183 10/12 5730

060 8 8 5708 W 262 11/28 5763 M

U 3466643 4/11 4779 3804083 2/16 5703 F 292 2 14 5772 F

F 3470743 6/22 4790 999 11 15 5691 H 363 7/24 5791 U

W 3479743 2/11/4815 939 6 12 5675 W 424 4/6/5808 W

S 3485843 10/25 4831 929 9 15 5672 H 535 8 27 5838 M

T 3487843 4/16 4837 848 7/13 5650 W 585 5/5/5852 W

3503053 12/07 4878 818 4/26 5642 S 636 4.22.5866 U

3515153 1/24 4912 3774773 11/17 5622 H 646 1/16/5869 S

3517153 7/16 4917 3773773 2 21 5620 F 676 4/4 5877 W

U 282 12/6 4947 696 696 9/25 5882 M

M 414 1/26 4984 686 11/30 5608 U 717 6/25 5888 M

F 535 3/14 5017 656 3/6 5606 787 8/26 5907 M

U 585 11 21 5030 636 12/18 5597 H 939 4/7/5949 H

T 636 11/7/5044 626 6 27 5592 S 999 9/10/5965 F

= 696 4/12 5061 464 10 01 5589 3913193 11/10/6001 S

S 868 5/16 5108 434 5/25 5545 F 161 1/27/6010 W

W 898 8/2 5116 323 3/8 5537 M 181 7/20 6015 M

T 909 8/7 5119 282 10/17 5506 W 242 4/1/6032 H

W 919 5/3 5122 222 7/26 5495 F 272 6/18/6040 M

U 949 7/20 5130 212 2/20 5479 H 313 9/9 6051 S

3601063 4/12 5147 171 5/26 5476 F 383 11/8/6070 S

S U 7 9/15 5163 161 3/5 5465 U 919 424 H 1/29 6082

F 181 2/4 5194 090 6/9 5462 M 949 464 1/11 6093 U

282 3708073 12 31 5442 S M 1/13 6284 979 484 F 7/14/6098

3621263 989 4/5 5440 U 10/9 U 6236 989 646 11/11 6142

898 4 27 5415 H 707 7/25 6159

808 9/27 5390 H S 838 6/6 6195

737 10/05 5365 S U 919 8/10 6217

707 4/28 5346 H H 949 10/27 6285

3646463 2/9 5338 U

3643463 7/20 5271 H

3635363 5/13 5263 U

3627263 3 9 5241 S

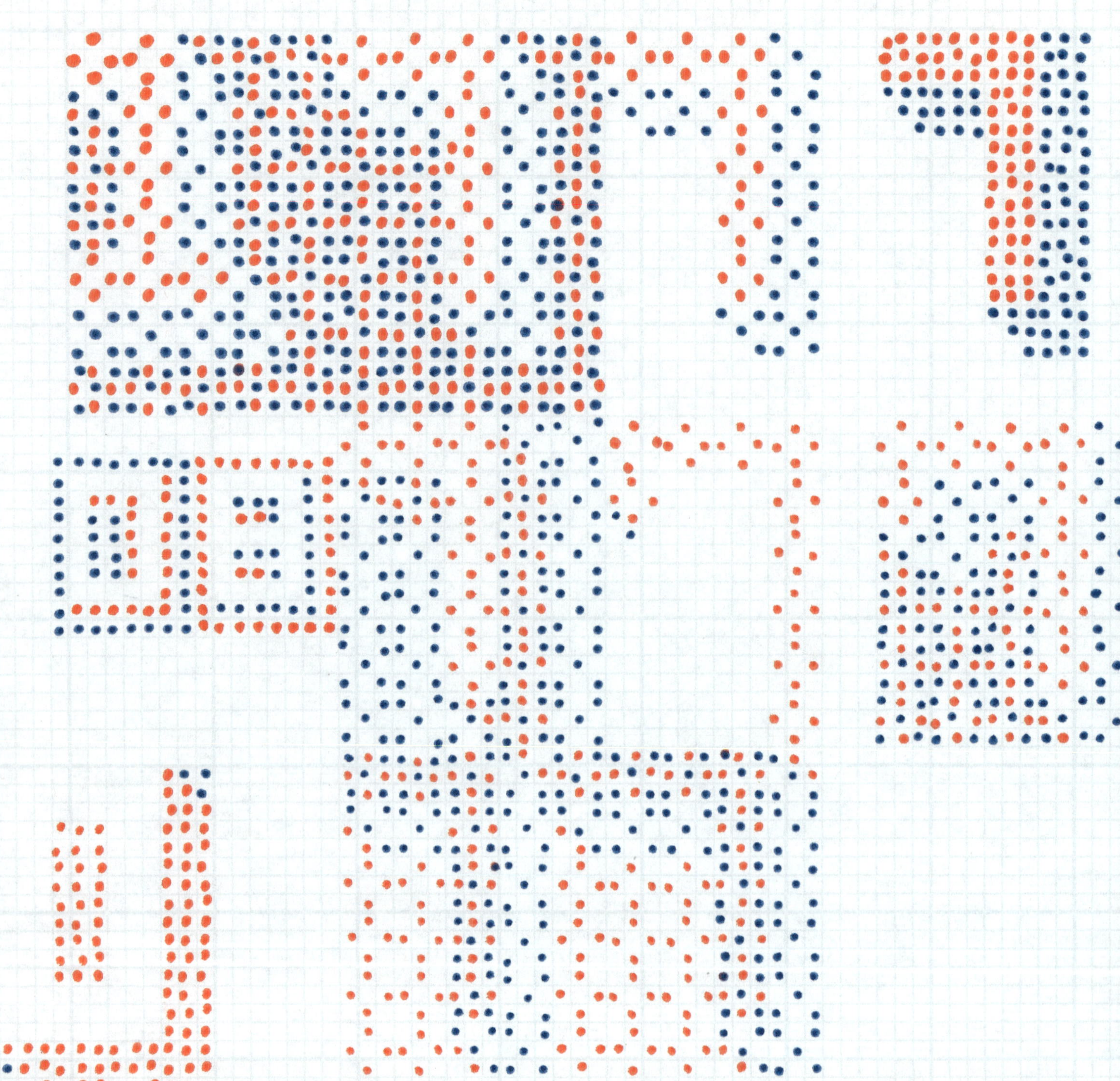

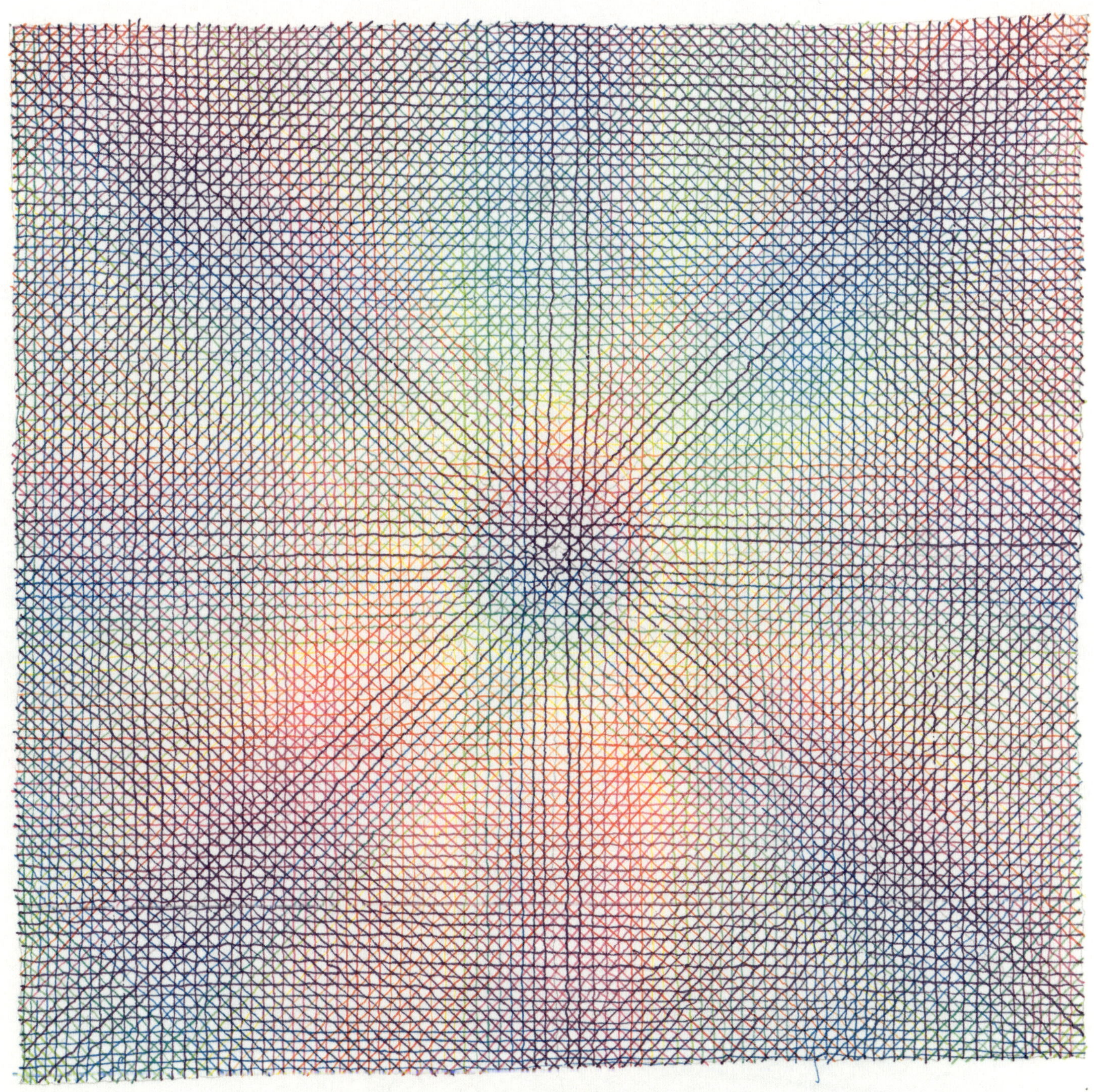

3001003	~~3443443~~
3002003	~~3444443~~
3064603	3589853
3065603	3590953
3072703	3591953
3073703	3708073
3211103	3709073
3212103	3716173
3222223	3717173
3223223	3721273
3285823	3722273
3286823	3762673
3364633	3763673
3365633	3768673
3391933	3769673
3392933	3773773
3424243	3774773
3425243	3792973
3443443	3793973
3444443	3863683
	3864683
	3997993
	3998993

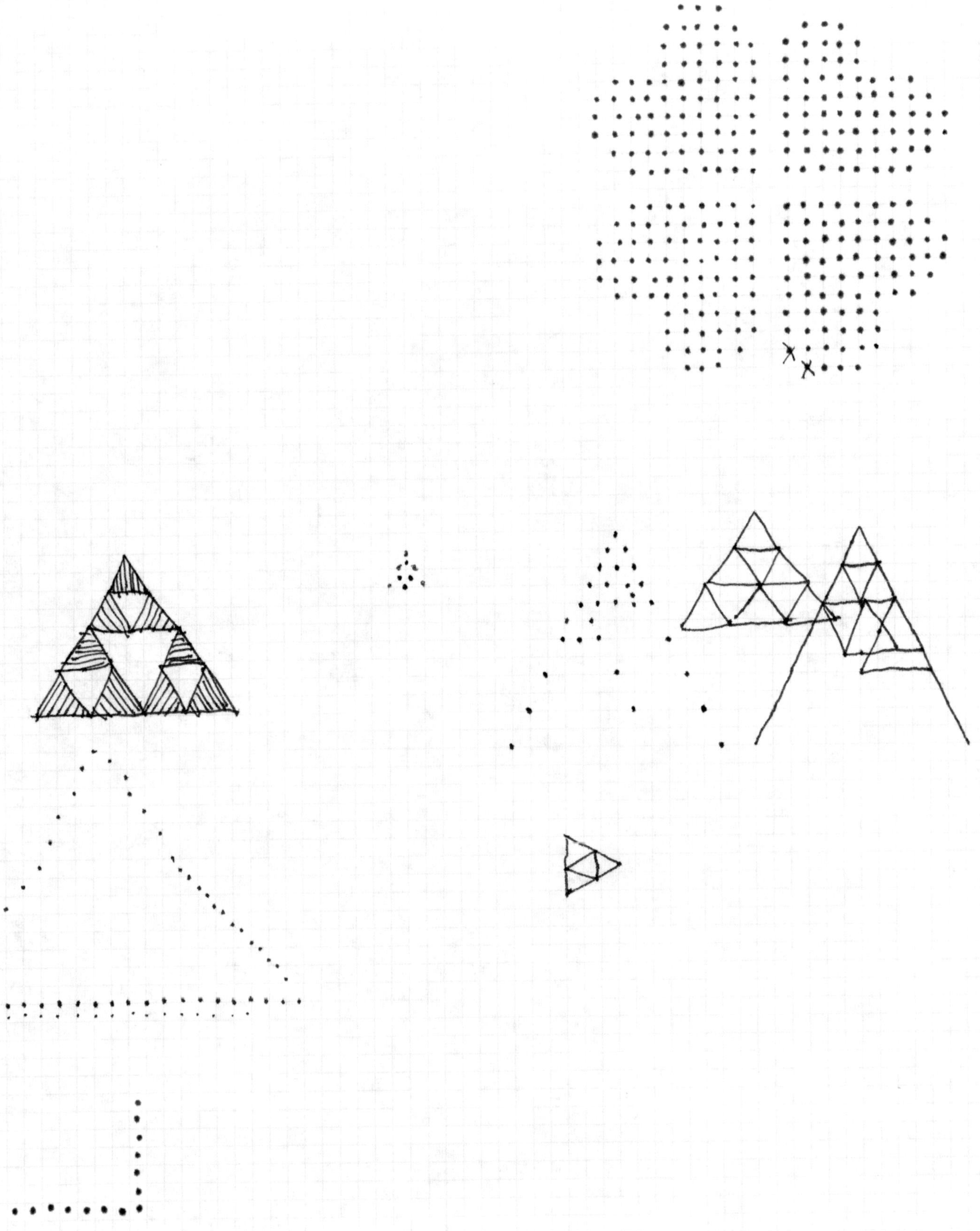

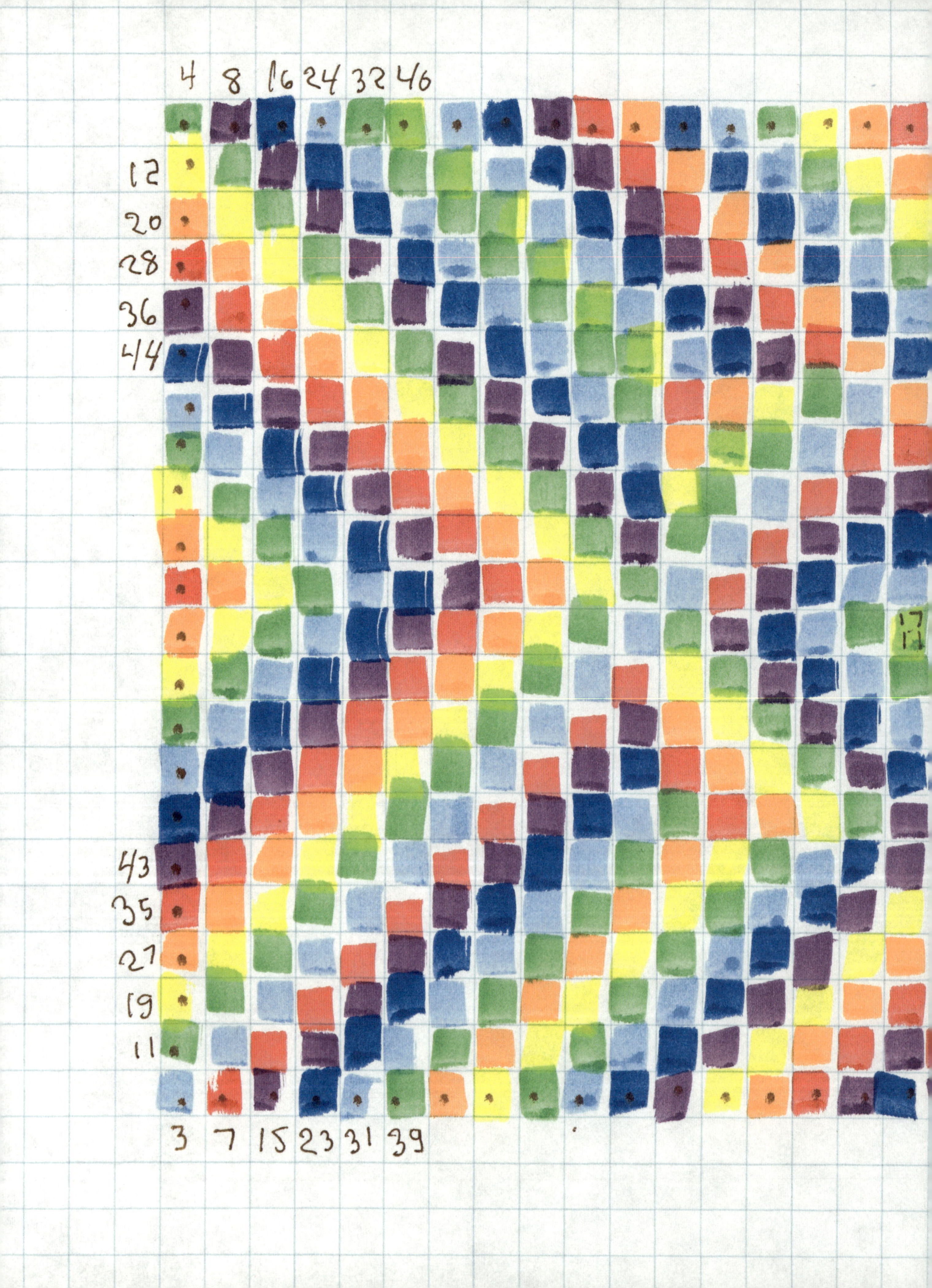
4 8 16 24 32 46
12
20
28
36
44
17
43
35
27
19
11
3 7 15 23 31 39

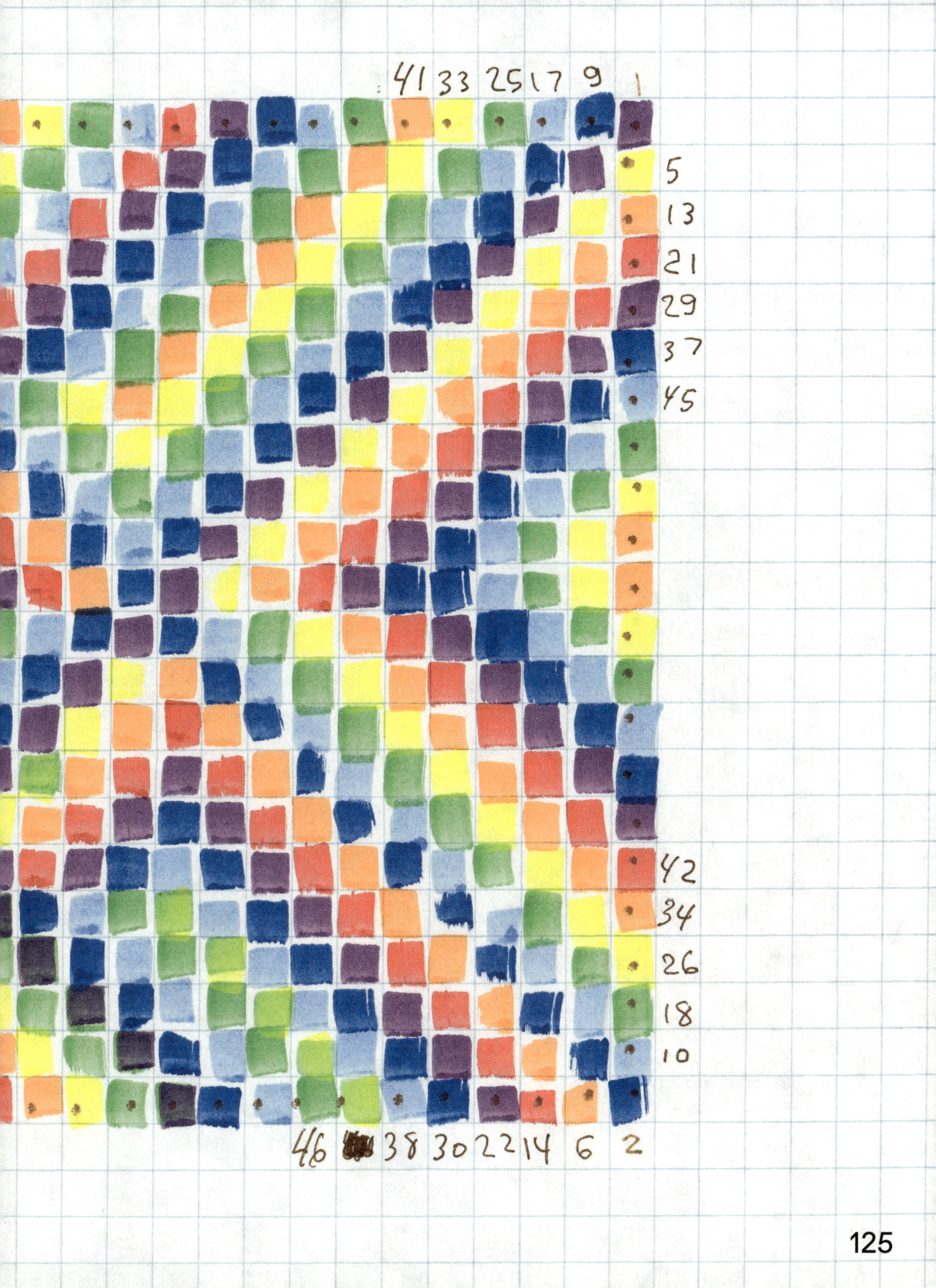
41 33 25 17 9 1
5
13
21
29
37
45
42
34
26
18
10
46 38 30 22 14 6 2

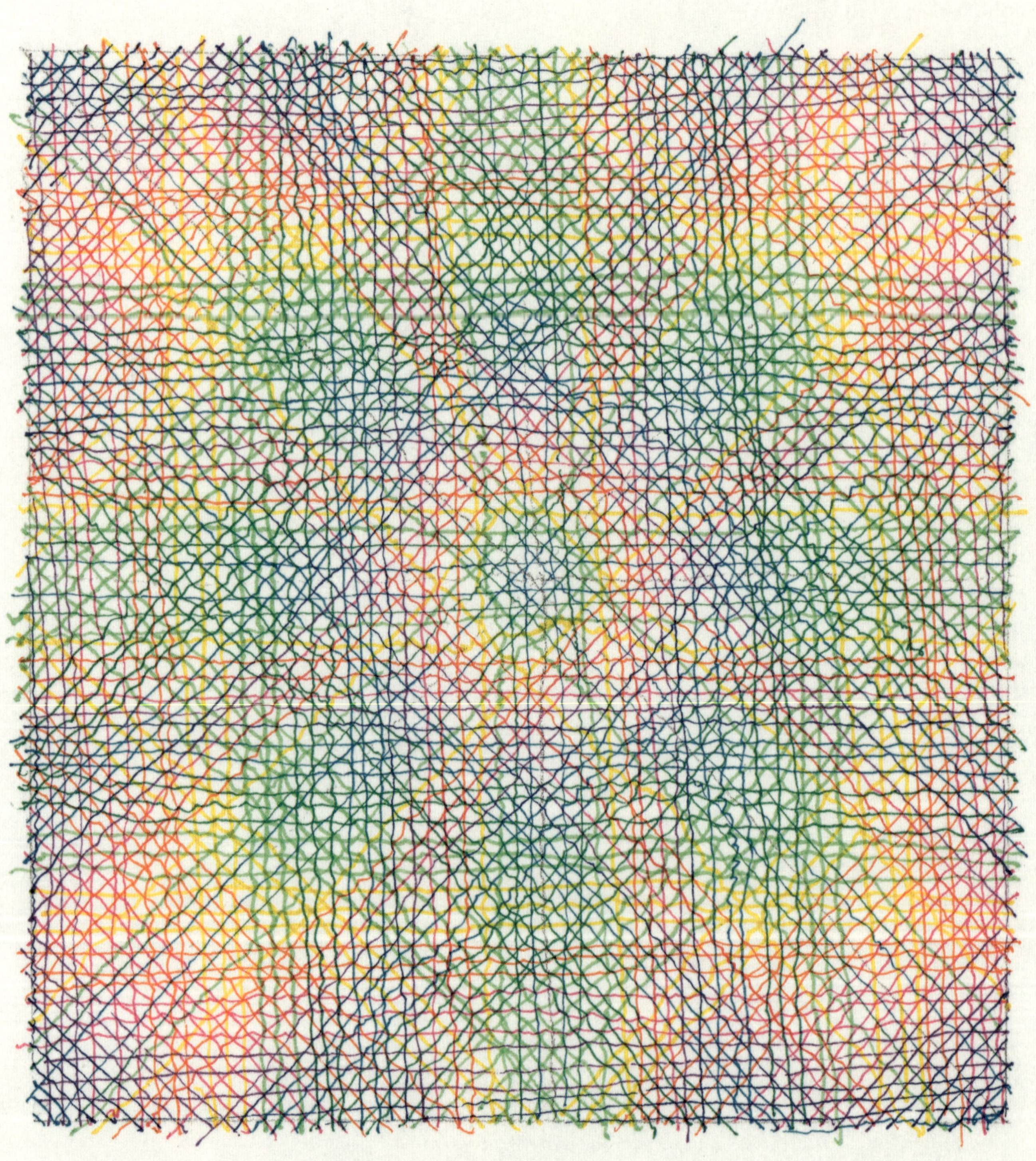

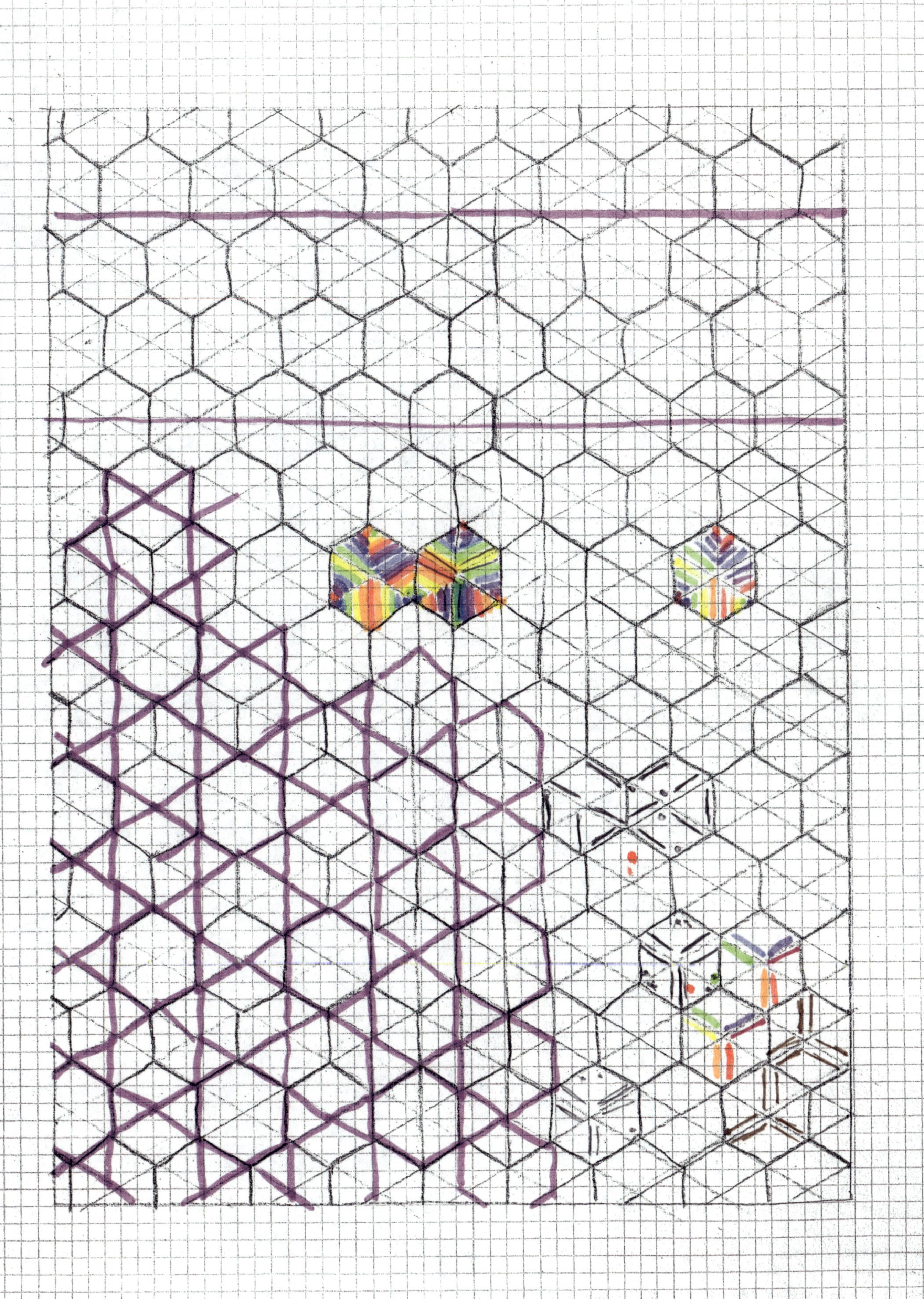

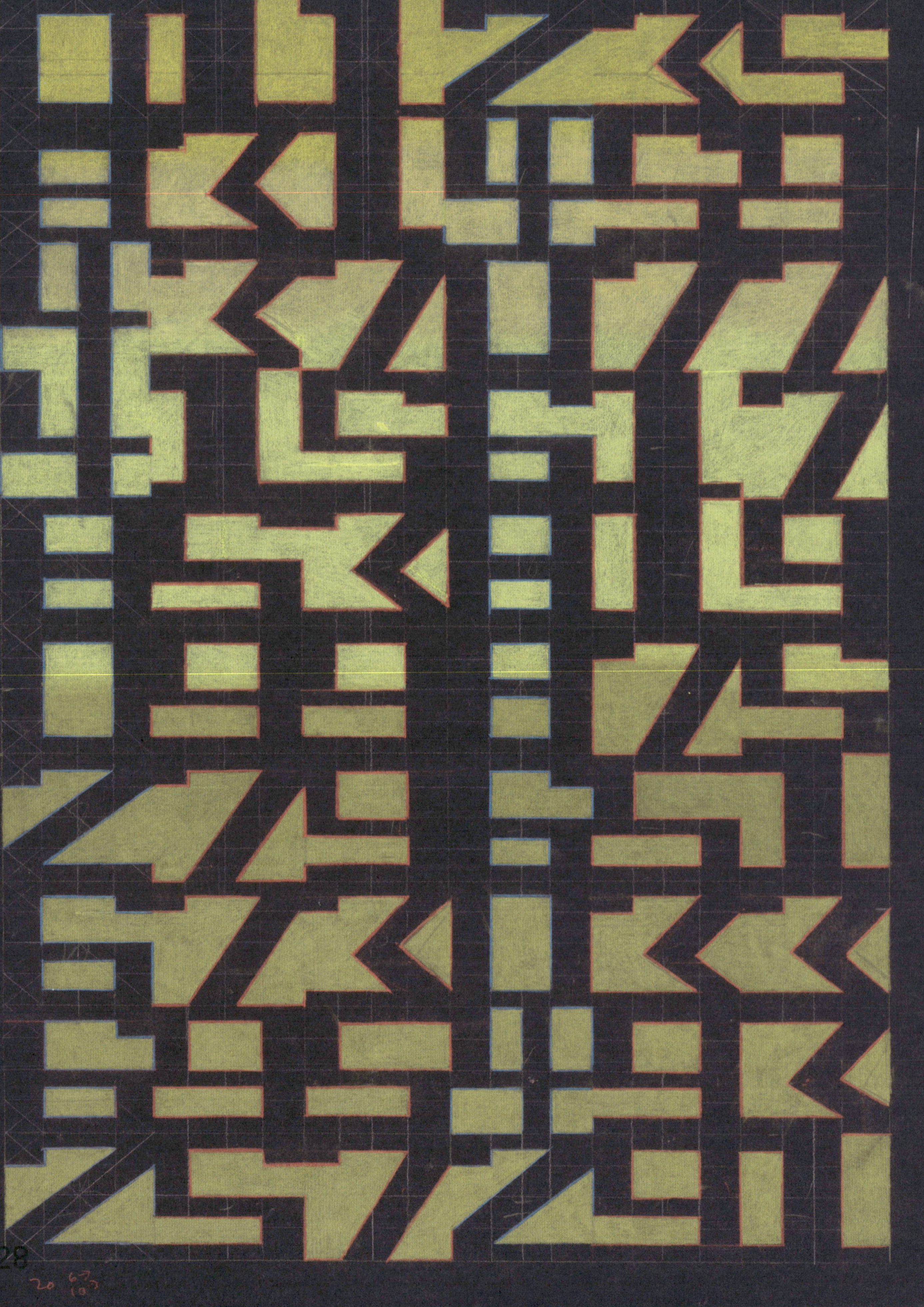

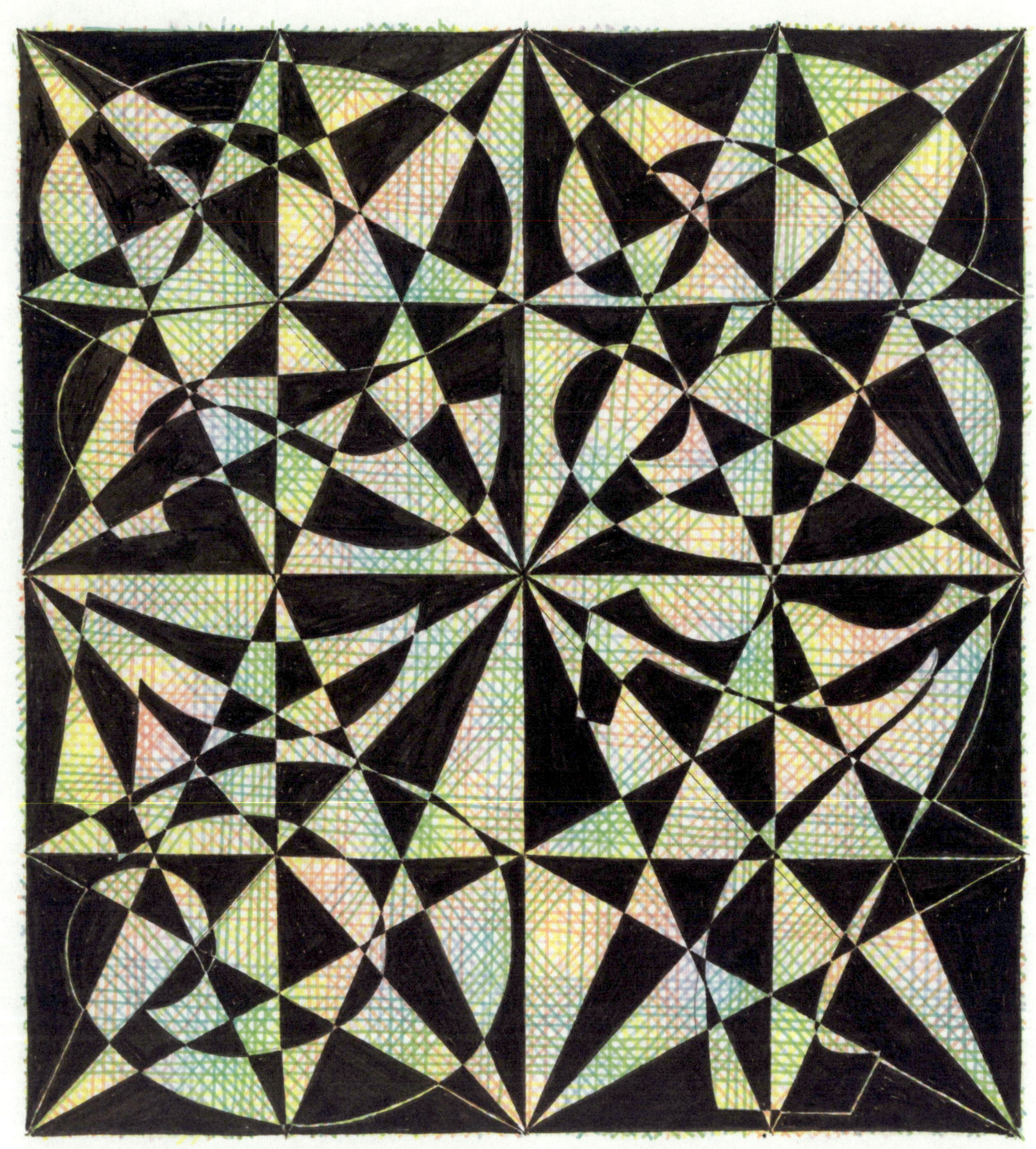

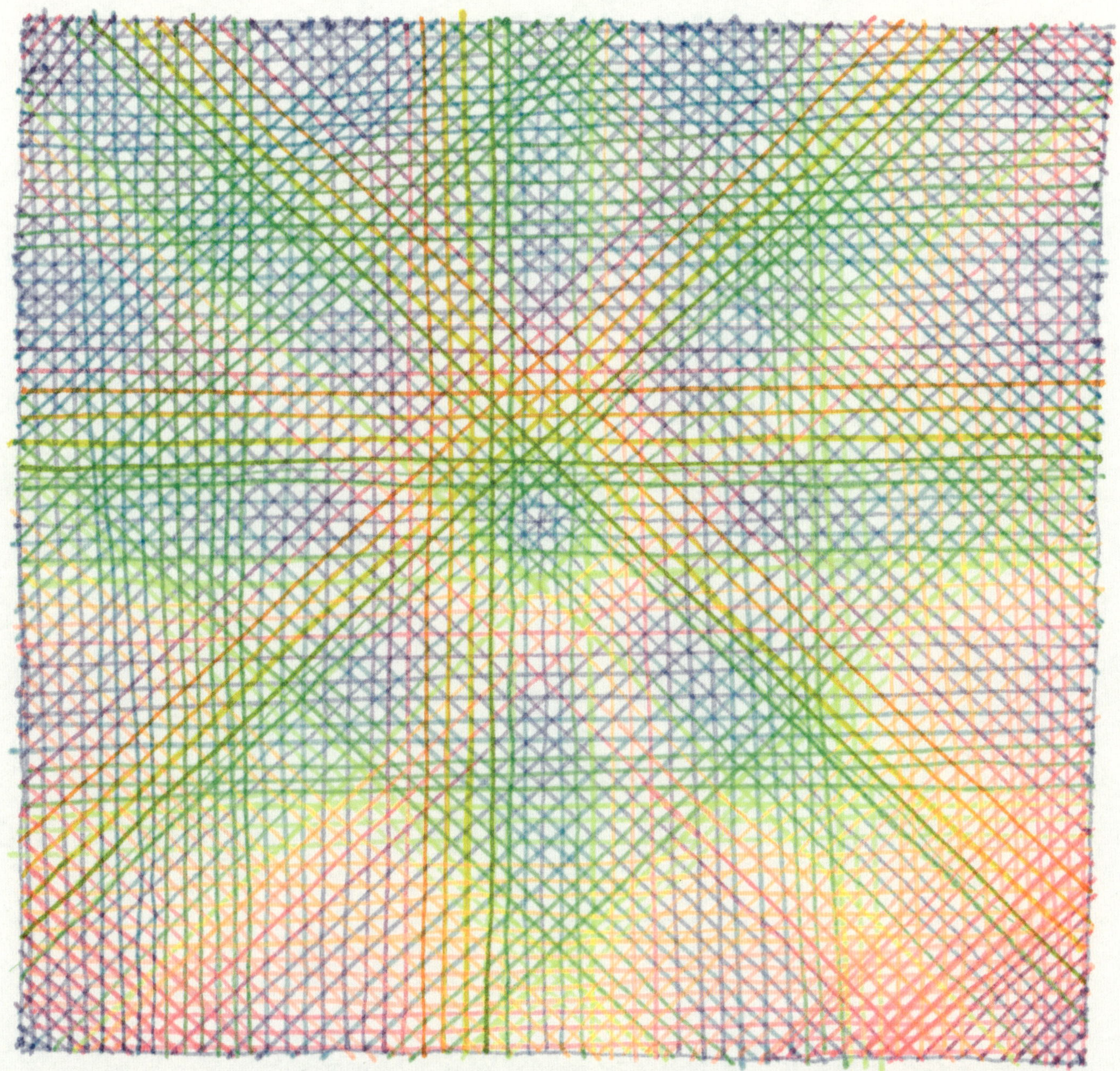

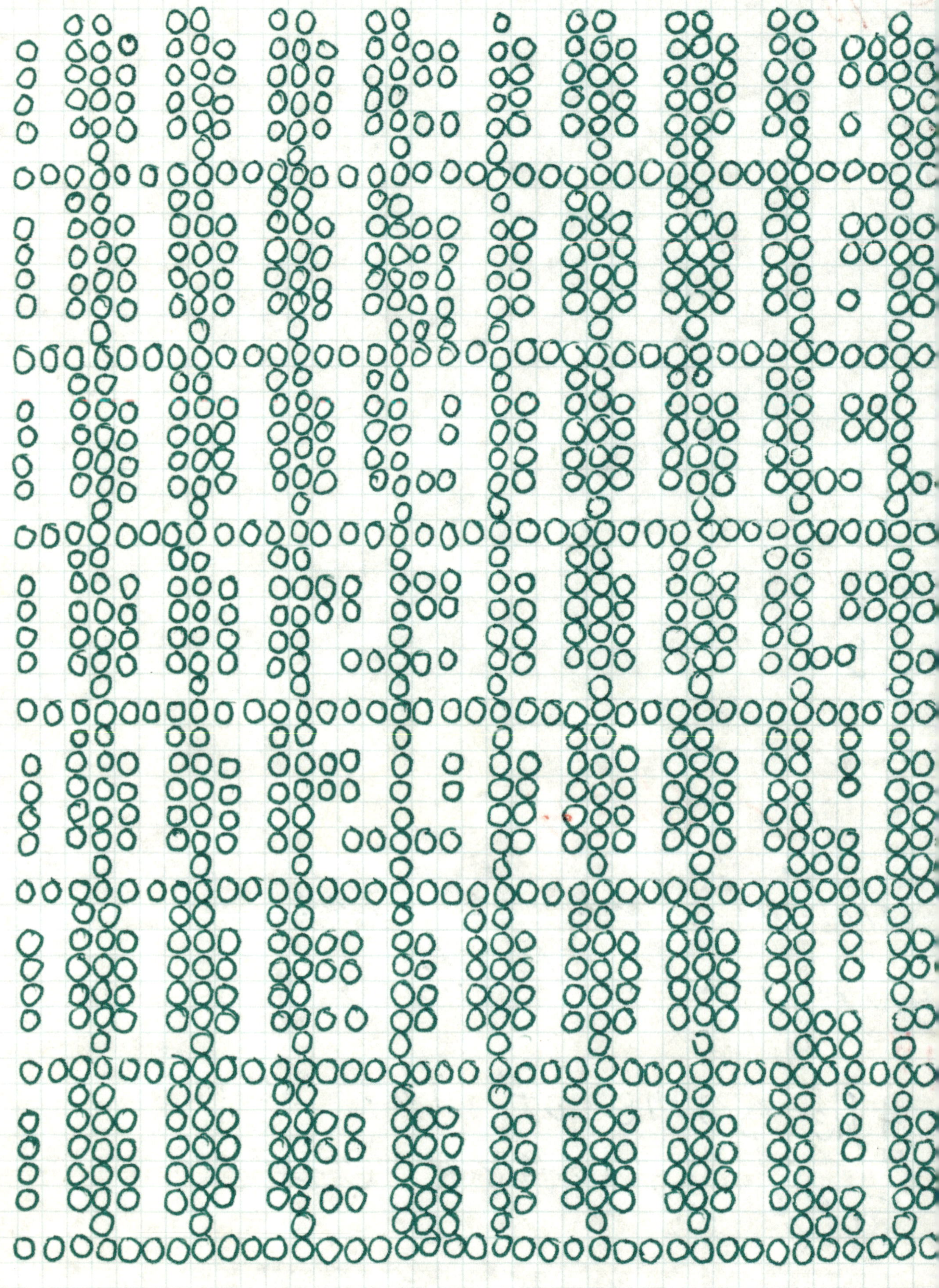

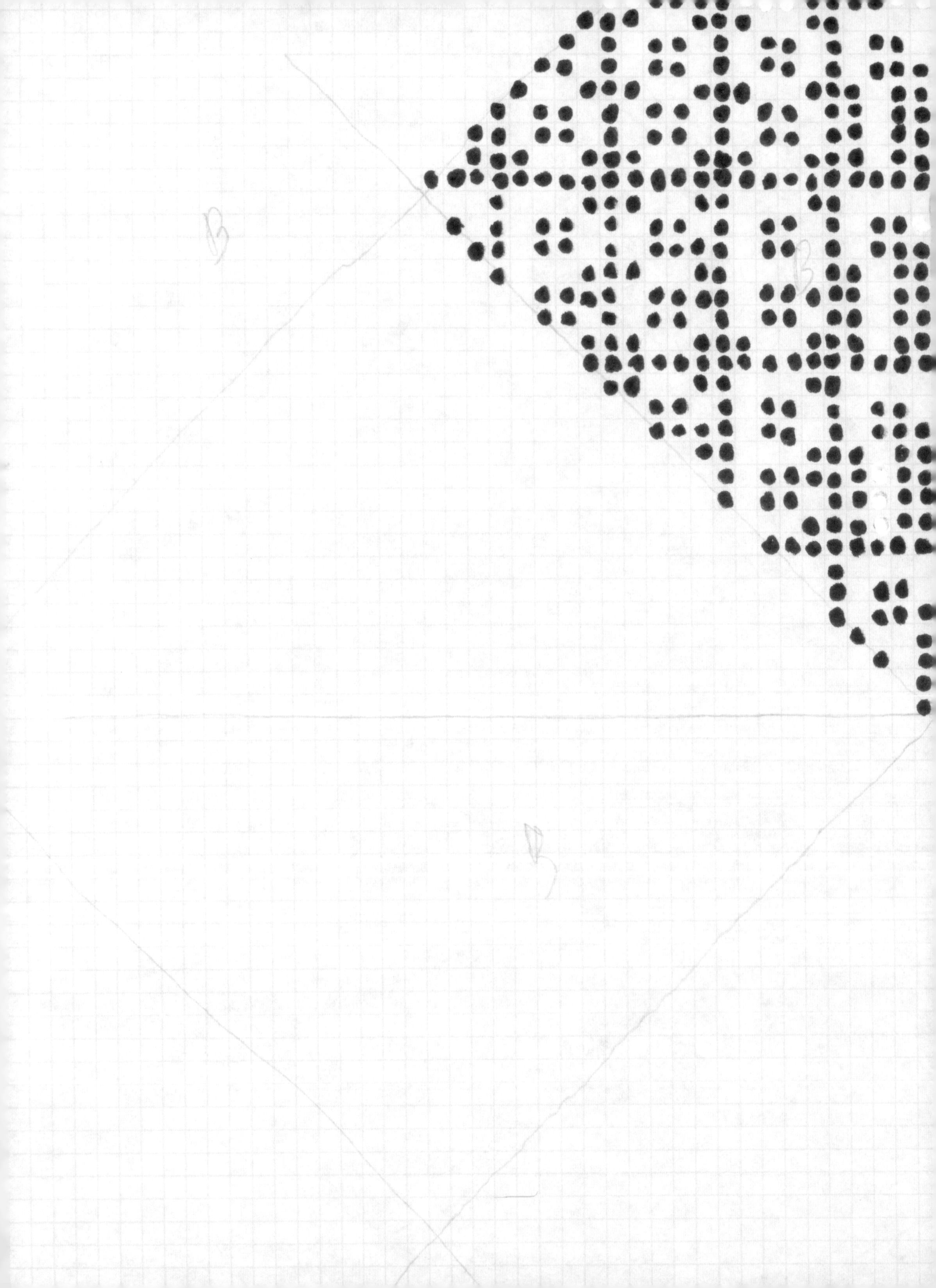

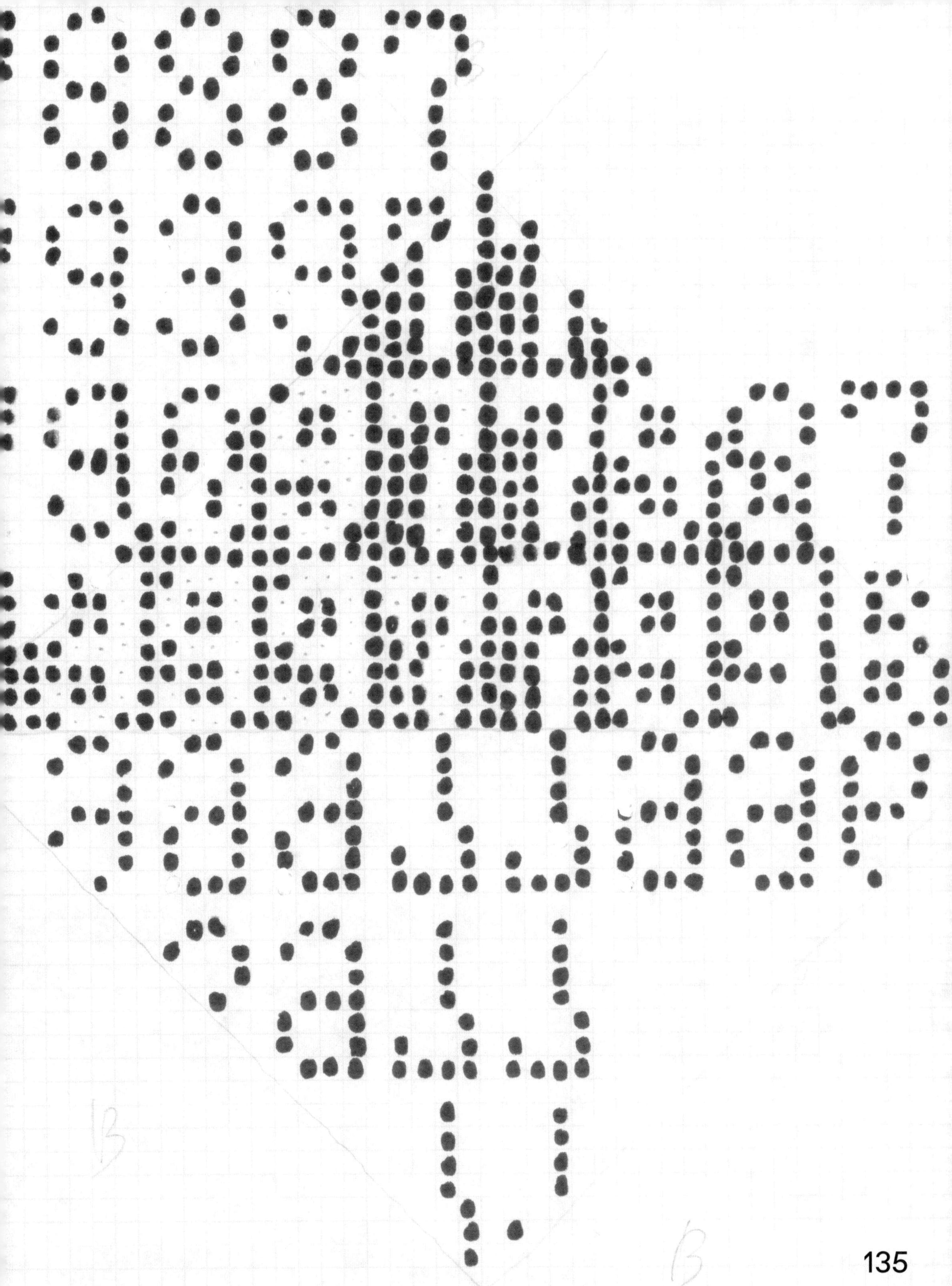

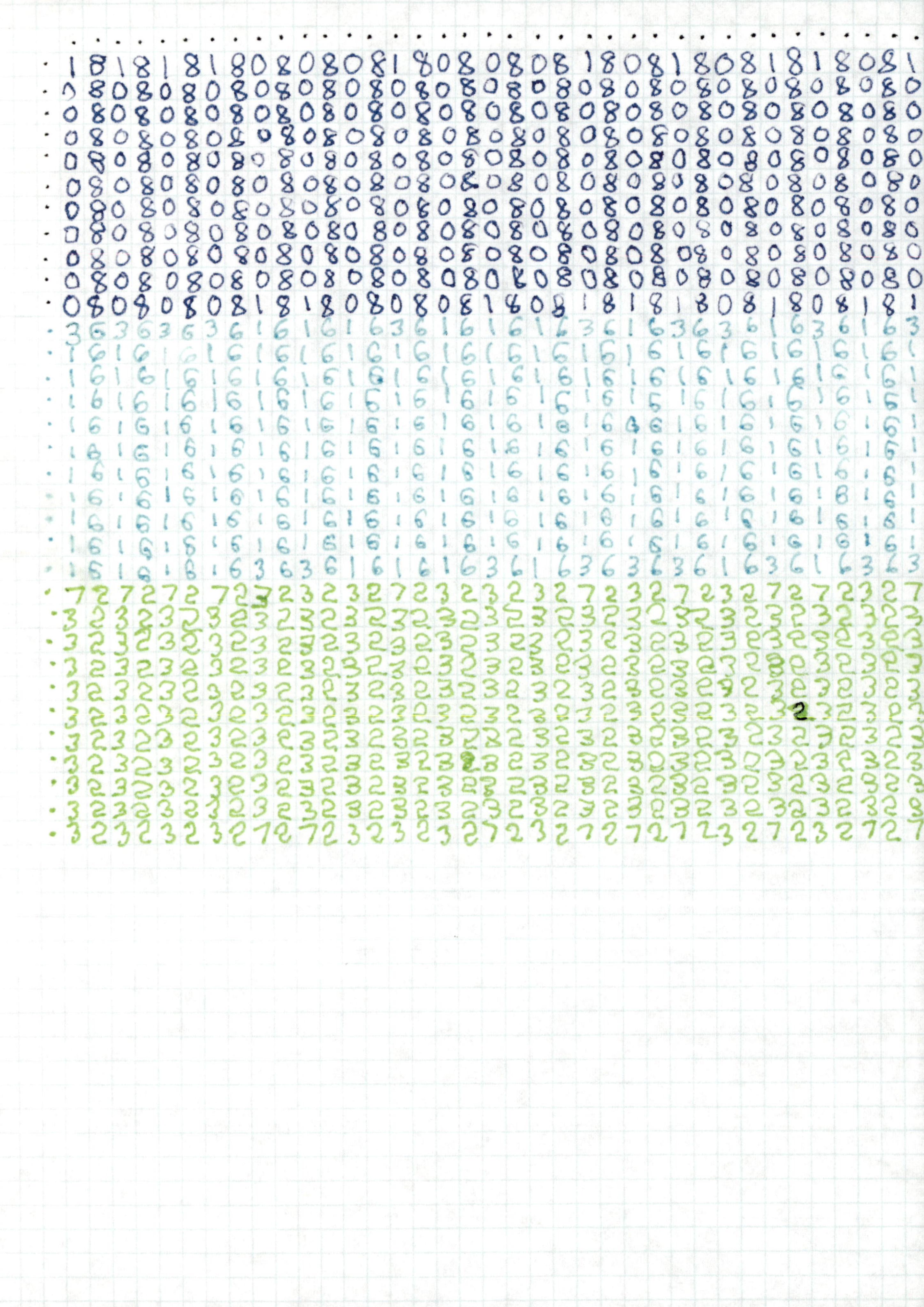

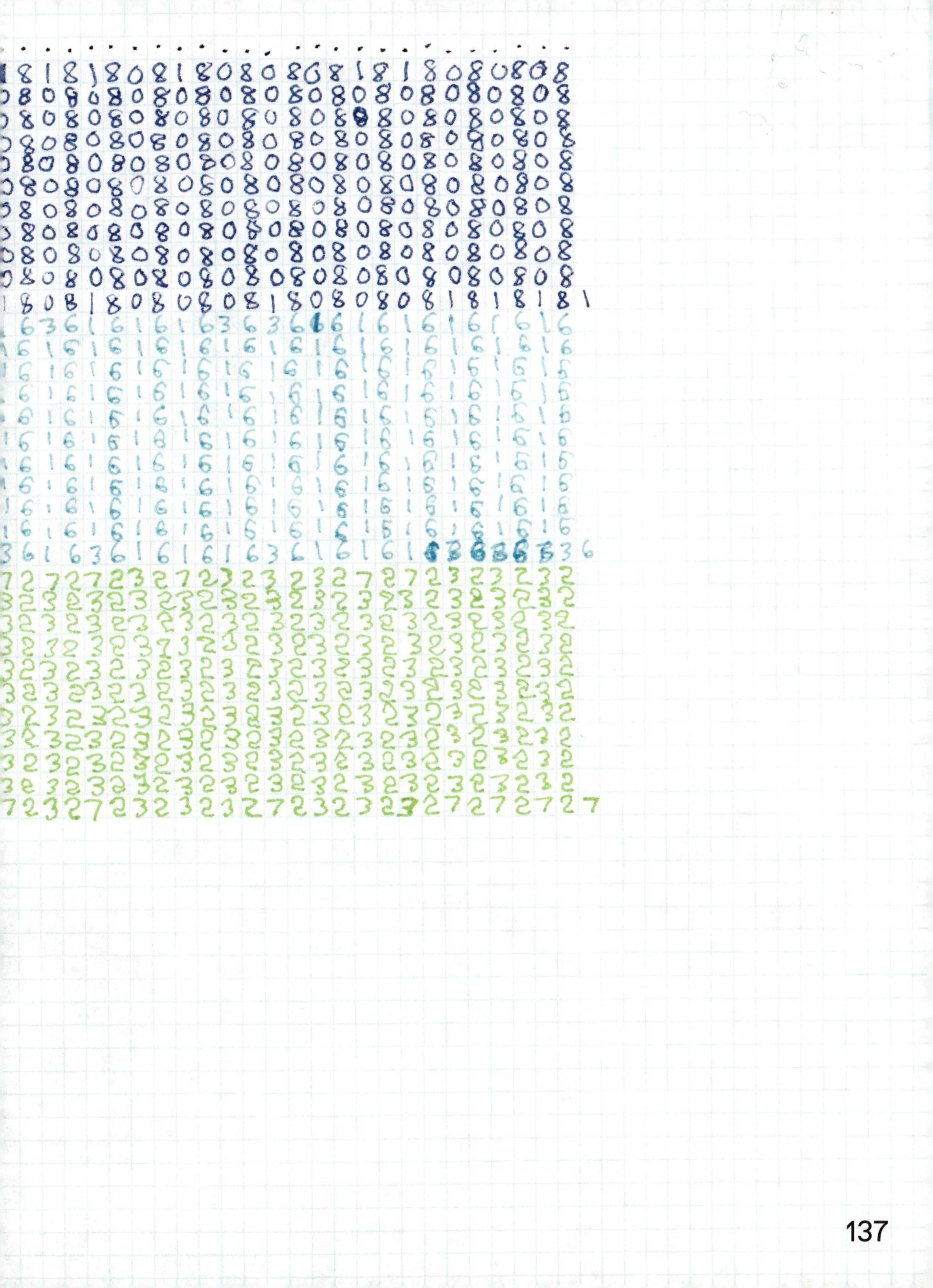

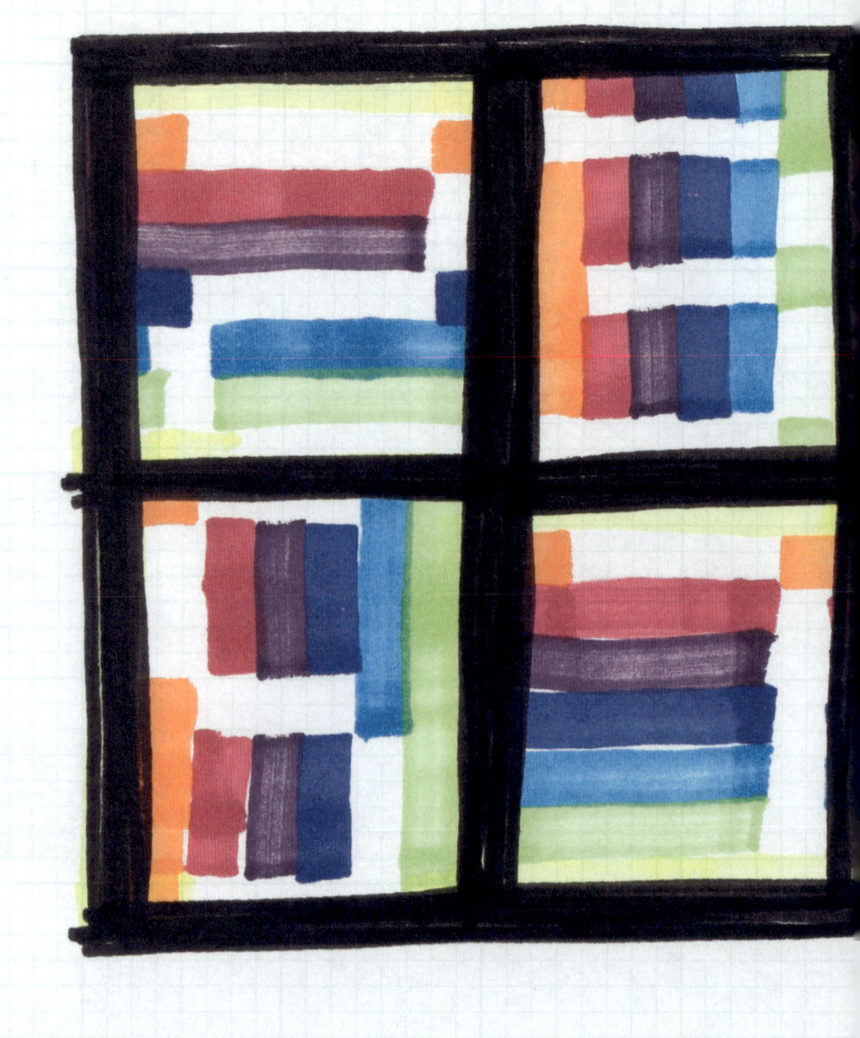

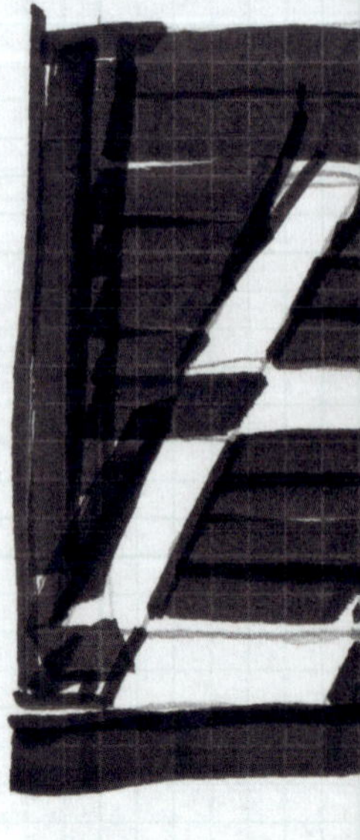

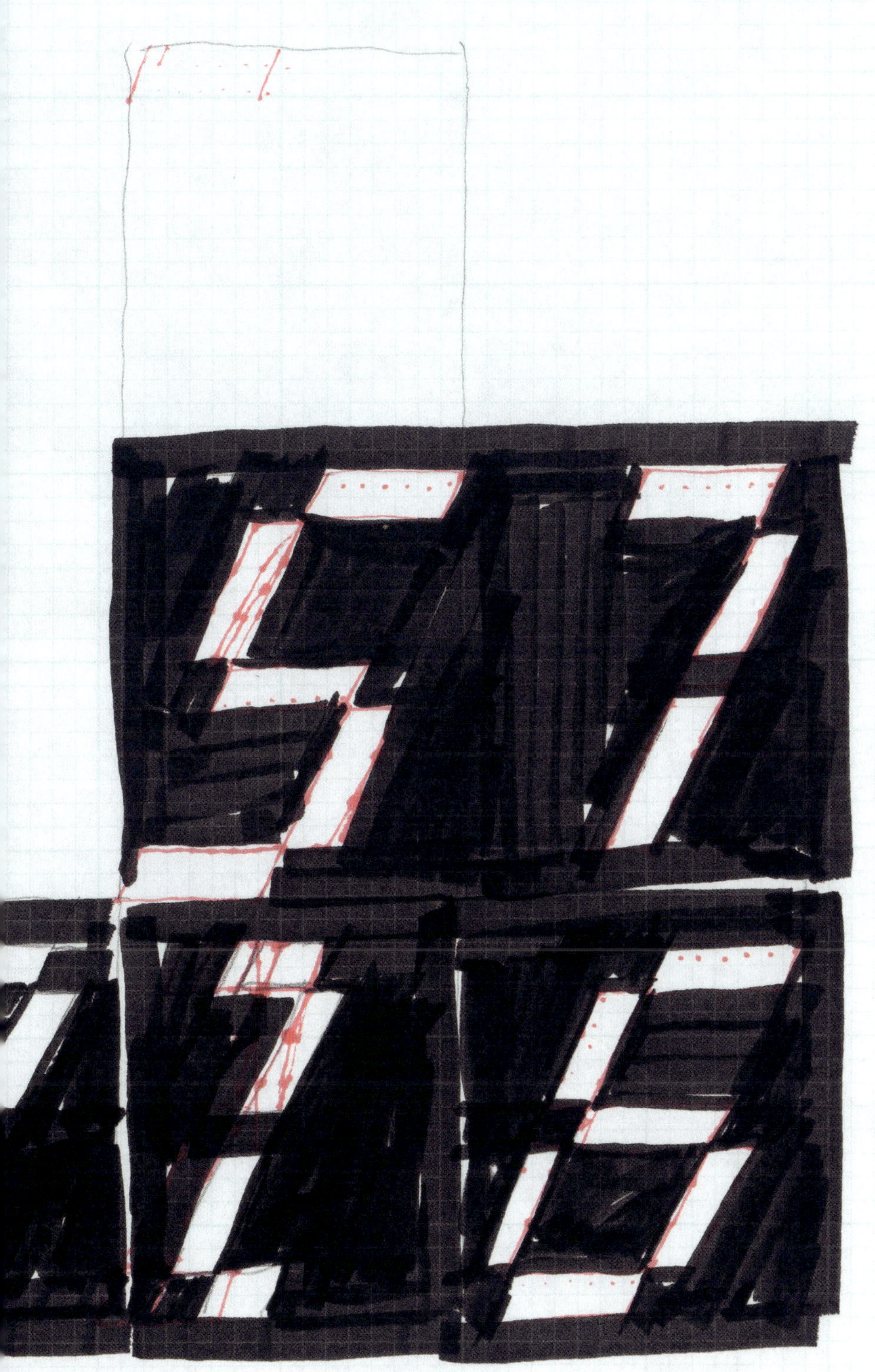

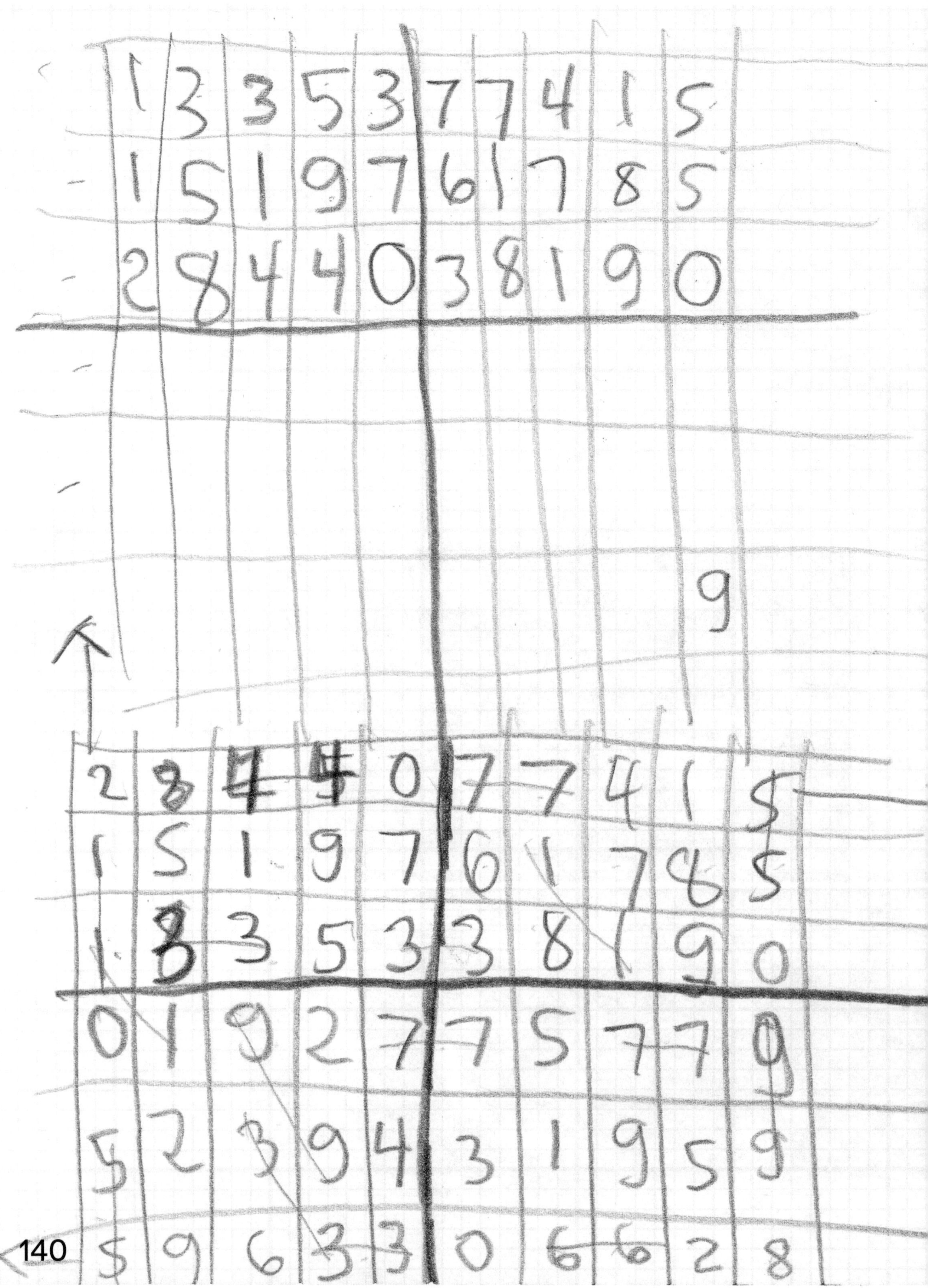

What follows are the first 100,000 digits of the number e. These digits were computed by Robert Nemiroff (George Mason University and NASA Goddard Space Flight Center) and checked by Jerry Bonnell (University Space Research Association and NASA Goddard Space Flight Center). There were computed during spare time on a VAX alpha class machine over the course of a weekend. We do NOT guarantee the accuracy of these digits. Although these digits have been checked once we encourage others to check them as well. We believe these are the most digits ever computed for the number e on or before 1 May 1994. We have computed at least 5 million digits of the number e and several digits of the the square roots of integers as well. These are available on this mosaic server:
(URL:http://antwrp.gsfc.nasa.gov/htmltest/rjn.html).
We welcome comments.

- Robert Nemiroff and Jerry Bonnell

e -

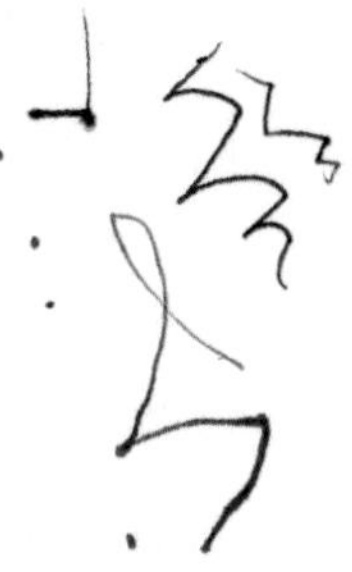

2.718281828459045235360287471352662497757247093699959574966
967627724076630353547594571382178525166427427466391932003059
921817413596629043572900334295260595630738132328627943490763
233829880753195251019011573834187930702154089149934884167509
244761460668082264800168477411853742345442437107539077744992
069551702761838606261331384583000752044933826560297606737113
200709328709127443747047230696977209310141692836819025515108
657463772111252389784425056953696770785449969967946864454905
987931636889230098793127736178215424999229576351482208269895
193668033182528869398496465105820939239829488793320362509443
117301238197068416140397019837679320683282376464804295311802
328782509819455815301756717361332069811250996181881593041690
351598888519345807273866738589422879228499892086805825749279
610484198444363463244968487560233624827041978623209002160990
235304369941849146314093431738143640546253152096183690888707
016768396424378140592714563549061303107208510383750510115747
704171898610687396965521267154688957035035402123407849819334
321068170121005627880235193033224745015853904730419957777093
503660416997329725088687696640355570716226844716256079882651
787134195124665201030592123667719432527867539855894489697096
409754591856956380236370162112047742722836489613422516445078
182442352948636372141740238893441247963574370263755294448337
998016125492278509257782562092622648326277933386566481627725
164019105900491644998289315056604725802778631864155195653244
258698294695930801915298721172556347546396447910145904090586
298496791287406870504895858671747985466775757320568128845920
541334053922000113786300945560688166740016984205580403363795
376452030402432256613527836951177883863874439662532249850654
995886234281899707733276171783928034946501434558897071942586

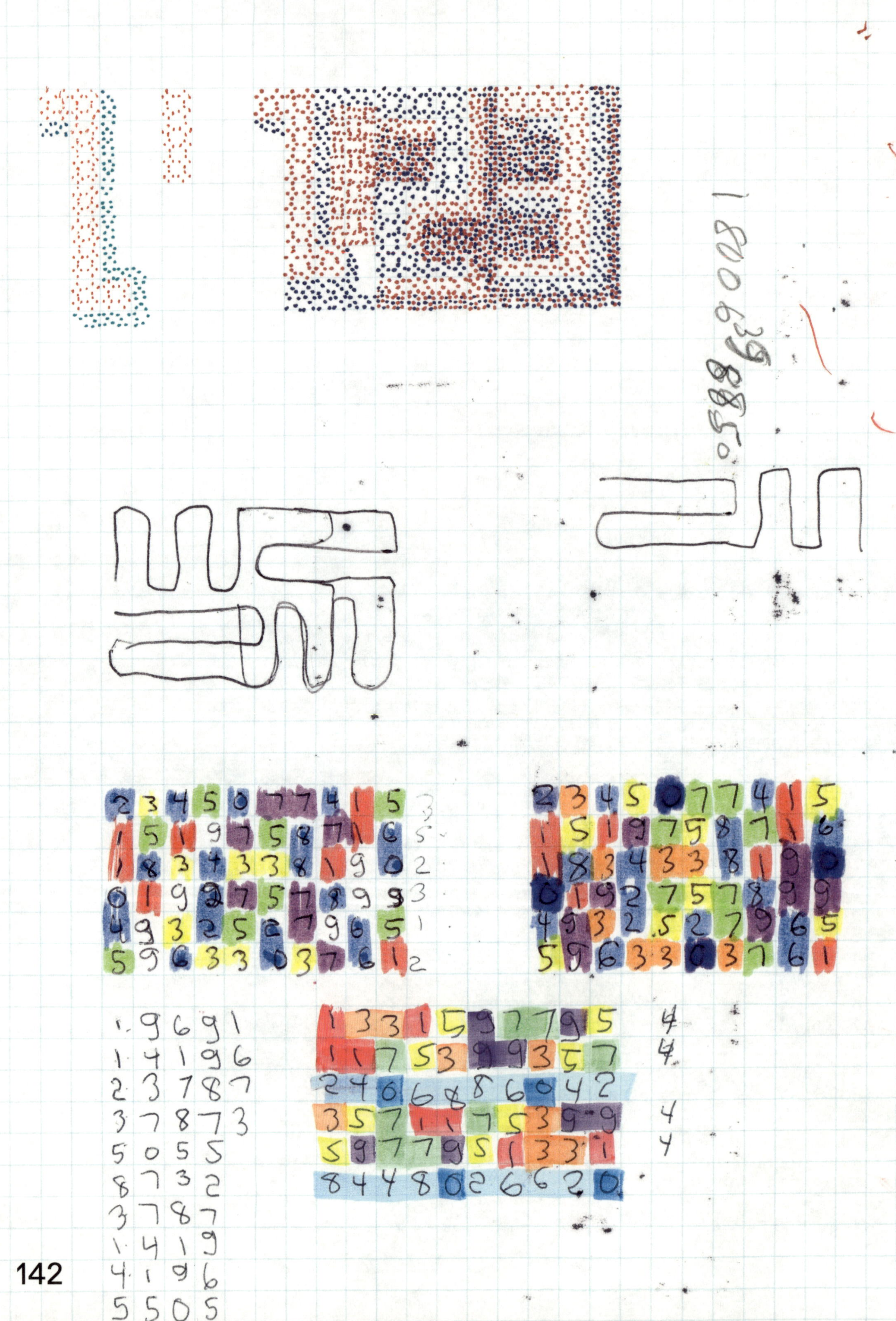

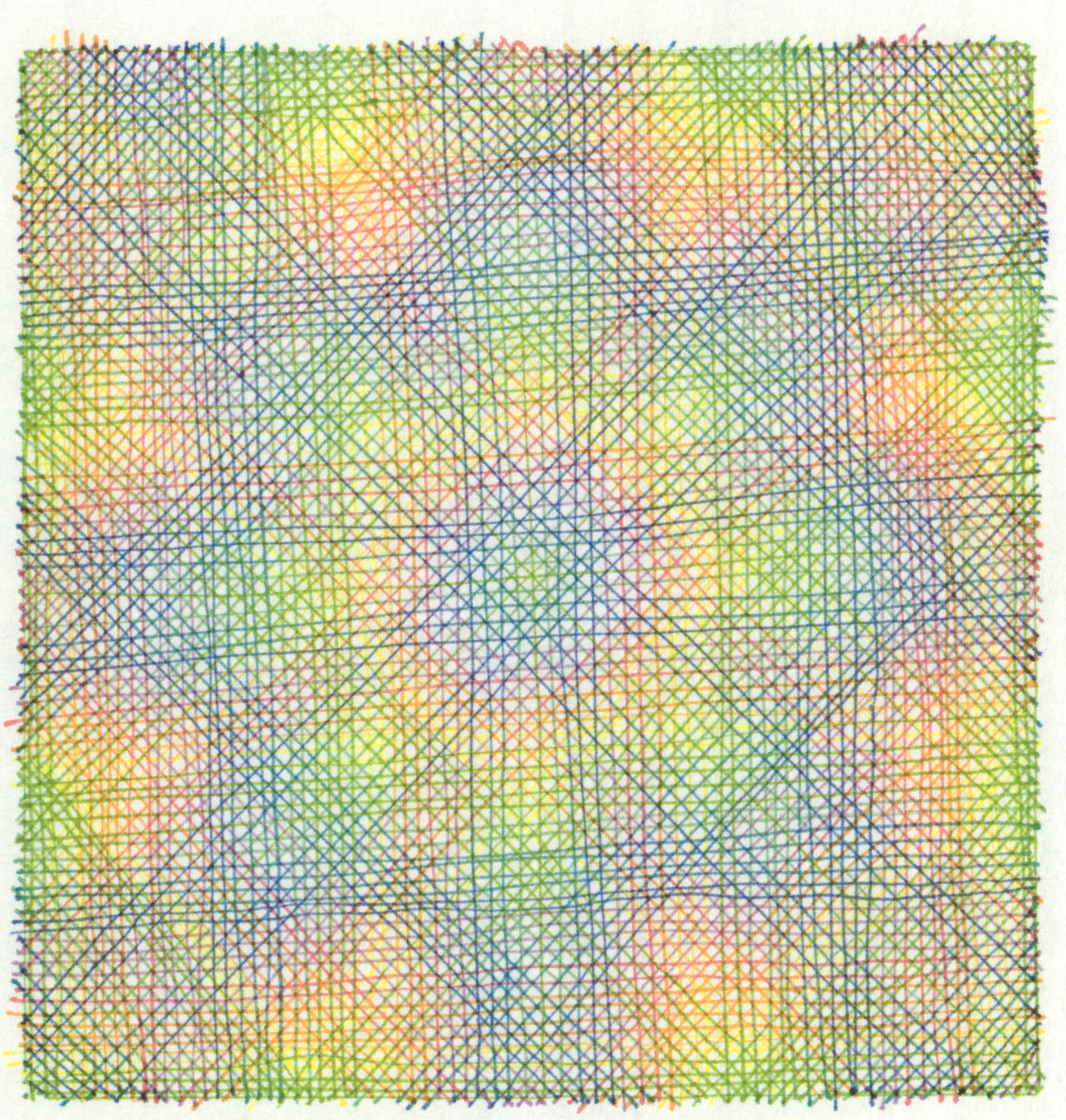

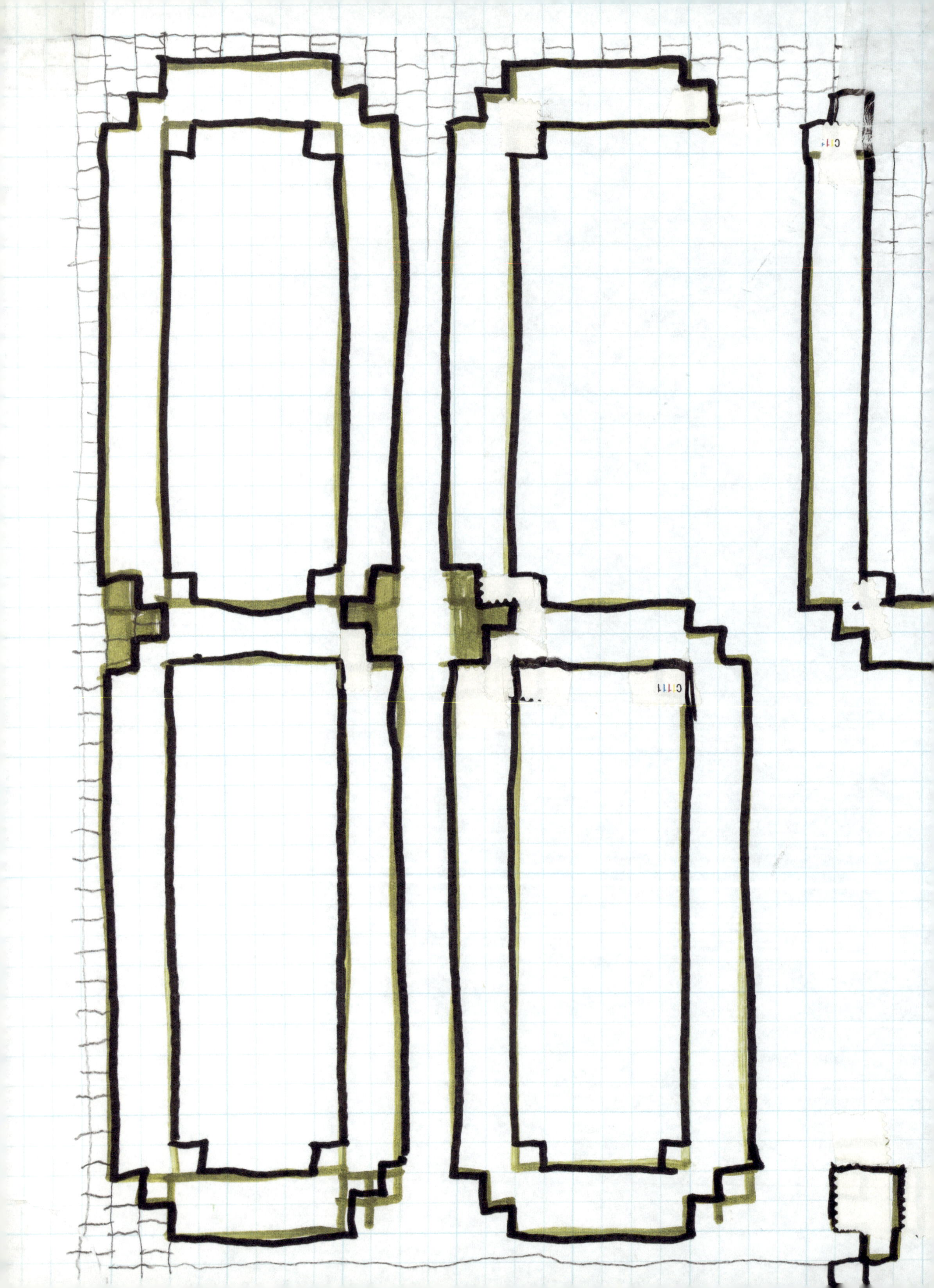

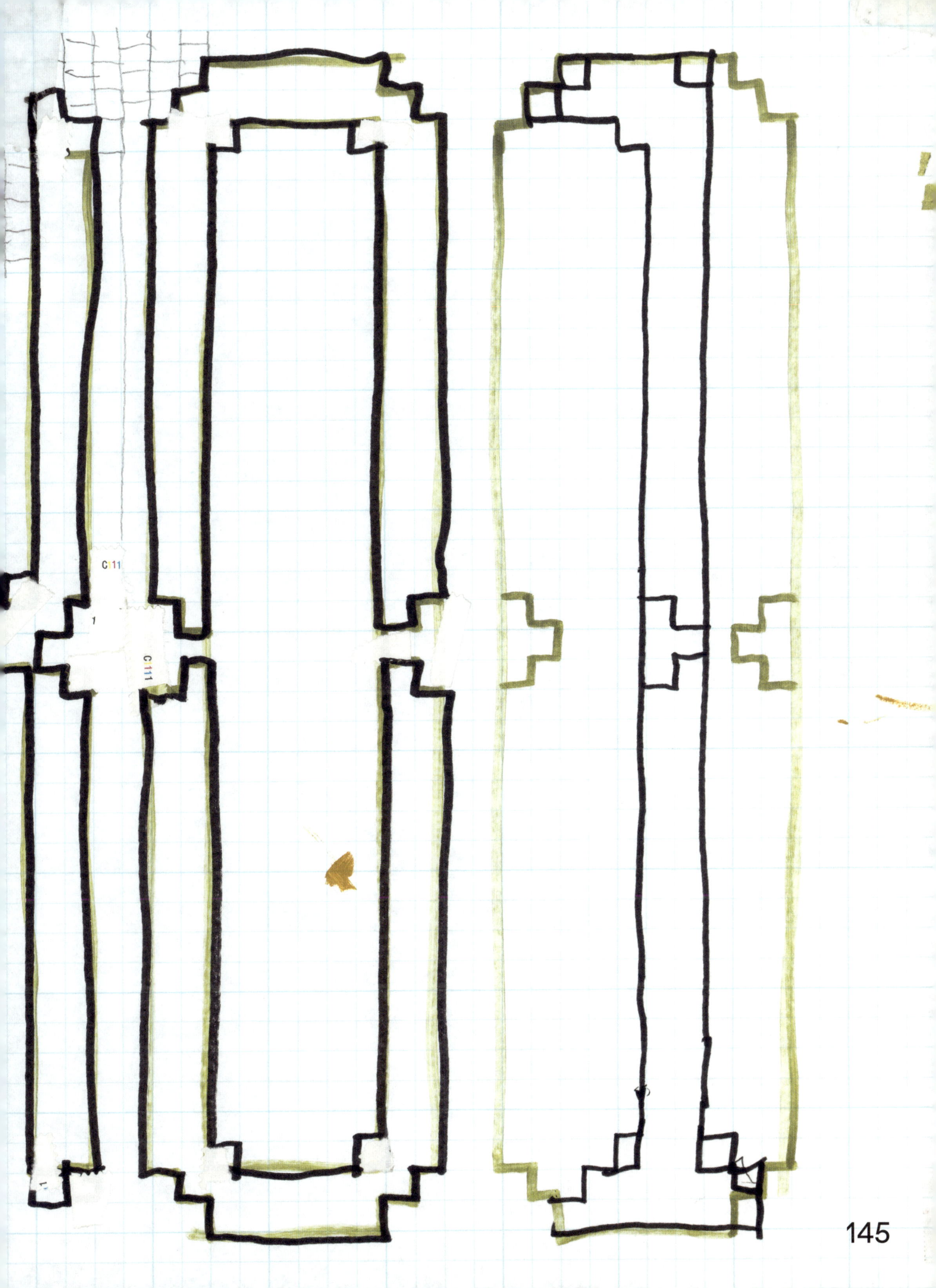

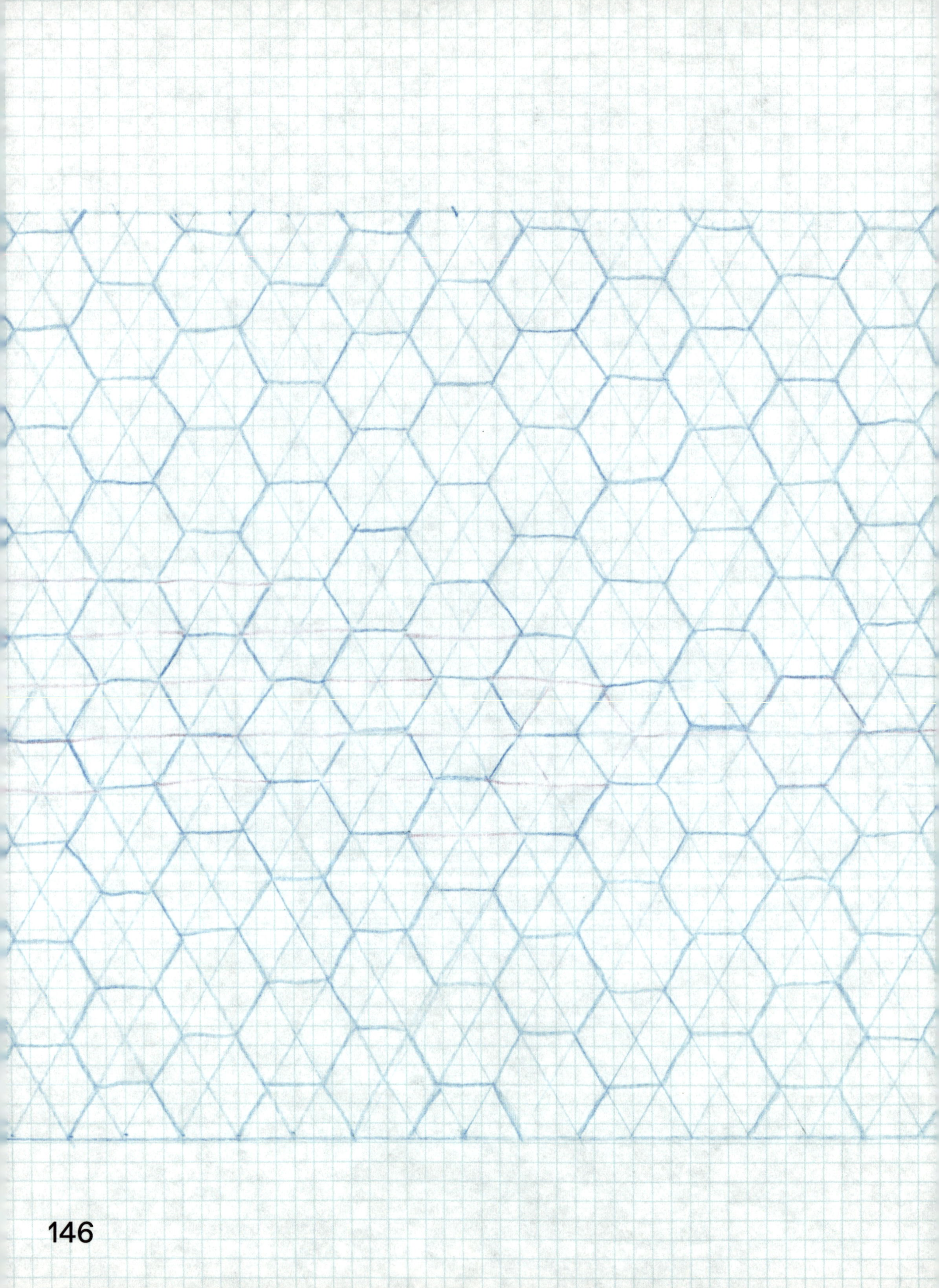

CHAPTER ONE 1963 R.R. LA – FL

TWO Ms. JOHN 1973

THREE ~~Happy Hour~~ REDDING LOUNGE 1983

FOUR O.C. SOCIAL DISTORTION

FIVE SFAI ~~[illegible]~~ 1989

SIX ATLANTIC OCEAN

SEVEN OCTAGON 1994

~~EIGHT CLOWN PICKLES [illegible]~~

NINE CARRY THE ONE 1999

TEN ~~[illegible]~~ CANADA 2003

~~[illegible]~~

~~[illegible]~~ ELEVEN CROSLEY 2010 44 HOPE ST.

~~[illegible]~~ 33 RUSSELL ST.

THIRTEEN not dots / DR. FARBER 2013

FOURTEEN NOT DADS

XV MAGIC SQUARES

6teen TRIANGLES

17 9.15.18 19992-30103

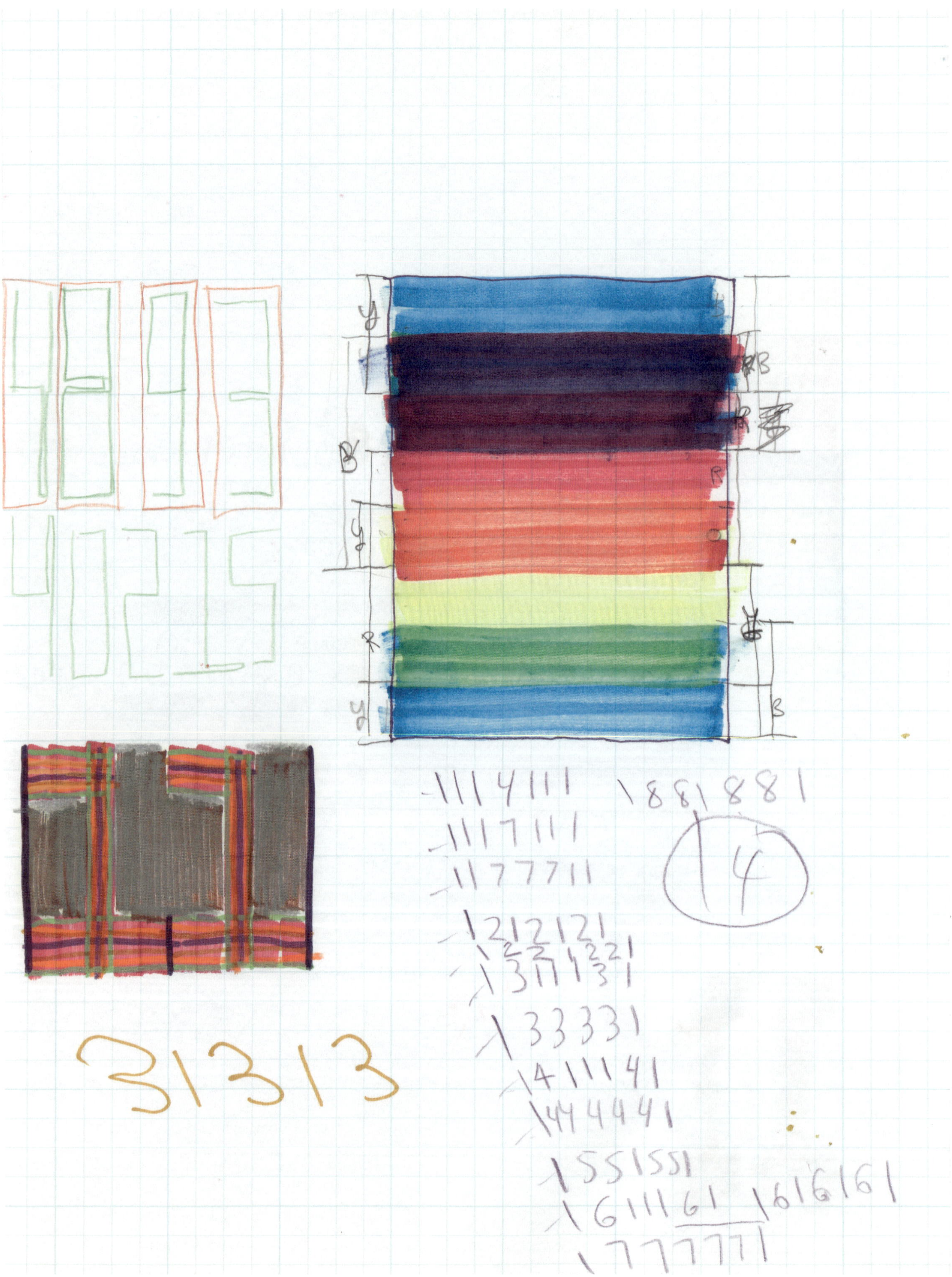

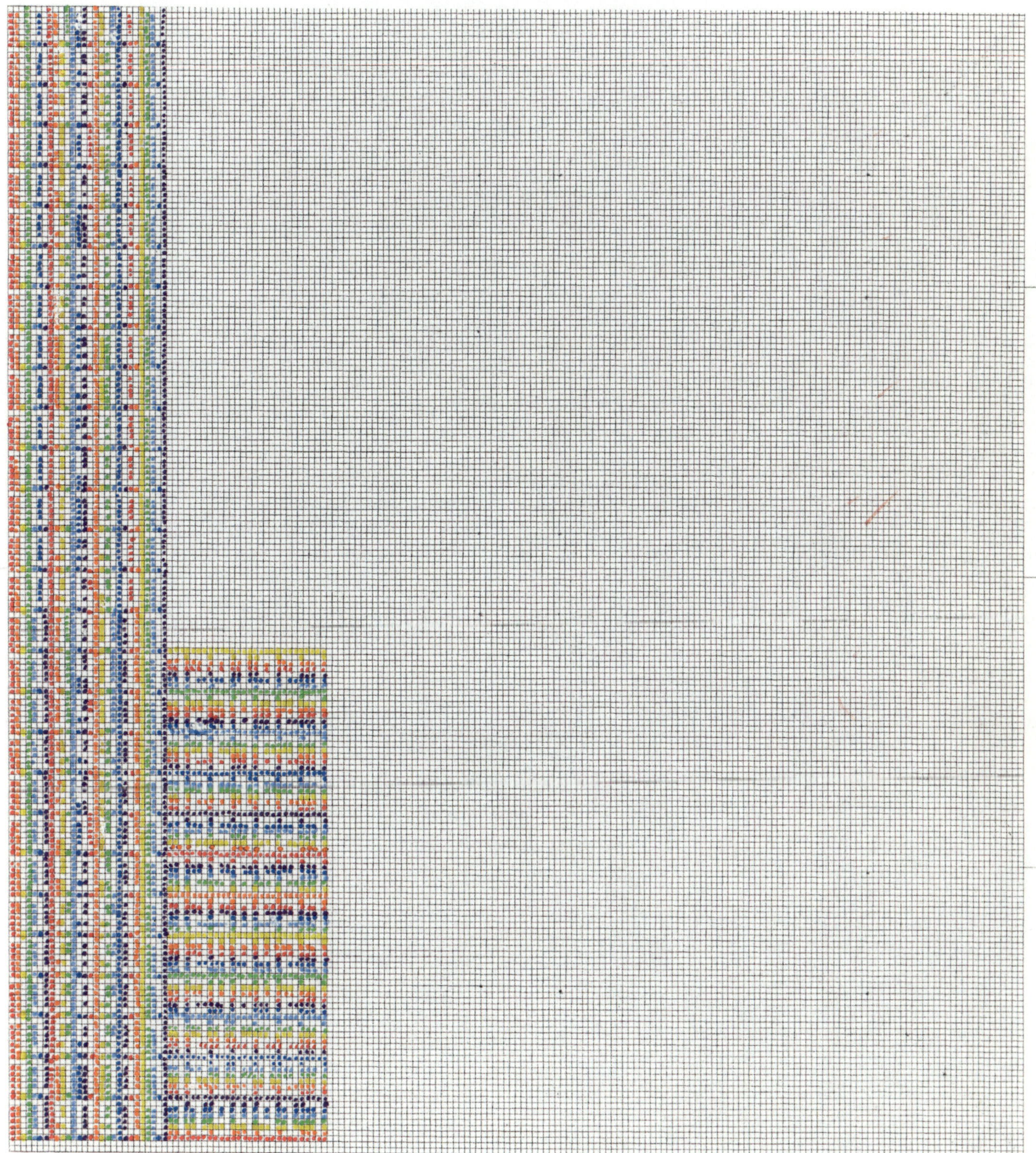

PROBLEMS W/ PAINTING

- FATIGUE
- BOREDOME
- IMPULSE CONTROL
- PRODUCTIVITY
- SKETCH TRANSLATION
- MENTAL STATE AMPLIFIED
- LONLINESS
- VOICES
- REPETITIVE THOUGHTS
- DRIFT
- TIME LOST ON FAILURES
- LOSE PERSPECTIVE
- BACK ACHE

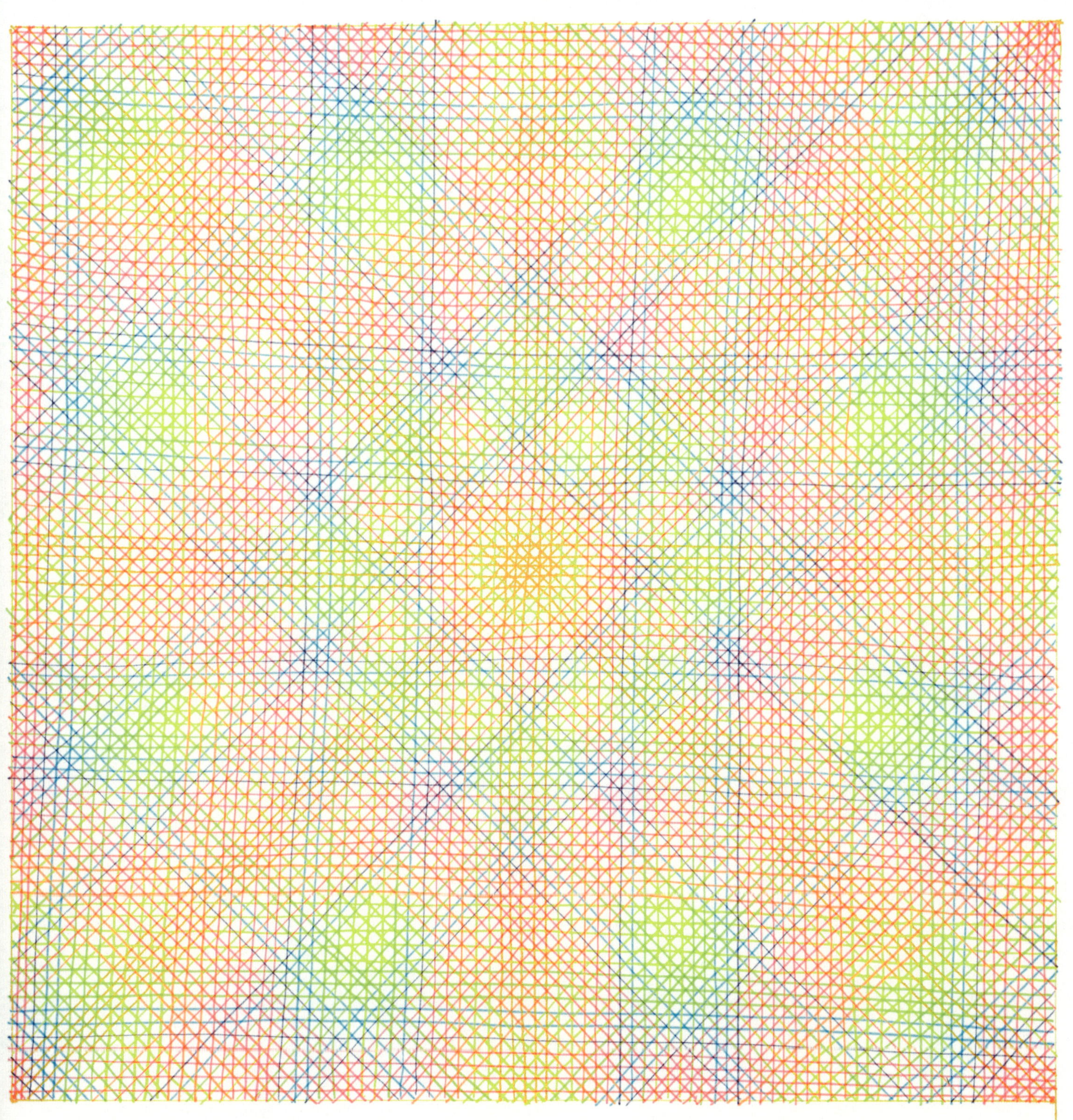

1. When do you want to die?

2. Wha t is your best day of the week? Why?

3. Do you know which day you were born on?

4. What is your date of birth?

5. Do you wear a wa tch? Why/Why not?

6. When is time your friend?

7. How ma ny hours would you like in a day?

8. Do you have a least favorite month?

9. What is your favorite season? Why?

10. Do you keep a diary? if yes, since what age?

11. Do you know anyone who studies time?

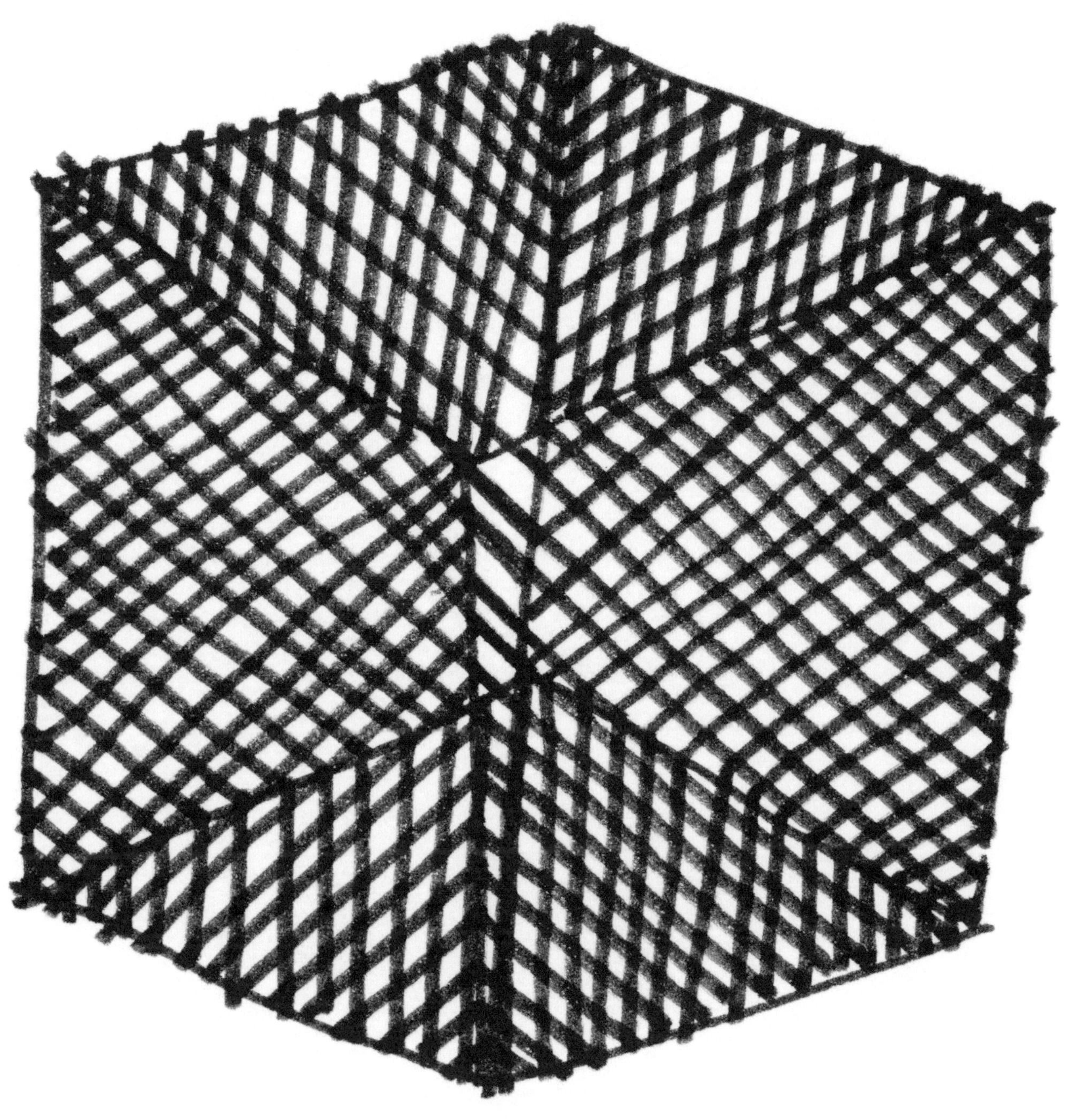

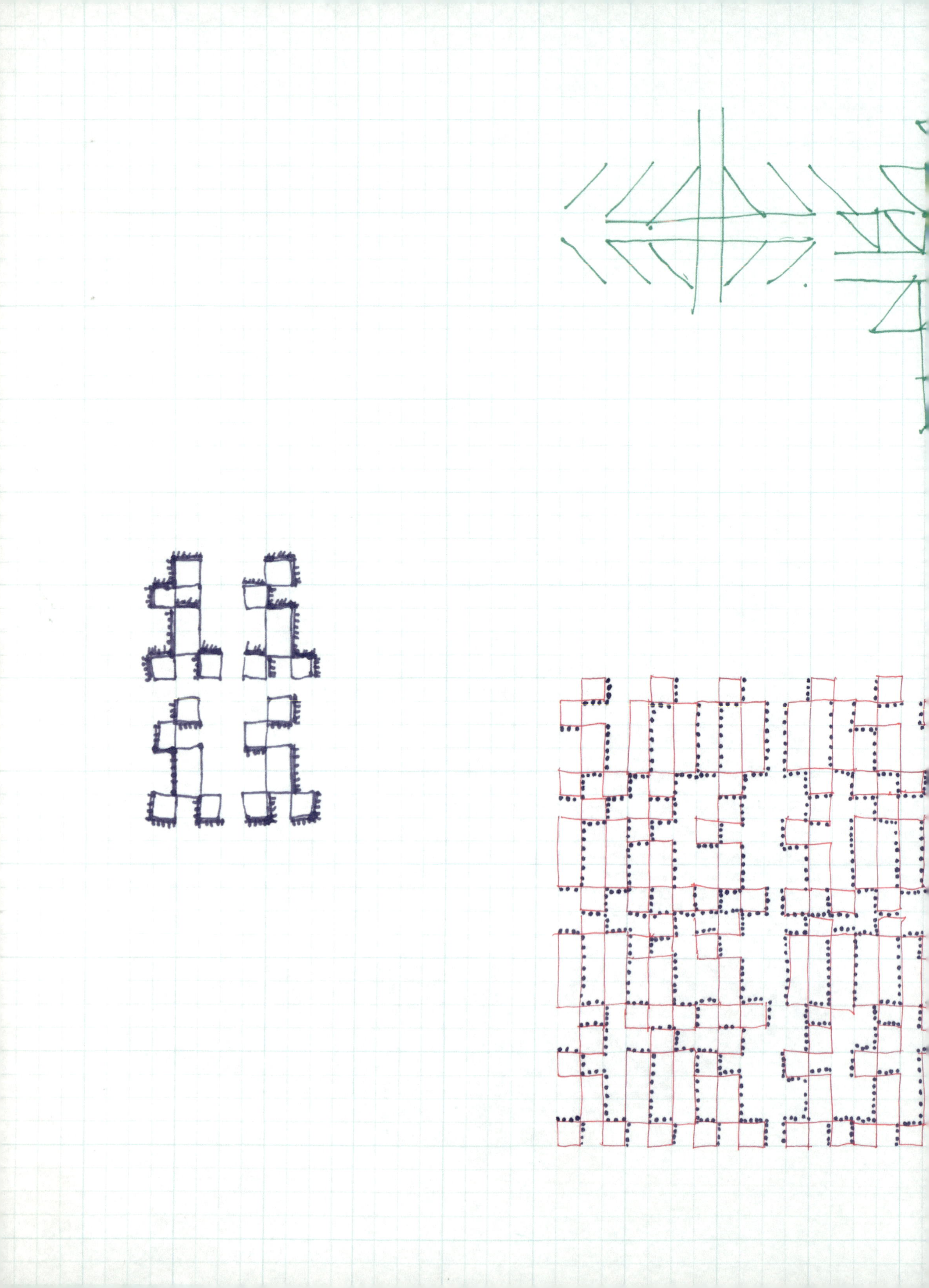

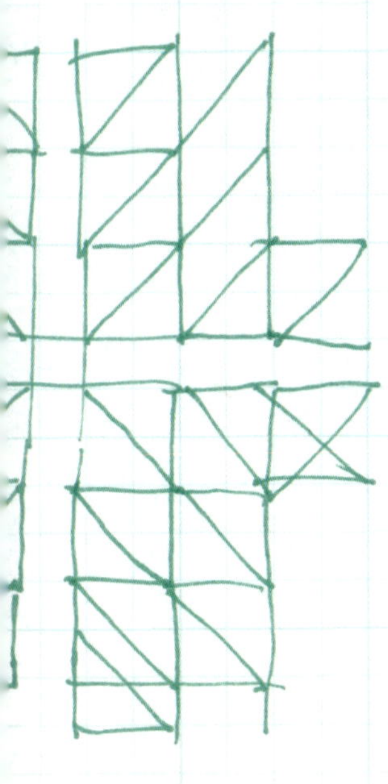

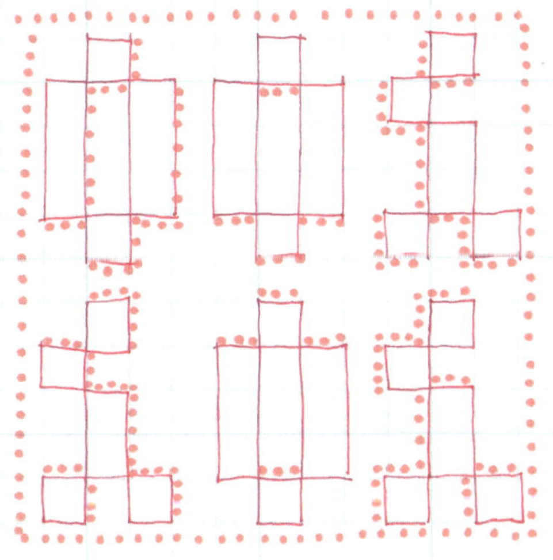

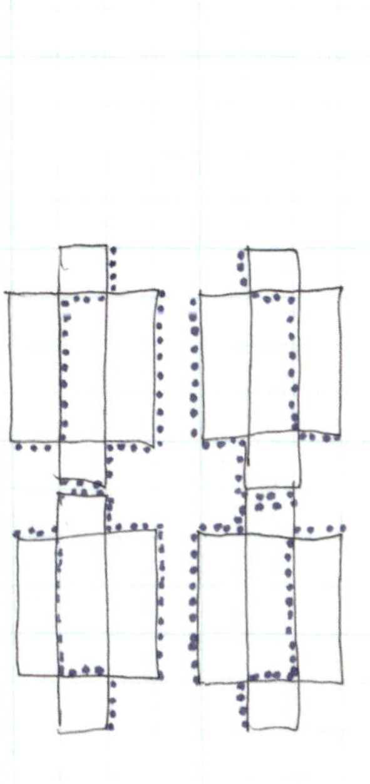

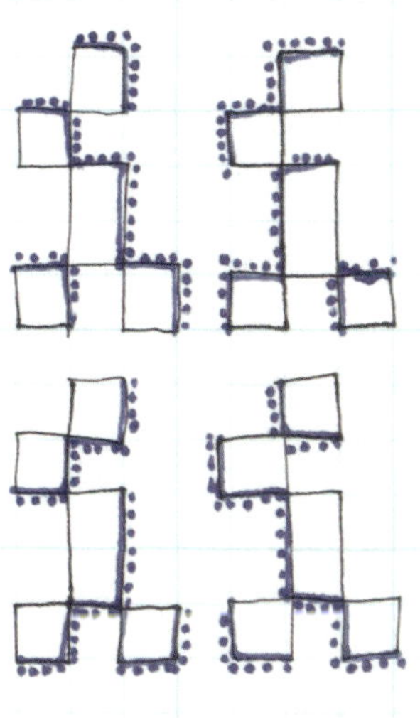

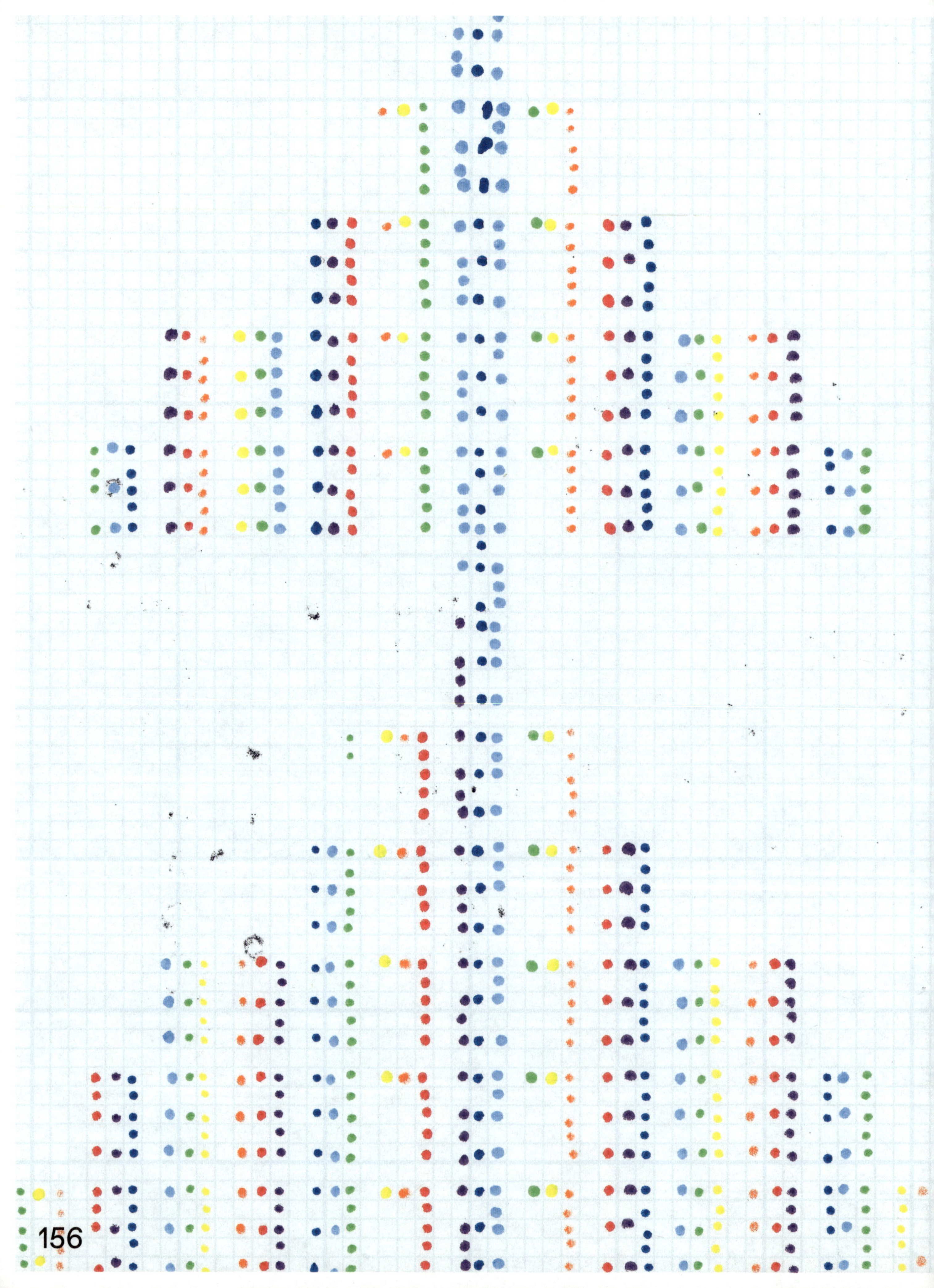

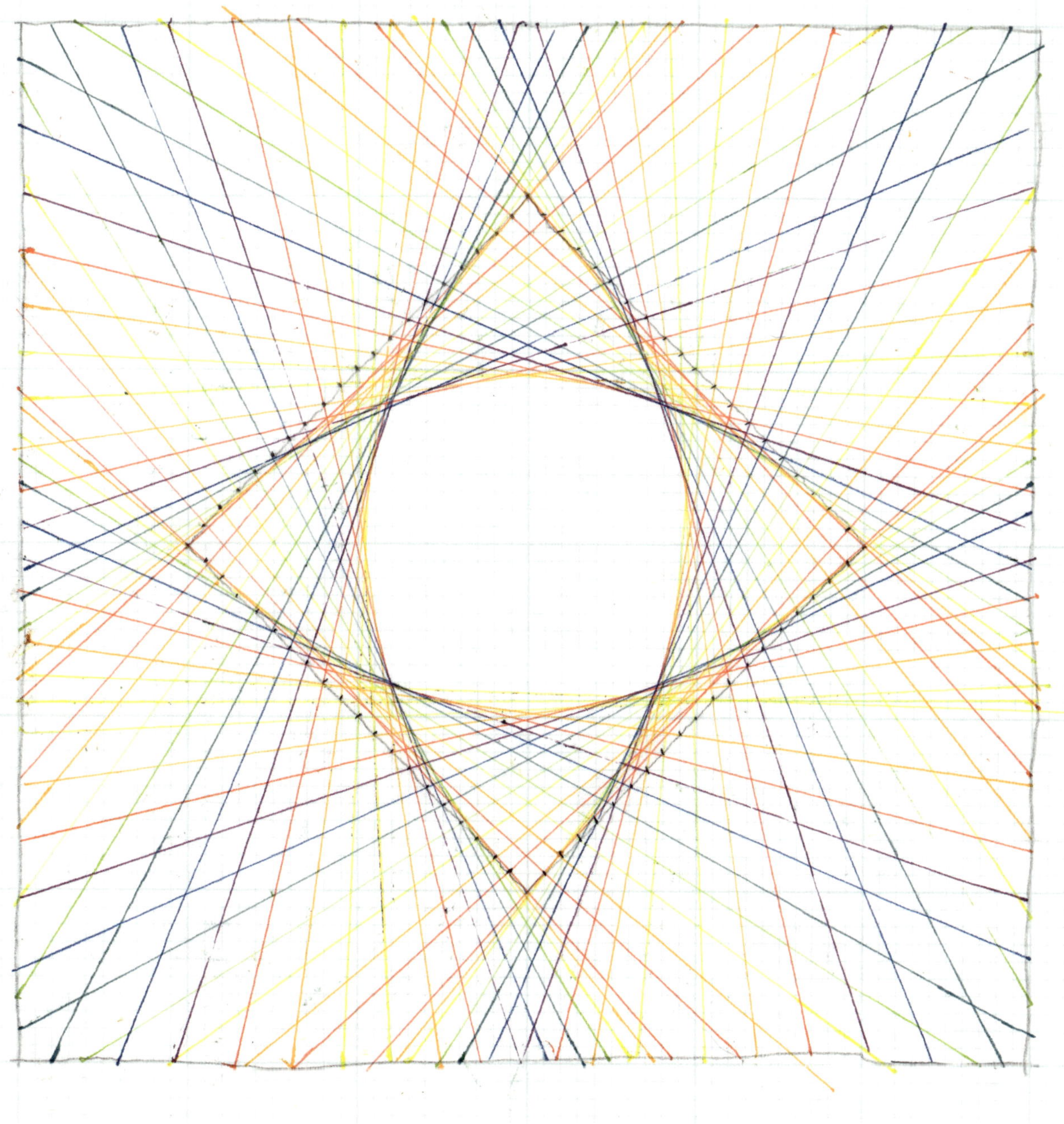

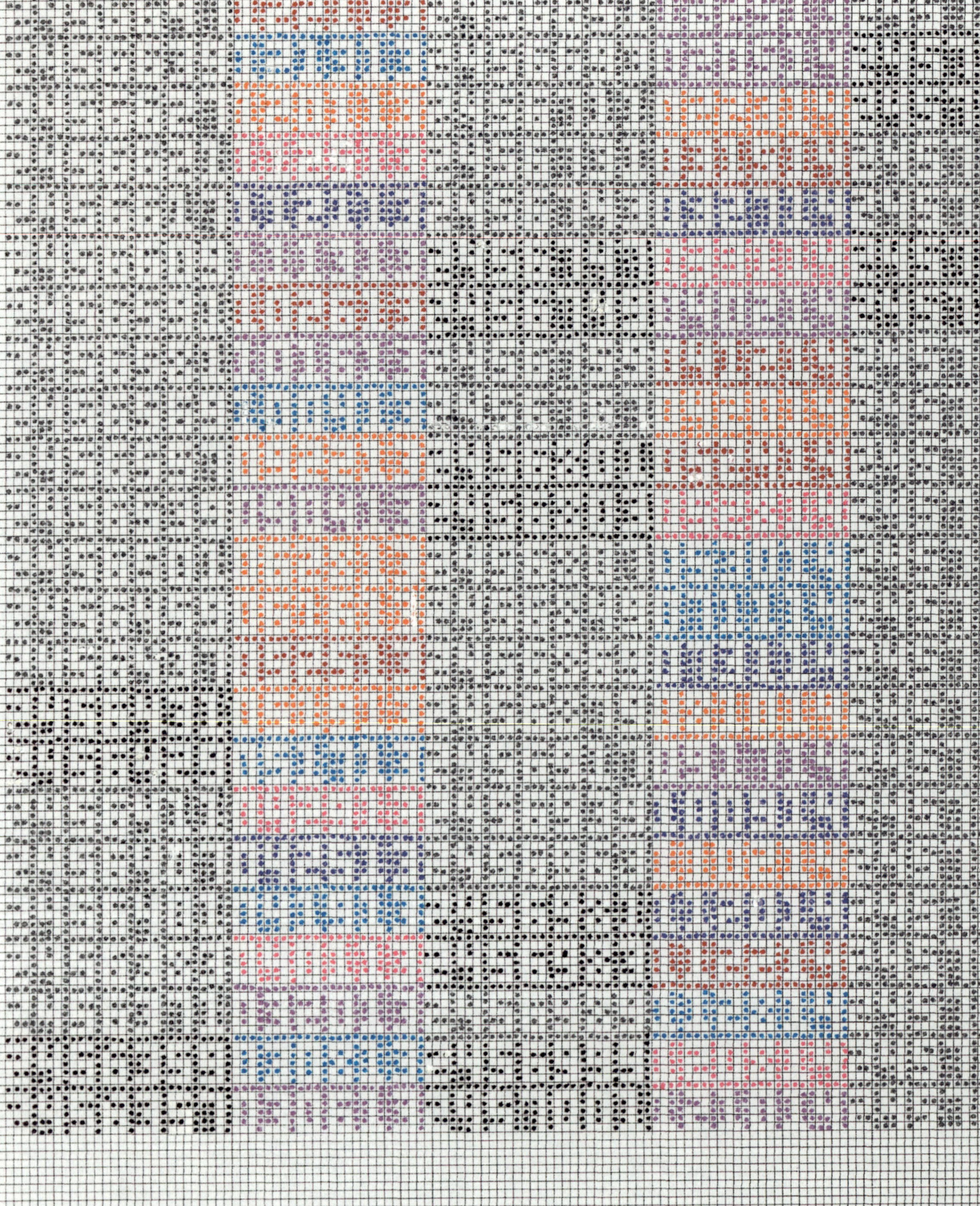

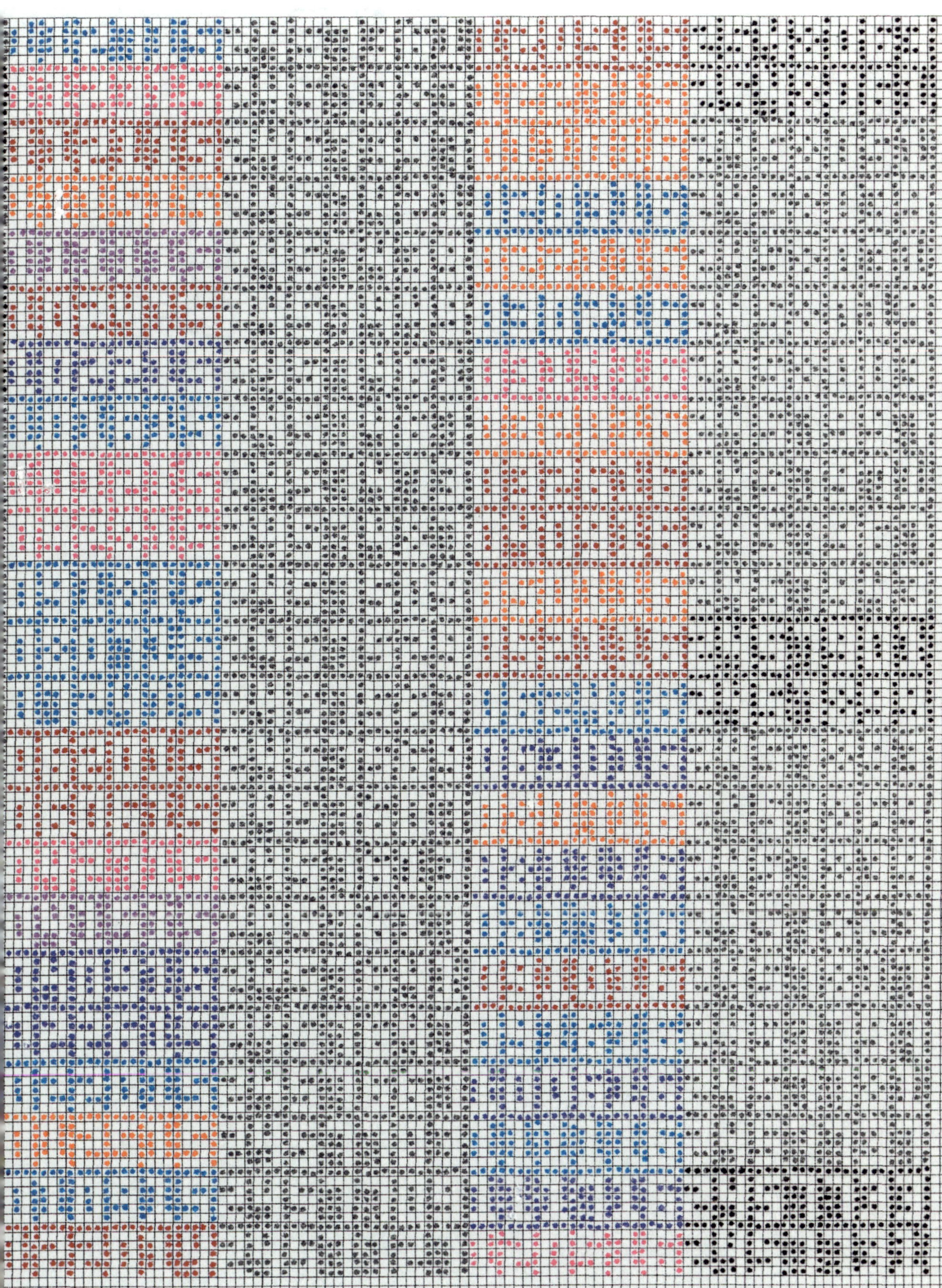

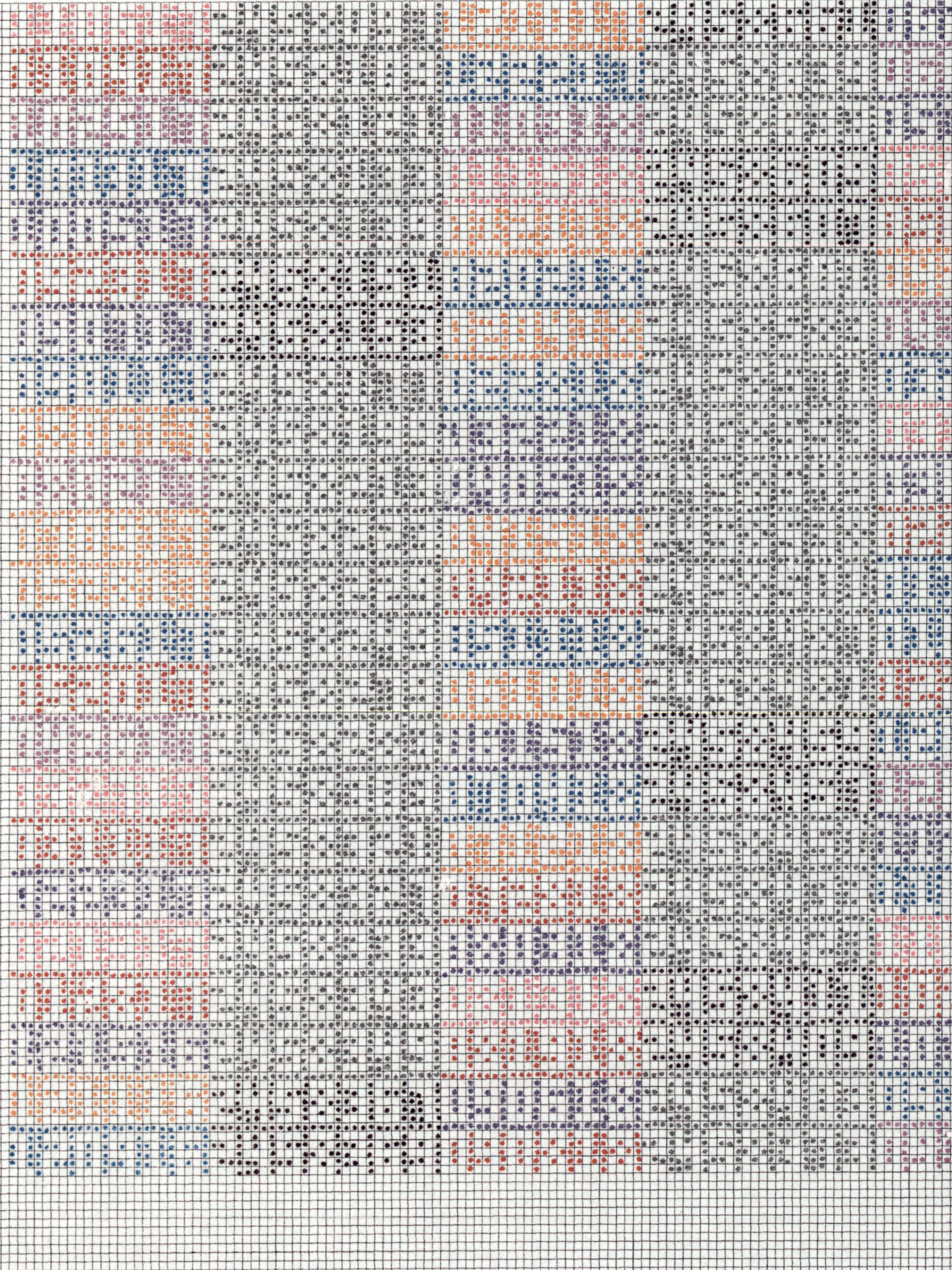

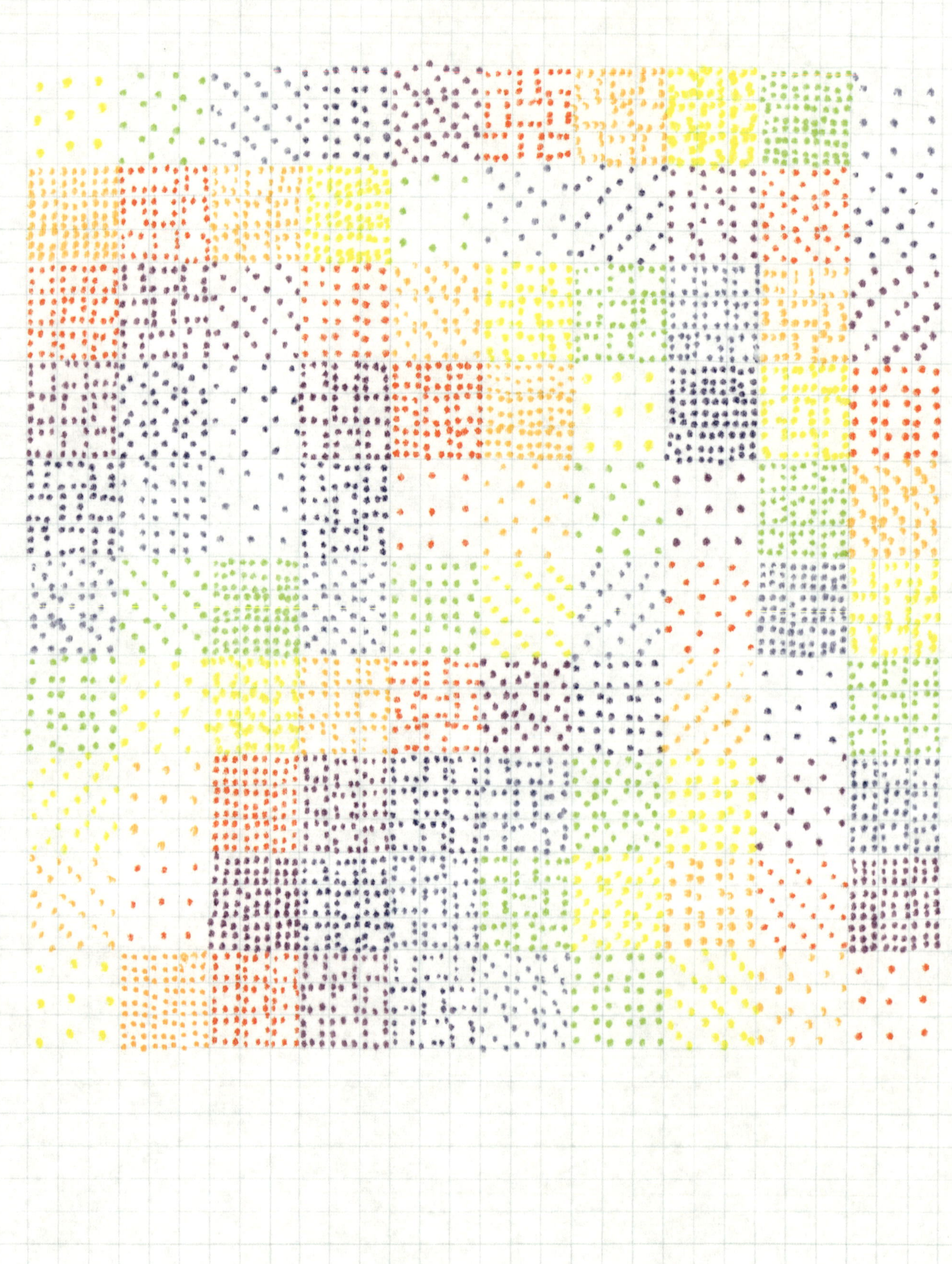

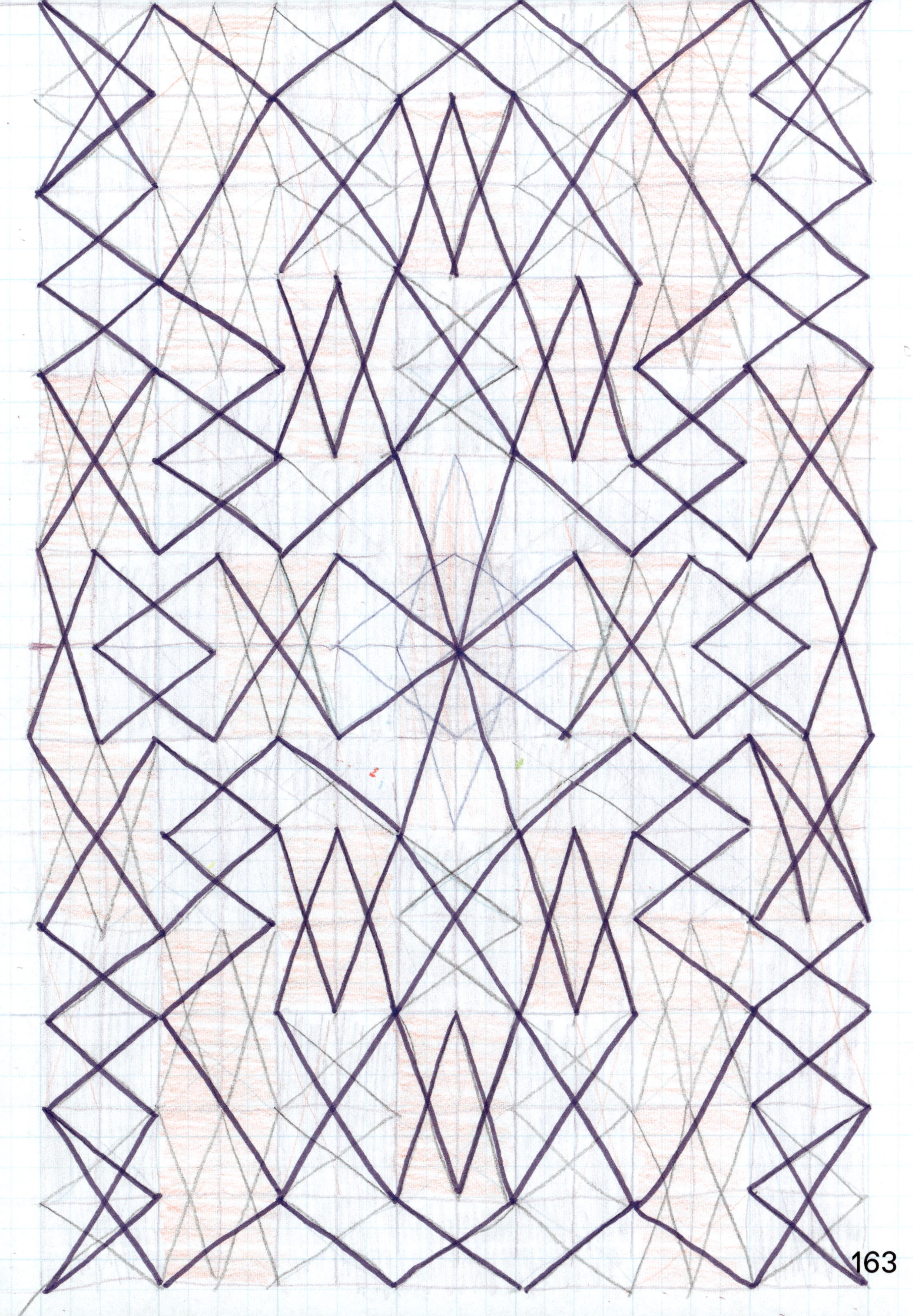

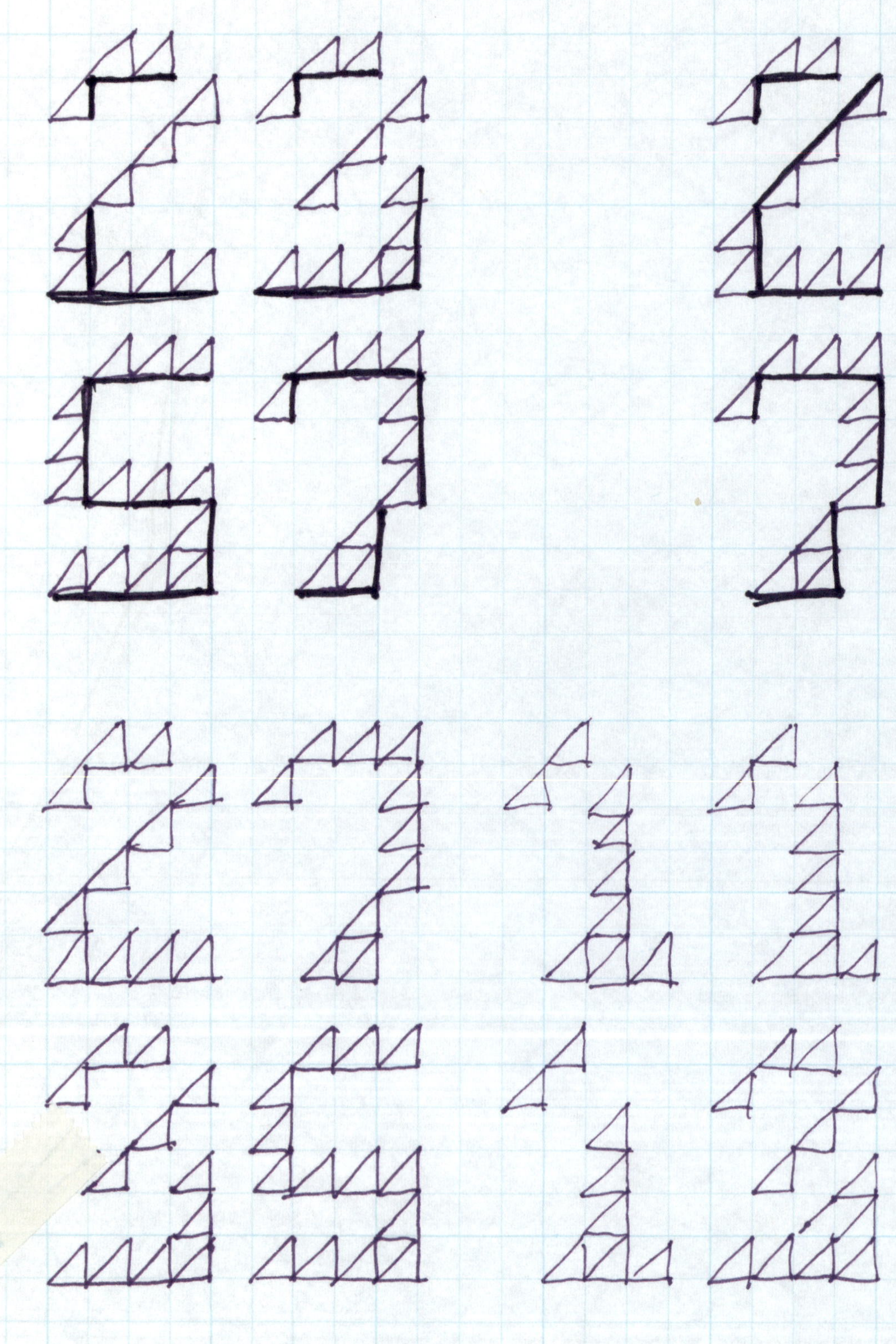

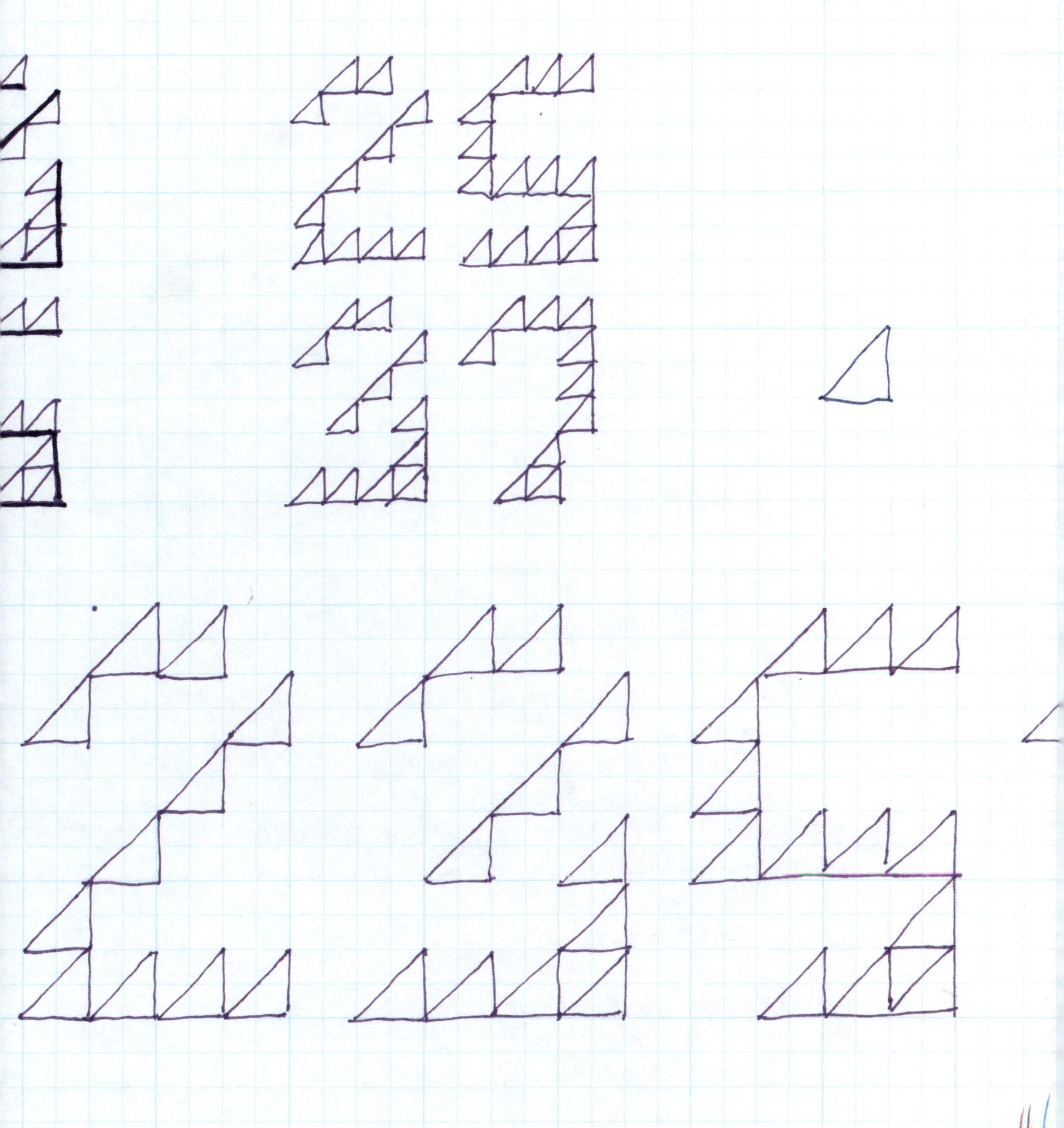

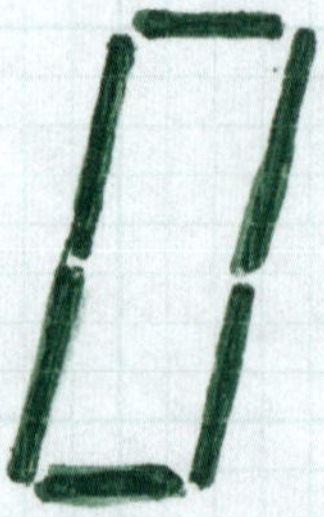

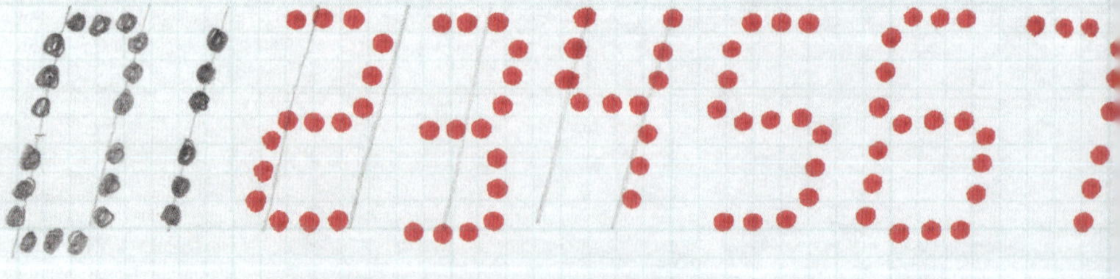

0

0123456

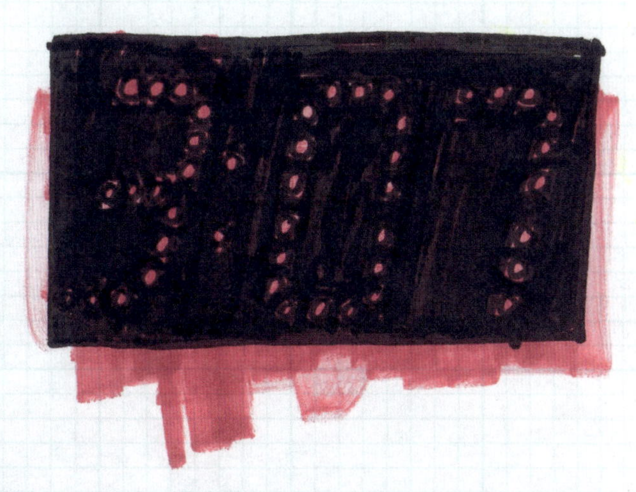

3400043	3310133	3291923
3411143	3315133	3288823
3417143	3319133	3286823
3424243	3321233	3285823
3425243	3329233	3283823
3427243	3331333	3272723
3439343	3337333	3267623
3441443	3343433	3260623
3443443	3353533	3256523
3444443	3362633	3252523
3447443	3364633	3245423
3445443	3365633	3241423
3452543	3368633	3236323
3460643	3380833	3223223
3466643	3394933	3222223

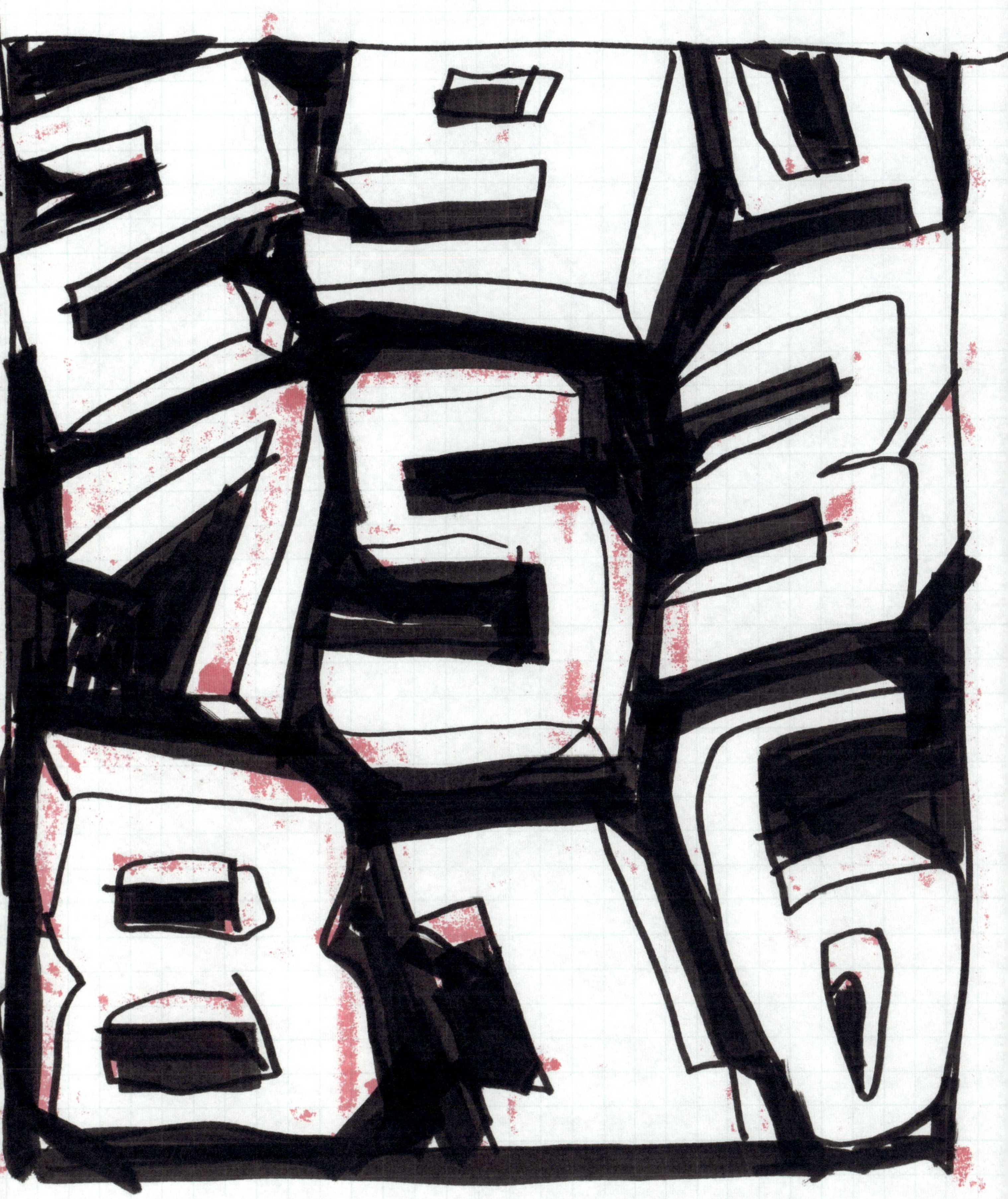

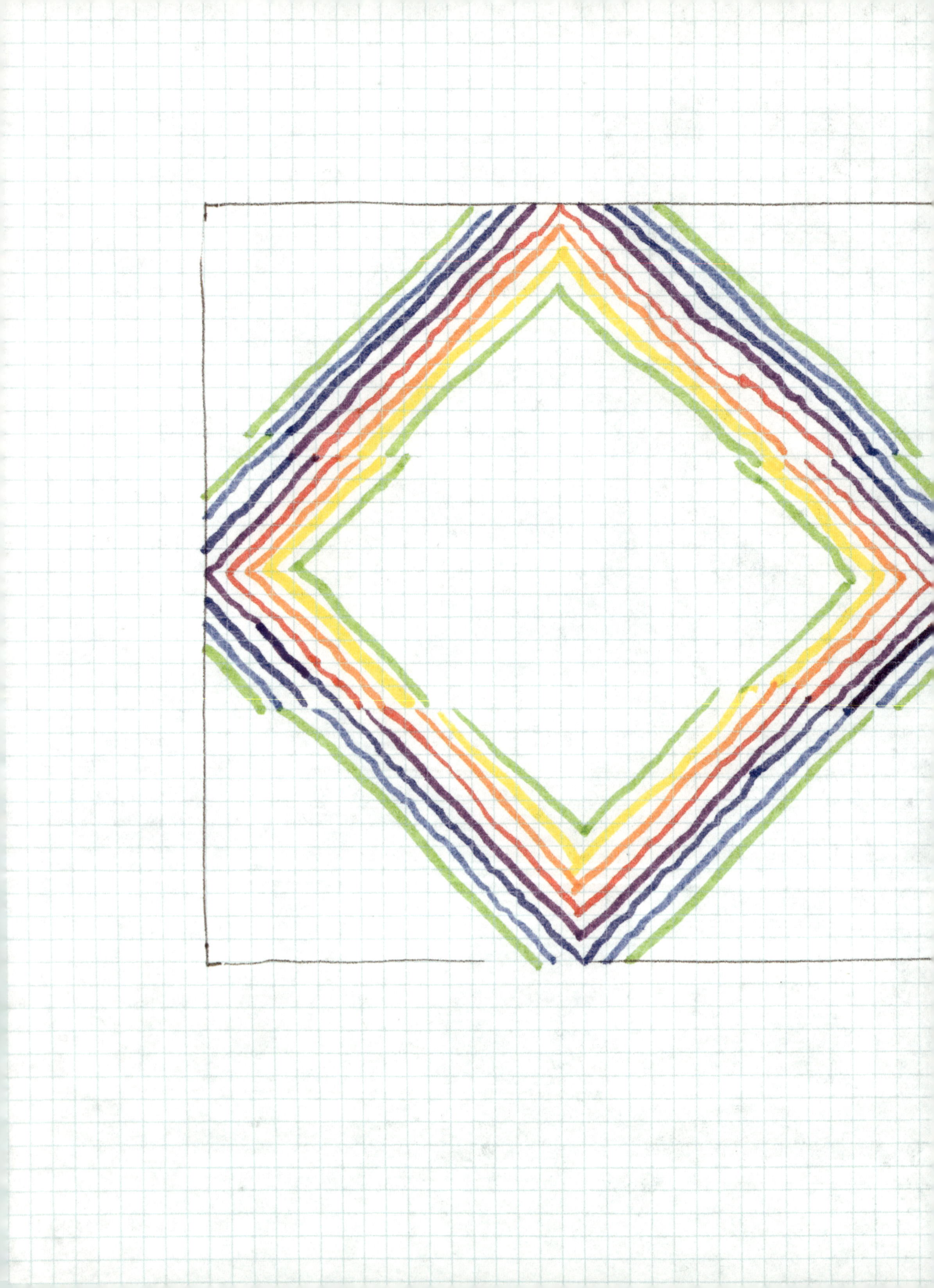

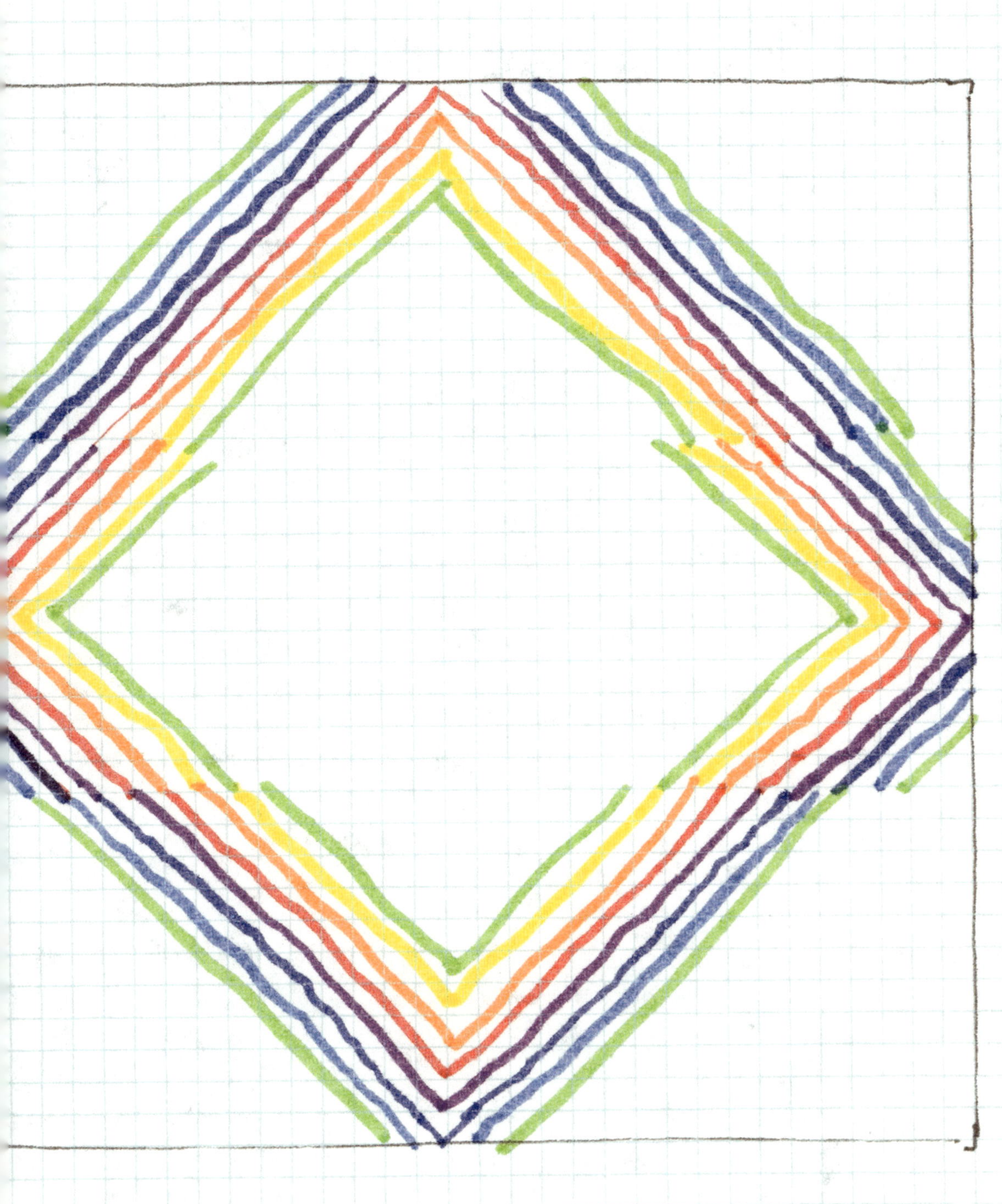

DAYS ALIVE
EM ROONEY

WATERING THE GODHOLE

XJ says maybe she's going to try to start believing in God. And that the thing about believing in God is actually a problem with the words "Believing" and "God." And furthermore the whole concept of "belief" and the whole concept of "god." We're on top of a dune in a sea of white. *How are you supposed to believe the thing you're bathing in? Are we not in a bathtub of God right now?*

I flew to New Mexico where Xylor is the current Frederick Hammersley Visiting Artist in residence at the University of New Mexico in Albuquerque. I thought being near her while I wrote would help me start (process and tackle) this essay. I write from here now.

Five days after I arrived we decided to take a road trip—a loop that would take us from Albuquerque to Carrizozo to the White Sands National Monument and finally back to Albuquerque. Our drive, and what I saw and learned while on it, will lend some structure to this essay. It is one of two loops—the one that Xylor and I successfully closed. The other loop is unclosable. It has to do with how and why an artist's work is interpreted the way it is. Specifically, with Xylor's paintings, this question becomes a bow, curved by our contexts and drawing closer our shared feminisms, one that is still being written and cannot yet be closed.

Writing about another artist's work, the work of a living artist, an artist you know, says, "I was there," or, "I know." There is a way that you become a part of their "I." Why else would anyone write?

Two nights ago at dinner, I brought out a torn notebook page with a handful of questions. They were questions that I could have speculated on in the privacy of the page, like "How do you feel about dying?" or "When did you stop using white grounds?" but since I'm here to immerse myself in her, and her work, since I'm here—why not just ask? It took her about forty minutes to answer each question, and when I left to return to my Airbnb for the night, I felt like I'd spent the day at the library doing research on my favorite topics. Smile endorphins coursed through my veins. We talked about her travels in Turkey, the leather scene in San Francisco, her introduction to feminist thought, class, color, religion, the body, and the progression of her work and her life over the past almost forty years.

What follows is a collection of arc segments from each loop.

PEER REARING

I've been reading essays from the *Paintings for the Future* monograph I bought from the Guggenheim after several people demanded that I observe the Hilma af Klint show in relationship to Xylor's work. The essays in the book remind me that the purpose of most criticism has been to historicize the work posthumously, and if that artist is a woman, define the artist as either reflective of the dominant discourse or in opposition to it. You might imagine a bunch of dingbats in three-piece suits swinging around a study in the dark, piñata chasers trying to whack the leather-bound books off the shelves. It can be random and haphazard, or it can be studied and selective. In either instance, the writer has been graced with distance from their subject and freedom of movement, freedom from the circumstances that melded their subject so definitively.

Contemporaneity with one's subject doesn't necessarily avoid the formation of prescriptive interpretation either. Right before coming here, maybe in some remote or distant mode of preparation, I read Rilke's *Letters to a Young Painter*, a series of letters he sent to Balthus, the son of the painter Baladine Klossowska, Rilke's longtime friend and lover. Rilke, no stranger to intergenerational relationships, began to support and mentor Balthus when he was thirteen years old. When Rilke was a young poet, he had been Rodin's secretary, and it is during this time that he produced the writing which would later become "Letters to a Young Poet" (based on his correspondence with nineteen-year-old Franz Xaver Kappus), despite the fact that Rilke (only in his late twenties) was in the process of being deeply indoctrinated with his elder Rodin's advice: Don't eat much. Never have cushions on your seats (beds and night are for sleeping, and the sleep should be light). Don't marry, don't have kids, avoid sex. Work, work, work. The historical record, meanwhile, tells us of Rodin's hypocrisy, his inability to follow his own advice. Rodin went to fancy dinners, ate himself portly, and had multiple lovers. But Rilke, under Rodin's tutelage, left his young wife and child. In his later years, he lived alone in a castle, obsessed with the isolation required to make his last work of great mastery. He pushed Baladine out of his life and suffered terribly from loneliness. His letters, especially the ones to Balthus, suggest regret at his self-imposed loneliness, yet prove how generative its contradiction was: he spent hours and even days on end writing to loved ones and, although he blamed his lack of productivity on this letter-writing, his correspondence became some of his most enduring work.[1]

The allegories of Rilke and Rodin became instrumental in creating the myth of genius: an artistic solitude, a poetic self-exile incubating the pain necessary to ferment genius, rather than a less productive pain of specific lived circumstances, which, in Rilke's case, included the atrocities of World War I, and unaddressed leukemia. How has this myth created by Enlightenment-period male artists been passed down? And how does it affect Xylor and me, our ideas about camaraderie and mentorship?

Getting training and guidance from your elders is quite literally at the crux of human survival, and for artists, it is just as practical. Younger artists align themselves with older, more powerful ones for access, guidance, and relevance. Older artists benefit from younger ones because of their patience, flexibility, interest, and excitement. This is all fairly obvious and commonplace, yet what is less documented, let alone mythologized, is what happens when an artist rejects the solitude principle. Even the notion of fraternity, through its order of similarity, is exclusive.[2]

Younger artists, older ones, her peers, her neighbors, her friends and neighbors' children, and a menagerie of animals are the beneficiaries of Xylor's generosity. Friendship, for her, becomes an "art of life, a form of the everyday."[3] She has built a comfortable life for herself, and her paintings have not suffered. Instead, they have gotten better and better with time. Is it really surprising that meeting your social, physical, and emotional needs makes a dedicated artist's work better, not worse?

It seems important to remember, and remember again, how many of our ideas about artistic world-building were made by men. They were made to reify and perpetuate heteronormative and oppressive social doctrines that designate men as the sole creators of their circumstances, pushing women—their kith, their kin, their cohabitants—out of the field of intellectual production and into the roles of captor, savior, and/or consolation.

AGNES MARTIN

Like the elephant in the adobe hut, Xylor brings up Martin while we're lying in the sand facing in opposite directions (me toward the sun, XJ away from it). We're talking about artists who've picked up and moved to the desert. Agnes Martin comes to mind right away and, because she's an artist who has been brought up in relationship to Xylor, I ask, "What do you think about Agnes Martin?" *Who doesn't want to sit in the glow of a room filled with those?* The seemingly unanimous love of Agnes Martin does not stop at Xylor. Their paintings share a love of yellow, the grid, and a certain type of godliness. Yet what we discuss is the sentimentality, evident in Martin's paintings and their titles, that was pushed into overdrive in her public appearances, her self-statements. Her isolation and self-aggrandizement, her quirky asexuality, became a schtick performed to the point of tedium. It is a coin or token, the other side of which is the evisceration of self, a predictable and historical endgame.

"If you wake up in the morning and you feel very happy about nothing. No cause. That's what I paint about. The subtle emotions that we feel without cause in this world."[4] That is a refreshing and generous idea, and I value its purpose. It is an idea embedded in the context of her life, in a particular set of circumstances that can never be recreated. But I find much more value in—and this too is a result of my place and time—the way art can, through subterfuge, be charged with cause, and inexplicably hold huge emotions without badgering didacticism. This is where Xylor has landed with her work, on an adjacent launch pad to Martin's.

HILMA AF KLINT

There are some significant similarities between Xylor and Hilma. The one that seems most obvious to people is the one I'd like to repudiate right off the bat: that they are both strangers or outsiders to their time. Although there is enough literature to dispute or to fill out the idea of af Klint as a sage witch, making painting through the power of conjured spirits and working in a cultural landscape utterly devoid of other abstract work, the idea stubbornly, if conversationally, persists. It is not so dissimilar from the persistent soundbite that Xylor is obsessed with numbers—driven

1 Rainer Maria Rilke, *Letters to a Young Painter* (New York: David Zwirner Books, 2017).

2 Céline Condorelli, "Too Close to See: Notes on Friendship, a Conversation with Johan Frederik Hartle," in *Self-organised*, ed. Stine Hebert and Anne Szefer Karlsen (London: Open Editions, 2013), 65.

3 Ibid.

4 *Agnes Martin: With My Back to the World*, directed by Mary Lance (Corrales, NM: New Deal Films, 2003), DVD.

by the spirit of math. In actuality, they are both formally trained artists, practicing in the day-to-day, in a field dominated by men. What really is the difference between "The Five" (af Klint and four other women with whom she performed séances and channeled spirits) and your cohort of female/queer friends? Of course, you find your coven when commonality with your peers has been robbed of you in a male-centered economic and social kinship structure. Of course, you seek alternative faith when the violence of Christianity isolates its worshippers for their sins. Of course, you seek holistic measures of healing through nature when Western medicine alienates and others your body.

Are af Klint's spiritual, theosophical, and physiological practices and interests that different from a community of women who happen to also be growers, hen-raisers, healers, and beekeeping death doulas (i.e., lesbians)? I think the answer is no. It is tiring, cruel, and obnoxious to perpetually other artists who make spacious worlds for themselves away from the patriarchal one above the glass ceiling.

Fuck off, you dickheads! It's cozy in the greenhouse.

WHAT IS THE TOTAL SITUATION OF MAKING ART?

In Daniel Birnbaum's essay on af Klint titled "Another Canon, or Why Have There Been No Great Women Artists?" he re-asks the question originally posed by Linda Nochlin in her 1971 essay "Why Are There No Great Women Artists": *What is the total situation of making art?* Nochlin had suggested that a "total situation" of making art could only exist within an "institutional structure, determined by specific and definable institutions be they art academies, systems of patronage, mythologies of the divine creator, or museums."[5] Instead of disputing Nochlin's terms Birnbaum reaffirms that, indeed, it is not at all strange to dream up your own networks and architectures when all the others are exclusive and "dominated by men." He does nothing, however, to formulate a corrective to the idea of the "total situation" as laid out forty-eight years ago by Nochlin.

Nochlin suggests that only fully resourced artists can become total. In this scenario the ability to turn your life into your life's work is an option only for the economically advantaged artist, or the insane one.

We might begin to reconsider this binary (total vs. not-total) by asking: Who can see? Can feel? Can hear? Can care? What is totality? A black hole? A womb? The idea of turning everything you do into your art is neither an elitist nor an outsider mentality. It is a constant fact of life and it exists in three forms: as feminism (caring for all living beings), as plagiarized feminism (capitalism),[6] and as a no-way-out singular mode of existence (one that we typically ascribe to prolific, untrained, or neurologically atypical artists). Xylor is a feminist. For a feminist, being a fully resourced artist can mean being a *contributor* to the building of a world which forges collective empowerment.[7]

At SFAI in the early nineties she was taught by Mary Gaitskill, Dorothy Allison, Sarah Schulman, Kathy Acker, and Diane di Prima. (Also Five.) Quite a coven of outsiders.

CONFIDENCE IN PAINTING

Xylor, because of her exposure to late modernism and the conceptual art movement, is unburdened by representation. Neither is she an abstract painter. Her paintings are neither figurative nor symbolic. In this last distinction exist two huge fissures in the connection between her work and af Klint's. But there are important similarities. For both painters, the sum of the painting is greater than its parts. For both painters, the power of the work emerges through touch, the labor of each artist. For each, though especially for Xylor, the marks are notational, they are in the service of the whole. There is a type of "filling in." There is no real question of expressivity; we don't have to wonder, like the majority of painters working in the criteria of expressionism or representation, what feeling went into a brushstroke. There is presentness and there is intentionality and that is all. And yet the paintings transcend their parts. In each work, there is a belief in painting. Mark-making is guided by reverence toward, not just the powers of the multiverse, but also art history, and their respective—and very real—places in it.

EE Miller, Xylor's longtime lover, wrote this to Xylor after seeing the af Klint show: "She is yer granny systematic idiosyncratic hubris vagina and working inside

5 Daniel Birnbaum, "Another Canon, or Why Have There Been No Great Women Artists?", in *Hilma af Klint: Paintings for the Future*, Tracey R. Bashkoff et al. (New York: Guggenheim Museum Publications, 2018), 210.

6 Maggie Nelson, *Women, the New York School, and Other True Abstractions* (Iowa City: University of Iowa Press, 2011), xxi. Nelson quotes Claudia Rankine and Alison Cummings, "Afterword and Conception," in *Fence* (Spring–Summer 2000), 125–26. In the introduction to her book Nelson looks at the New York School poets' "Feminine Identifications" and wonders via this Rankine/Cummings quote what happens when power is maintained in male-dominated culture through the usurping of a feminine that is partitioned from "feminist inquiry": "Does the triumph of the detail signify a triumph of the feminine with which it has long been linked? Or has the detail achieved new prestige by being taken over by the masculine, triumphing at the very moment when it ceases to be associated with the feminine?" The link I make here, is that through cooptation capitalism, and patriarchy are the same, and all ideas tied to feminism—from the details up—that maintain or reinforce patriarchal power structures or that aid in the production of capital are both capitalist and patriarchal, and neither are feminism.

7 Ideas about friendship and work from Céline Condorelli, "Too Close to See," in Hebert and Szefer Karlsen, *Self-organised*, 71.

the godhole." *Hubris vagina* is the key phrase here. It is actually not only their confidence in painting that links them but also miraculous pride in their superior genitals.

XYLOR AND OTHER ARTISTS

Sol LeWitt
Alicia McCarthy
Cathy Opie
Giotto di Bondone
Richard Tuttle
Hanne Darboven
Anne Truitt
Hilma af Klint
Roman Opalka
On Kawara
Dorothea Rockburne
Agnes Denes

THE TRIANGLE

> "One can almost say that the megalithic man was obsessed by the desire to discover and record in stone as many triangles as possible which were right angles and at all three sides integers."
> —Alexander Thom[8]

> "The ultimate polygon that every plane can be reduced to is a triangle; therefore we should look to the triangle for our essential sets of relationships."
> —Plato[9]

XJ started painting the triangle as a way to see if she could physically resolve the emotional problem of triangles. Her, Her Sister, Her Mother. I have that same triangle. Since 2013, the triangle has been part of her painting vernacular. One recent work-in-progress utilizes a typeface she calls "postal font," taken from a sign hanging in her local post office advertising the "stamp yearbook" of 2014. XJ could not find the typeface anywhere else in the yearbook. So from these four numbers (2, 0, 1, 4) she created the rest of her numerical alphabet.

TIME & COUNTING

> "Numbers interested me because they are so available. Everybody counts things. Everybody measures things. It's our way of ordering the world around us ... It is all just there. I use it. Those numbers don't mean anything other than themselves.

8 Lucy R. Lippard, *Overlay: Contemporary Art and the Art of Prehistory* (New York: Pantheon Books, 1983), 82.
9 Ibid.

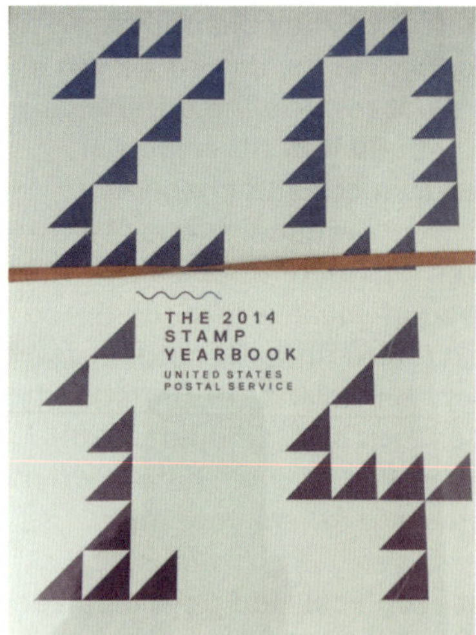

> You could ask me what number means, but I don't know."
> — Mel Bochner[10]

> "By the mid-1960s there had emerged a group of artists, mostly sculptors, whose intentionally unevocative cubes, modules and grids, mathematical systems and permutations, diagrams, mechanical 'working drawings,' and inventories were based on yet another New Realism—'what you see is what you get.' Their goal was 'wholeness.' Through literal conjunctions of number and language."
> — Lucy R. Lippard[11]

In Lucy R. Lippard's 1983 essay "The Forms of Time: Earth and Sky, Words and Numbers" she ties the work of Ad Reinhardt, who studied Eastern and Islamic art, to religion as a critical derivative of it, saying that he "admired the former for its rejection of linear progress and the latter for its rejection of pictorial and relational composition—in other words, he admired both for their formal neutralization of time and space." In 2019, the annulment of the specificity of time seems radically misguided and antiquated. Dates provide the quickest proof. Here's just a handful of years from American history which are both meaningful in and of themselves, and significant for posterity: 1865,[12] 1870,[13] 1920,[14] 1963,[15] 1965,[16] 1968,[17] 2001,[18] 2008.[19] Xylor's frequent use of Julian Day Numbers (the continuous count of days since 4713 BC, used mainly for astronomy, and for software calculations to count elapsed days between two events) reifies the idea that every *day* might be significant.

10 Ibid., 80.
11 Ibid., 79.
12 The abolition of slavery.
13 African American men granted the right to vote.
14 American women granted the right to vote.
15 The assassination of JFK.
16 The assassination of Malcolm X.
17 The assassinations of Martin Luther King Jr. and Bobby Kennedy.
18 The September 11 attacks.
19 Barack Obama elected first black president of the United States.

There is a kinship here with On Kawara, whose dates are both banal and deeply signifying. In Kawara's practice, his dates are only about the passing of time until we recognize one of the dates as historically significant. We think about Kawara, a longtime resident of Lower Manhattan, painting in his studio on September 13, 2001. The date is a marker of so many images both collective and personal, and we can imagine plumes of dust blowing around his studio.

This, for me, is part of the magic of both Kawara's and Xylor's paintings; though they are there to speak to time (its arbitrariness, its endlessness, the inevitability of death) they also invite you to consider the artists' body, as an object moving through time. We find bracketed time (the time it took to make the painting) compressed on the panel and shifted into a type of ever-presentness, or some total *now*, as we stand in front of it. Through their labor, their "spending time," we can imagine a nurturing space. This enveloping feeling is common to drawing as well—I'm thinking of Vija Celmins's drawings and her relationship to Sisyphean labor, or Xylor's two-year effort to draw a perfect freehand circle, or her prismatic drawings.

Numbers can be charged with varying degrees of significance. I will never think of the number 3 without thinking of my sister, born on January 3. Or 10 for the month that both my mother and I were born. 1983 is the year I was born. I am 7,244 days younger than Xylor—that is, nineteen years and ten months exactly. Today, March 19, 2019, it is fifty-four more days until Xylor sees her cats back in Greenfield, Massachusetts.

Xylor's numbers oscillate across her painting panel (like running code on a screen), relaying selected mathematical phenomena, but even these are not random—she has favorite numbers and sets of numbers. In her recent painting *Mani/Pedi*, a list of her favorite eleven-digit prime number palindromes is presented in four separate solid-color columns. The red column begins with ones, yellow is threes, blue is sevens, and violet is nines. They have meaning because she has given them meaning, in some ways, through her love of them. In other paintings, numbers have been selected for concretely personal reasons, someone's passing or someone's birthday.

Her numbers aren't meant to be used, they are not math problems. This failure to become a working total is part of what makes each drawing and painting so distinctive even as they consistently utilize similar parameters (a grid, a pattern, a magic square, prime palindromes). There is no cynicism, nihilism, or irony in Xylor's paintings and drawings. Instead, what you might absorb, or what might radiate out from within or behind a grid of numbers off one of her metallic grounds, is love. Like in *Jupiter's Square* (2019), where bricks of gold and silver fade into shades of metallic pink as they get closer to the numbers. Her paintings, through their very existence, their devotional radiance, transform time spent into love.

I've heard her talk about her drawings and sketches like gestation and labor: beautiful to some, grotesque to others, but bloody either way. What happens through the act of painting, in this analogy, is Xylor's paintings become objects of worship like the Virgin Mary—with all her concomitant horrors absorbed and held rather than erased.

GENEROSITY AND DEATH

"We are 'thrown' into language, kinship structures, a given set of historical, social, economic, and geographical circumstances, and we are from the moment of birth given over to death. I think we have no agency until we have acknowledged the forms of finitude and determination."[20]

"All of the redemptive possibilities of looking, whether conscious or unconscious, inhere in the temporality of the look—in the fact that we never look for once and all but subject what we have seen to endless revisions and resemanticizations." —Kaja Silverman[21]

Xylor thinks about dying a lot. Every day when she leaves the house, she thinks about how to exit so that whoever might have to clean up after her, were she to die that day, won't be left with a mess. She leaves her studio every day with the paintings looking good—regardless of what phase they are in. Her moment-to-moment awareness makes you aware: you want to be around her in case she dies. If you're lucky enough to be her friend, you might find that she will care for you as though each moment could be her last. If you're working on a show you're likely to find tubes of paint arriving in the mail. If she thinks you're a promising painter, but you can't afford the right tools, she might buy you expensive brushes. Nothing is overbearing about any of it. Not in the paintings, or her actions; they both offer themselves to you in the form of an invitation to activate the potential of your own looking.

THE AJNA

Some of XJ's specific interest in perception may have come from vision problems she had as a child. She had to have eye surgery when she was six years old, followed by a series of appointments which tested her depth perception and vision to see how they may have

20 Rembert Hüser, "Crossing the Threshold: Interview with Kaja Silverman," *Discourse* 19, no. 3 (Spring 1997): 4.
21 Ibid.

changed as a response to the treatment. Directed by her mom's disciplined routines, Xylor performed daily eye exercises to strengthen the muscles around her eyes. Her vision remains doubled, which has an effect on her ability to perceive depth. She paints wearing magnifying glasses with prisms so that she can see, very clearly, each tiny section of the panel. Though this approach is different and more rigid than how she makes her drawings, the perceptual effects can be similar. *Back In Five Minutes*, a drawing from 2005, has a striking similarity to the painting *Threes* from 2015. They both use replicating diamond patterns to pull your vision back through space—you're viewing the precipice of a black hole. In each, the use of blacks and reds supplants void-fear with a homey familiarity. In the painting all perceived lines are painted-up-to instead of painted on—it is the underlayer that you perceive as a line, a line with the smoothness of pencil, marker, and pen. The paintings' dark warmth takes form as a simulacrum of what you see above the bridge of your nose, hovering in an unknown space, when you close your eyes after looking at a light.

JOY

She creates it more than she experiences it, I think.

MOBY-DICK

Xylor read *Moby-Dick* for two years straight. Xylor's first artist statement consisted solely of lines excerpted from *Moby-Dick*, collaged and reassembled.

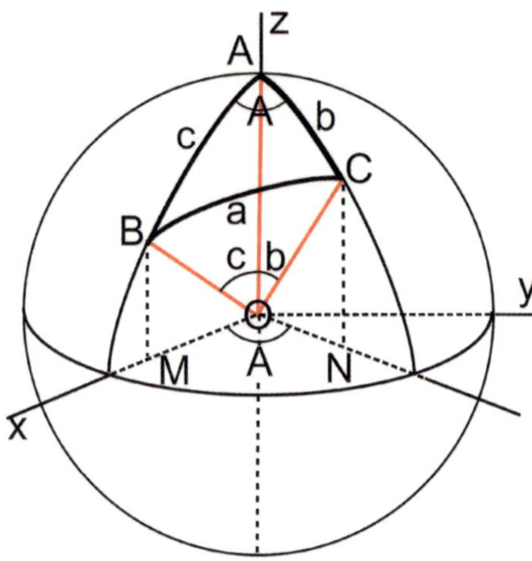

THE GREAT CIRCLE

In 1992, the year before Xylor finished college at SFAI, she traveled across the country from San Francisco to Virginia by train, then boarded a cargo ship filled with coal, a handful of passengers, and a crew, and headed for Europe. At some point, the captain decided to save time by using the Great Circle as a short cut across the Atlantic. The ship traveled about thirteen knots per hour and the trip took sixteen days.

The great circle is the intersection of a sphere where a plane passes through it at its center point—like the equator, except the great circle can be drawn at any latitudinal line. It can be used to find the minor arc as the shortest connecting path between two points on the surface of a sphere. As Xylor remembers it, this short cut cost them their smooth seas; a lot of passengers and crew got sick on a long stretch of deep swells.

Xylor, who had already begun to study sacred geometry, got the ship's third mate to write out the formula for the great circle in her sketchbook. You can imagine how cherished a drawing like this might be, given the circumstances.

Xylor's boat dropped her off in Rotterdam and she began her trek southeast across the continent. In Prague she serendipitously saw her ex-lover Deniz's writing scrawled on a message board at a café. Xylor left a note for her in return, and their romance recommenced. They left Prague for Greece, and eventually made their way to Turkey. In Selcuk, where they had gone to see the house of the Virgin Mary, Xylor lost her sketchbook. Deniz had gotten into an argument with the owner of their pension and as they hurried to gather their belongings—rushing—to catch a train to Cappadocia, Xylor remembered her sketchbook on a bench in the courtyard at the pension. It was almost completely filled with drawings and the captain's notes from the sea journey. Devastated, she thought she might never draw again. Instead, she used a stick and made ephemeral drawings in the dirt for the duration of the trip. This is when she began two years of trying to draw a perfect circle, a practice born from the realization that her body made the best compass.

"The Circle of Earth" is Xylor's favorite passage from the Old Testament. In Isaiah 40:22 Isaiah says, "It is he who sits above the circle of the earth, and its inhabitants are like grasshoppers; who stretches out the heavens like a curtain and spreads them like a tent to live in." It has long been thought that in saying "the circle of the earth" Isaiah is referencing spherical earth. If we were to believe this, it would mean Isaiah, said to have lived seven hundred years before Christ, and the ancient Israelites, knew that the earth was not flat.

SPACE

I asked Xylor why she wanted to go to the Very Large Array, mainly because I had no idea what it was. "It's just like about seeing the Universe?"

Right, except now it's referred to as the multiverse because there are multiple universes.
"How does it make you feel to know how insignificant we are?"
Better. Extremely calmed and reassured.

The last town before the Very Large Array (a massive radio astronomy observatory) was the town of Magdalena. We'd been planning to drive on, westward, past the VLA into the Madre Mountains near the Alamo Navajo Indian Reservation and back east toward Albuquerque, completing the loop. People at the Magdalena gas station advised against this route because of the elk and the snow and the long, windy, dark dirt roads that were not showing up on our maps. We'd been driving through what seemed like an endless valley for two days—mountains changing and repeatedly unfolding before us, and dry, brushy shrubs changing from green to beige to green again. At one point, driving through White Sands National Monument, we noticed how the sky seemed to be pulled down, like blinds, over the distant mountain ranges, making the rock formations look purple and disrupting the atmospheric illusion that the air begins where the mountain ends. Blue, blue, blue, blue, blue, blue, indigo, purple, WHITE.

When we arrived, we stood at the base of the ninety-five-feet high, eighty-feet-wide satellite in the middle of a twenty-five-mile-wide field, with more satellites stretching out in three directions as far as the horizon line. Beyond that was an elaborate and varied set of ecosystems, visible and felt. Lava and gypsum, red rocks, evergreens and snow. Dry, expansive skies and wet, enclosing, active ones, all within our field of vision. I could feel the cellular structure of my body changing in response to this all-ness.

THE MOON PAINTING

The next morning Xylor figured out how to bring White Sands into a painting she was working on, *9th Order Magic Square for the Moon*. The ground is yellow with hues of green seeping through, almost as if the first ground had been green, and then covered with yellow. The numbers in this painting utilize the same "postal font" but are slightly bigger than an average Jane-sized digit (if such a thing exists), and the triangles are lovingly painted with alternating warm and cool whites.

PAIN AND THE MEANING OF COLOR

Xylor can be grim in her orientation toward the world. In many ways she sees the world for the shitty place it is, and as a deep empath, is weighted down with its sorrows. She has experienced a lot of pain. I'd been sitting at her kitchen table all day writing and thinking about her and her work so her arrival struck like an apparition from my psyche and startled me. She was distraught as she pulled out her earbuds and told me about the terrorist anti-Muslim attack on mosques in Christchurch, New Zealand, that left fifty people dead. Her effort to pull herself together seemed almost as if on my behalf, or as if to stop one mini-cyclone of pain among a much larger storm system.

There is a way that our daily experience of pain makes grooves in our neurological pathways. We can imagine these grooves as a kind of counting, the rhythmic negative dimension on a rolled-out swatch of corduroy. The inverse of these grooves, the raised velvety parts, might be the tracks in Xylor's paintings, the movement of color, and texture. In this phenomenology, the eye is not your only receiving organ. There is a somatic experience. To be in the presence of Xylor's paintings is to be held in their hum, and there might be some way that their repetitive patterning has a similar effect as purring for a cat; the vibrations actually restore damaged tissue.

XJ paints with translucent colors so every mark reveals what is behind it. What color you perceive is influenced by its surroundings, and this flutter between perception and aura can alternatively create a kind of vertigo, especially when the paintings are really "working." I've wondered if the rainbow so often used in Xylor's paintings might not directly be about healing, and if she is aware of the correlations between the neurological experience of color, light, and serotonin. Eileen Myles said the paintings were medicine and I think that's right. They heal like hypnosis, or MDMA.

Like a lot of artists, the specific colors Xylor uses in her work are sometimes circumstantial. They might be based on the color ground (which she decides on based on how much she wants to challenge herself with any given painting), the light in her studio, the colors in a new pair of sneakers. She has strong feelings about color (all you have to do is go thrifting with her once to observe this). Currently, my nails are painted yellow, her favorite color, so that I can be connected to the idea of her through my fingertips while I type.

One of her few yellow (or mainly yellow: the paintings are never monochromatic) paintings, *Magic Square for SPSP-5385*, from 2015, is evocative of a beehive, with black patterned dots that suggest dimensionality. The title honors SPSP, the abbreviated name for her cat Shadyl or ShadylPushkeSparklePlenty, whose days alive stopped at 5,385 (fourteen and a half years) when he was hit by a car in Xylor's neighborhood. Here, her favorite color is reserved for the sacred rituals of death and mourning, two of the most reliable forces of change.

XJ is also tuned into the colors of chakras. Yellow is the color of the solar plexus which is the chakra of intentionality and intuition. Indigo, Xylor's other favorite, is the color of the third eye chakra, the chakra of imagination and clarity of vision.

The way colors come together might look like a print from the seventies, or the patterns on the backs of seats in buses, a disco floor, a disco ball, or a digital street sign on a foggy LA morning, or a bank sign on a midday afternoon. There are also quilts, and leather, and the colors of the galaxy. The colors of sunset, the shades of the night. The colors of Christ in his earliest depictions, gold under red, and later ones with rococo Eastery pastels. Her colors move back and forth through time and space. They span centuries.

It's no surprise that light is very important to Xylor. The use of color in Xylor's paintings comes, in many ways, from a Californian experience of light. Here in New Mexico, the light everywhere is severe, even when it is completely overcast and gray, as it has been for the past several days.

FORM=FEELING=FACT

Throughout the course of our trip, I was so overwhelmed with the physical landscape and the time-travel narrative of Xylor's life that, at times, my fascination would put up a wall between us. A conversation Xylor and I had about cutting, therapeutic pain, and S&M broke through this wall, and is still, as I write, generating new sense memories. She told me how the first cut she ever made into her flesh was across her cheekbone. Many years later, after more than a decade of cutting and covering herself in tattoos, she tried to close the loop by making her final cut in the same place her first cut had been, where she could still see the scar. I was driving, and so I was looking forward when she took her thumb and ran it along my cheekbone in the place where she had made the cut on her own face. And with this quick touch came a simultaneous flash of warmth in my sacral chakra and in my mind's eye.

"YOU BELONG TO WHAT YOU INHERIT AND CAN TRANSFORM." —CAROLEE SCHNEEMANN[22]

Xylor makes machines that make machines. Each painting invents its own idiosyncratic system for building itself. But each device is needfully generated. None are rote, or phoned in—there is real physical labor at stake, and purpose. The phrase "broken machine" is exactly the language Xylor uses to describe what happens when she begins a painting from the outside and moves inward only to realize that the pattern will not resolve itself at the center. The painting *40Love* (2019) is a broken machine that Xylor chose to leave open and unresolved at its center. Its undulating green triangles point toward themselves and backward in space to an interminable lime-green center. The painting could be visually broken down into four parts folded over themselves like a box, and from this perspective, the box appears to glow with green light from inside, Anahata green, the color of the heart chakra. Looking at her paintings, I'm reminded of the massive metal lathes beached on the sprawling first floor of my old studio building in Newburgh. One person worked in the shop among these mostly dormant machines. They were beautiful, and they'd built themselves by lathing their own parts.

GRATITUDE

I got a lot of support in the writing of this essay, and in keeping with its spirit, I want to recognize everyone who helped. Thank you to Marissa Bluestone and Celeste Dupuy-Spencer, who weighed in and read the essay several times. Thank you to Chris Domenick and Emily Davidson who also read and edited several versions and engaged me in expansive conversations about the writing and its purpose. Thank you to RJ Messineo who, through many phone conversations and several phases of edits, helped shape the ideas and hold them true to her ideas about Xylor and her paintings. And thank you to Lee Relvas, who edited this essay like she might carve one of her wooden sculptures. She uncovered buried hints of patriarchy within even what I thought of as my most feminist declarations, and revealed my own ideas to me, like a new piece of writing. <3 <3

22 Joyce Beckenstein, "Carolee Schneemann on Five Decades of Meat, Harnesses, and Innovation," Hyperallergic, October 20, 2017, https://hyperallergic.com/406640/carolee-schneemann-on-five-decades-of-meat-harnesses-and-innovation/.

A NOTE FROM A DEVOTED FAN
JOHN YAU

Let's cut to the chase. I have been a fan of Xylor Jane's art for more than a decade, having first come across a folder full of her works on paper in the crammed flat files at Pierogi Gallery in Brooklyn. I remember going back to the gallery soon afterward specifically to look at the work and being even more enthralled the second time. It soon became a habit that whenever I went to Pierogi, I would make a point of checking to see what of Jane's I might find in the flat files.

In 2009, shortly after I began writing about art for magazines again, I reviewed her show *Xylor Jane: N.D.E.* at CANADA for the *Brooklyn Rail* (April 2009). "N.D.E." stands for "Near Death Experience," and Jane based the eleven paintings in the series on widely known descriptions of that phenomenon: your life flashing before you, bright lights beckoning you, a bridge you cross over, or a tunnel you enter.

In order to evoke these experiences, Jane used a palette limited to the seven spectral colors. Each color is applied as a dot of paint carefully placed in its correct square in a grid. The dot can be fat or tiny or even pointed. As strict and limited as her method might seem, the results are always spellbinding and mind-boggling. She never separates the act of looking from an awareness of time. She once did a painting based on the date September 14, 2018, marking the point when she had been alive on this earth for 19,991 days, which is a prime palindrome—a number that reads the same backward and forward but is divisible only by itself.

When we look at a painting by Jane, we see ourselves seeing it—we see it and see *into* it. We contemplate our relationship to time and infinity.

This is one aspect of Jane's genius. A number that can only be divided by itself becomes an expansive visual possibility.

This is the connection that I made in the first review:

> Not surprisingly, Jane's dots of paint recall William Blake: to see the universe in a grain of sand. Her dots are analogous to colored grains of sand, which she uses to patiently construct visual schemes that seem at once open and opaque, dense and accessible. I found myself poring over the paintings like a watchmaker or cartographer, noticing the specificity of each dot, its physicality recalling that it was put there by hand, that it is evidence of attention and a lover's delicate caress. Moving back and forth in front of the paintings, drawing away and stepping closer, as if afflicted with myopia, I was reminded that research in pure science or mathematics could be an act of devotion driven by curiosity. Jane is never less than completely responsible to each inch of the surface, never inattentive to any part of the painting.

Reading this earlier observation, as well as the review of a later show at CANADA, which I wrote for Hyperallergic Weekend (June 3, 2012), I began thinking that I still have not said nearly enough about this artist's work.

Whenever I think about Jane's paintings, I am dumbstruck by the myriad passions, preoccupations, devotions, and interests she brings to her ongoing inquiry into the mysteries of being alive in time, within an infinitely expanding universe. What further strikes me is how lightly she wears the knowledge she has accumulated across her years of research into numbers, the occult, religious art from Giotto to Barnett Newman, science, and much else. Despite all the heady stuff she gets herself into, Jane never seems to show off how much she knows—which cannot always be said of the great Alfred Jensen.

Rather, what drives Jane's work, as well as makes it so particular, is the seamlessness with which she joins her demanding painting practice to her deep currents of curiosity, joy, fascination, and devotion to knowledge and visual mysteries. Stylistically, she has brought together pointillism's dots, Josef Albers's color studies, op art's pulsations, and the structure of grid painting in the service of something that far exceeds the historical scope of these styles. She has achieved this by pushing their focus on the visible world to extremes, while redirecting it toward the invisible and occult, that which is hidden from us. I don't think I am alone in saying that I don't simply look at Jane's work. I luxuriate in its celebration of wonderment. I am enthralled by it.

Consider Jane's methods and subjects, which she continually tweaks and refines. Her palette of seven spectral hues is applied to square or nearly square wood panels that have been carefully gridded. Her painting vocabulary consists of two elements: a dot, which she lays as precisely into the grid's square cell as a jeweler fits a stone into its setting; and a triangle, which she positions tightly into one corner of a cell. Working with this basic vocabulary, she has made paintings consisting solely of dots, a combination of dots and triangles, and solely of triangles. No two paintings are alike.

One of her ongoing interests is tetradic numbers, which are also known as four-way numbers. A tetradic prime is made of tetrads and divisible only by itself. The first few tetradic primes (11, 101, 181, and 18,181) are palindromes of 1, 8, and 0, which are also the only numbers that remain the same when flipped upside down or mirrored. When she makes a painting using these elements, such as *727 Digit Tetradic Prime* (2010), the results are hypnotic. I don't think I am the only viewer who drifts between consciously reading the numbers and being mesmerized by the structure and color.

In 2009, Jane began paintings in response to Barnett Newman's Via Crucis series, which consists of the fourteen Stations of the Cross (1958–66). In an interview with Mack McFarland that appeared in *BOMB* (April 12, 2012), she stated:

> I saw Barnett Newman's about ten years ago at the Philadelphia Museum of Art and thought, geez, someday I am going to do a set. And I was so psyched to start them after my show *N.D.E.* in 2009. I am committed to doing #5 again each year. That was the most difficult one for me, Peter helping Jesus Christ.

Is it surprising that Jane has committed herself to an annual restatement of the most difficult subject of this monumental narrative?

Jane often creates the illusion of a line by means of dots, but she does not draw actual lines in her paintings because that would require her to reload the brush. She does use lines in her drawings, however. In an email exchange,[1] she told me about the moment when she began using line in what she categorizes as her "official drawing practice":

> my first one was in 2005 and they have been going ever since. they start at the center with the colour that represents the day of the week and they progress by drawing lines in the eight directions while turning the paper so the line is being pulled toward the heart. sat R sun O mon Y tues G wed B thur I fri V

Along with her line drawings, Jane makes voluminous notes for possible paintings, all of which are based on research. Science, mathematics, color theory, and painting are inseparable. Here are three quick things I learned from looking at the drawings and notes in her sketchbooks. First, if the logic of a sequence of numbers eludes you, this does not mean it is absent. Second, Jane is devoted to discovering what events or occurrences—however common (someone's birthday) or elusive, such as those recorded in "near death experiences"—can be transformed into paintings. The passage of time is central to all of them. Third, she makes all kinds of lists, from a series of questions one might be asked in an interview, to a sequence of numbers, to groups of phrases that I take to be personal word associations.

The range of effects she attains in her paintings is astonishing. The fields of dots waver between clarity and dissolution; they undulate, flicker, and continually shift. She sets her triangles within larger triangular fields, which she aligns at different angles so that they appear to collide with each other or collapse upon themselves. Strict order and impending chaos overlap to the point that they cannot be disentangled. By bringing together mathematics and op art, she pushes what has been defined as pure seeing from the literal domain into an imaginative one, shifting the historical strain of painting that originates with pointillism and the study of optics into a fresh place of speculation. The exquisite surfaces of her paintings are solely the result of the artist's rigorous approach.

Along with Blake's visionary proposition connecting the minute and the infinite, which I invoked in my first review of the artist's work, Jane's dots of color remind me of pixels and the dust of which we are made, and to which we will return. She is one of the few painters whose work I can describe as "cosmic." Her paintings are about time and our changing place in it. Each dot and triangle can be understood as a marker of time, which Jane uses to shape her passage through it.

The other word that her work brings to mind is "metaphysical." Her understanding of numbers has led her art into a very different perceptual zone than the ones the rest of us are likely to inhabit, or even be aware of. What does her understanding of a tetradic prime open onto? Where does it lead us?

What lifts Jane's far-ranging speculations into a place all their own is the paint—what she does with it as a physical presence and as a color interacting with other colors. Her visceral, hypnotic, thought-provoking art meets the viewer more than halfway without losing one iota of its mystery.

1 Xylor Jane, email message to author, March 4, 2019.

Xylor Jane
Notebooks

Published by CANADA, New York
and parrasch heijnen,
Los Angeles.

www.canadanewyork.com
www.parraschheijnen.com

Distributed by Artbook | D.A.P.
www.artbook.com

ISBN 978-1-942884-44-6

Edited by Dan Nadel

Designed by Joe Gilmore
www.qubik.com

Typefaces:
Maxi and Favorit (Dinamo)

Printed by Wilco Art Books,
Amersfoort, Netherlands